CODE
BLUE

CODE BLUE

Health Care in Crisis

EDWARD R. ANNIS, M.D.

REGNERY GATEWAY
Washington, D. C.

Library of Congress Cataloging-in-Publication Data

Annis, Edward R., 1913–
    Code blue : health care in crisis / Edward R. Annis.
        p. cm.
    Includes bibliographical references and index.
    ISBN 0-89526-515-X (acid-free paper)
    1. Medical policy—United States.   2. Medical care, Cost of—
United States.   I. Title.
    RA395.A3A66   1993
    362.1'0973—dc20   92-44875
                                                                              CIP

Published in the United States by
Regnery Gateway
1130 17th Street, NW
Washington, DC 20036

Distributed to the trade by
National Book Network
4720-A Boston Way
Lanham, MD 20706

Printed on acid-free paper.

Manufactured in the United States of America.

10 9 8 7 6 5 4 3 2 1

To Betty Starck Annis
Wonderful Wife and Mother of Eight

Acknowledgements

First and foremost, I thank my collaborator, Brent K. Pickard, for artfully putting my message on paper, and for meticulously researching and reconfirming every fact, every date, every statistic used in this book. My thanks also goes to Dr. Francis Davis, publisher of *Private Practice* magazine, who has for the past five years faithfully published my monthly opinion column. Many of those columns served as central themes of chapters in the second part of this book.

Contents

INTRODUCTION "It Was the Best of Times. It Was the Worst of Times."   3

PART ONE
THE GOLDEN AGE OF MEDICINE

1   Golden Years and Looming Clouds   11
2   From Sick England to Healthy America: Following the Path of Decline   22
3   Fighting for Noble Traditions   37

PART TWO
UNCOVERING THE HIDDEN TRUTH

4   Hiding the Truth: How the Press Does It   79
5   A Slit of the Wrist or a Shot in the Arm: Does Medicine Really Bleed the Economy?   112
6   Apples to Oranges: Comparing Old and New Technologies   128
7   Drugs, Sex, and Violence   145

8 AIDS: The First Politically Protected Disease   162

9 The High Cost of Living, the Higher Cost of Dying   179

10 Call the Plumber, We're Insured!   185

11 Paper Plague: The Sickening Saga of Government
Intervention   197

12 Toxic Torts: When Lawyers Make the Laws   220

13 What's the Solution?   242

NOTES   261

INDEX   269

CODE
BLUE

"It Was the Best of Times. It Was the Worst of Times."

Today's physicians live in two worlds. On the one hand we work in the wonderland of modern medicine, a gratifying and challenging world of achievement in research, education, and clinical practice. On the other hand we live each day cognizant that the health care system in America is faltering, on the verge of collapse. The same system that increased our ability to heal the sick and injured beyond belief is under siege by a bungling bureaucracy beyond our control. We have been thrust into the uncomfortable and adversarial world of politics. As a physician it seems appropriate to draw upon the words Charles Dickens used to open his *Tale of Two Cities*: "It was the best of times. It was the worst of times."

Reflect for a moment on the advances that have given contemporary society a quality of health care unimaginable in prior times. During my early years when I dreamed of becoming a doctor, I walked to school past signs on neighbors' doors warning prospective visitors that someone inside suffered from measles, scarlet fever, whooping cough, or diphtheria. Even more ominous were the red signs with only one word: "WARNING." I soon learned that someone inside was suffering from "consumption," the dreaded tuberculosis.

My mother was a bride at nineteen, a widow at twenty, and a mother at twenty-one; my father died of a ruptured appendix six months before I was born. In that day appendicitis was a little understood disease referred to as "inflammation of the bowel." I lost a baby half-brother to streptococcus. My aunt had a lifetime of deafness brought on by whooping cough, a disease that caused the death of one of every four of its young victims. Myself? I became deaf in one ear from a raging case of tonsillitis. For others, polio killed some and paralyzed many more during those days when "infectious disease" hospitals dotted the land.

Then, while I was still in medical school, the miraculous age of modern medicine dawned with the development of prontosil followed by the sulfas, penicillin, tetracyclines, and broad-spectrum antibiotics giving us the ability to control infections. These wonder drugs not only dislodged infectious diseases as the leading cause of death, but allowed us safely to pursue surgical treatments of injury (my hearing was restored through surgery), deformity, and disease. Next came immunizations to prevent smallpox, diphtheria, whooping cough, tetanus, polio, measles, German measles, and mumps.

The terrifying plagues of yesteryear are almost unheard of today. We are currently witnessing progress at an unprecedented pace. Laser technology, precision-imaging methods, and microscopic surgical techniques are revolutionizing diagnosis and treatment of cancer, heart disease, and, most dramatically, diseases of the brain, the nervous system, and the eyes. Genetic engineering has opened a whole new frontier in medicine every bit as promising as the momentous development of antibiotics.

But coincident with these remarkable achievements, there erupted an aggressive political climate that created burdensome and expensive bureaucratic intrusions into the practice of medicine. The current generation of medical professionals is buffeted by politicians, lawyers, and a hostile press. Until recently, public opinion polls showed that people had great confidence in doctors. Now, however, surveys indicate that this confidence is eroding, even as physicians gain the ability to provide better medical care than ever before.

More than a quarter century has passed since Lyndon Johnson's Great Society heralded, with extraordinary fanfare, that all people past a certain birthday, regardless of personal wealth, would be afforded the best medical care available through government subsidy. Along with the promise came, inevitably, a wasteful and disruptive bureaucracy that defied basic laws of economics, producing medicine's hyperinflation and fundamentally changing the relationship between doctor and patient.

The facts are shocking. So severe is this crisis that Medicare, though continuing to burden hospitals with untold administrative and inflationary pressures, has reduced reimbursements to less than the cost of treating patients. Over the last few years more than seven hundred of our nation's hospitals have been forced to close. Nearly a thousand hospitals nationwide are on the financially "endangered" list, a situation which makes it impossible to stock adequate supplies of drugs, retain qualified personnel, and buy new equipment or repair aging equipment.

The crisis in tort liability has forced over sixty hospital emergency rooms to close in the last five years. Just three years ago in my home town of greater Miami we had eight trauma centers to serve 2 million residents. Today we have two—one of which treats only children. From 1978 to 1985 lawsuits against manufacturers of whole-cell pertussis vaccines increased from one to 219, and the damages claimed increased from $10 million to $3.6 billion. And, according to Peter Huber, senior fellow at the Manhattan Institute for Policy Research, the "tort tax" accounts for 95 percent of the price of childhood vaccines. Ironically, the quality of American pharmaceuticals and the expertise of medical care has never been better.

And what of Medicare's future? The plan's own trustees have admitted that it will be bankrupt within ten years. Working American taxpayers (120 million of them) will see nothing for the money they have paid into the system year after year because the system, among other things, has been paying the medical bills for millions who were never required to pay their fair share, even those who could well afford it.

The philosophical flaws of the Great Society have festered, and the politicians who created the problems, with the aid of a biased and belligerent news media, are pointing fingers in all the wrong directions. They are mounting a final assault on common sense in an effort to gain complete control over the provision of medical care in America, and ultimately, to bring about rationing of life-saving technology and patient care in order to force medical costs down. This is the only way they can retain, and in fact greatly expand, governmental power.

The truth is that the problem is government, not health care. All of the current problems in the medical marketplace—hyperinflation, millions of uninsured Americans, excessive administrative costs—carry a "MADE IN WASHINGTON" label. Yet, the truth remains hidden to most Americans.

Rather than expose the truth, the news media tell us that the failure stems from the free market. Witness this from a May 1991 editorial in the *San Francisco Chronicle*: "The shambles that is our health system proves incontrovertibly that care cannot be left to uncontrolled private enterprise." Or this item by Loretta McLaughlin of the *Boston Globe*: "But it is also true that our laissez-faire approach to medical care fuels runaway costs." Uncontrolled private enterprise? Laissez-faire? As this book documents, health care has become the most regulated industry in American history, and runaway costs directly correlate to governmental intrusion.

In a free market, consumers, spending their own money, shop and negotiate for goods and services. But 80 percent of Americans' health care bills are paid by third parties—usually government or employers. This corruption of the marketplace is the fault of government: it taxes the income of individuals used to buy health insurance and exempts from taxation employer-provided health benefits; it taxes current workers to pay the medical bills of current retirees; and it taxes the savings of current workers so that they will be unable to provide for their own health care in retirement.

Would anyone question what would happen to the cost of automobiles if employers were obliged to pay for them on behalf of employees? It would not be long before Americans would lose their freedom to choose an automobile to serve their individual needs. That is exactly what is happening in health care as government tries to solve the crisis by forcing everybody into health maintenance organizations, or by dictating coverage under a government-administered system. Either way, Americans will have their health care purchased for them by faceless bureaucrats and third-party administrators. Imagine what would happen to the quality of automobiles under such an arrangement.

A free market still exists in one segment of health care: plastic surgery for cosmetic purposes. Predictably, plastic surgeons pioneered the use of safe, cost effective, ambulatory surgical facilities to attract patients who did not bear a blank check provided by their employers. Unlike the practice with other medical specialties, patients are quoted fixed prices ahead of surgery; differences in quality and price are deciding factors in the patient's choice. Credit terms are often negotiated and services are affordable not only for movie stars, but also for middle-class and blue-collar Americans, making plastic surgery a thriving industry across the nation.

As an octogenarian I practiced general surgery and family medicine in the era before government spoiled the free market—in the "golden years" of medicine. I also have a unique perspective on the situation, having been at the forefront of the fight to stave off governmental intrusion. The first part of this book is not intended as an autobiography, nor as my opportunity to say "I told you so" (although I did); instead, it is intended to chronicle the events and present the intellectual climate that brought about the current crisis. This review of events is especially intended for the millions of Americans who have not connected today's health care crisis to the collapse of socialism around the world.

The second part of this book attempts to uncover the root causes of the so-called health care crisis, and to show how we can go about fixing it. Perhaps my suggestions will seem out of step in the current political climate; perhaps my ideas will seem alien to those accustomed to the news media's campaign of "mythinformation." For those I cite Tom Paine. In the introduction to his famous Revolutionary Era treatise, *Common Sense,* Tom Paine wrote:

> Perhaps the sentiments contained in the following pages are not yet sufficiently fashionable to procure them general favor; a long habit of not thinking a thing wrong gives it a superficial appearance of being right, and raises at first a formidable outcry in defence of custom. But the tumult soon subsides. Time makes more converts than reason.

These prophetic words written in 1776 decried excessive governmental intrusion and regulations which progressively stifled fundamental freedoms, the freedoms guaranteed us by the Declaration of Independence. These same sentiments are applicable today as American medicine is threatened by the escalating actions which call for more legislation, more regulation, more government expenditure, more taxation, and less freedom for patients.

PART ONE

THE GOLDEN AGE
OF MEDICINE

———————\/\——————

CHAPTER 1

Golden Years
and Looming Clouds

When I was elected president of the American Medical Association (AMA), the only previous position I had ever held in the organization was that of "Chairman of the Speakers Bureau," although I must confess, I was a chairman who never chaired a meeting. As my story will show, I was given that title at the request of NBC News, and later I was made president of the AMA in an attempt to counter a cunning band of political sophists in Washington, D.C.

I am frequently asked how it was possible to become president of the American Medical Association at such a young age and with no campaign besides. But it's a fact; I never asked for the job, I never asked to be a candidate. How, then, was it possible for me to have beeen swept into office on the first ballot by a vote of over 2 to 1, when the only other candidate was a fine and deserving physician who had devoted years to bettering the profession on the AMA Board of Trustees? The answer lies in serendipity and the fact that I stand only five feet, nine inches tall.

As a student at Annunciation High School of Detroit, I had neither the physique nor the skills to make the football, basketball, or baseball teams. This left me only one choice for extracurricular activities: debate. Having volunteered for the debating team I quickly found that debaters were required to defend both sides of controversial questions. It was in those early days, too, that I came to realize that on matters controversial, strong arguments could be supported by either the negative or the affirmative. Because the questions were controversial, one could develop some very cogent arguments to defend either position. Because of the visibility my debating career provided, I was elected president of my senior class.

By the time I entered premedical school at the University of Detroit, the Great Depression had hit and my parents' savings had been lost in a failed bank. But luck intervened, and I attained a position as student-instructor in the department of biology, due to my public speaking experience, limited though it was. I was also lucky to find employment during the summer months in an ice factory where I worked seven days a week for fifty cents per hour; this made my college education possible.

Busily engaged in the premedical curricula, I had no time for such courses as speech, but I did join the Philomathic Debating Society as a diversion from my studies in science. Later, as a lark in my senior year, I entered an oratorical contest intended primarily for students of speech and law. My subject was a plea for wholesome family life because even then family values were waning, even then some children were growing up without the guidance of a mother or father. I emphasized that the success enjoyed by each succeeding immigrant group of America was marked with strong family traditions—the one common denominator. Having picked my theme, my delivery was passionate—I believed in what I was saying—and I was awarded the oratorical gold medal. I knew that although there are two sides to every debate, as a physician in the years ahead I would only speak to advocate positions in which I truly believed.

Having completed my premedical studies and obtained my Bachelor of Science degree, I was accepted at the Marquette University School of Medicine, which I entered in 1933. Shortly after the school year got under way, while walking back to my rooming house, I passed the school of speech. For fun, I went in and asked if they ever let medical students debate. The answer was yes, if they're good enough, and I joined the debating team. I continued to hone my oratorical skills, and though I could no longer travel to other cities, I debated a number of major universities at the Marquette campus. This activity gave me enough prominence among the student body that, in addition to being made president of the Phi Chi medical fraternity, I served for two years as president of the Interfraternity Council for Marquette University.

During my junior year as a medical student, luck interceded again and I obtained a position as an extern at Misericordia Hospital in Milwaukee. The hospital had approximately two hundred beds plus an additional fifty beds for young women who were unmarried and needed prenatal care as well as delivery services. Misericordia had neither residents nor interns; one other physician, Walter Giffin, and I were the only externs, which provided us the opportunity to work every night handling emergencies, assisting in the operating room, and delivering a great number of babies.

In those days the mortality rate for patients suffering from pneumonia was approximated 50 percent, and even higher during winter, because we had no means to treat infections. Patients, most often elderly patients, with broken hips were put into a body cast extending from under their arms down and including both legs to relieve the pain. Many of these patients would accumulate fluid in their lungs which became infected because of immobility, and great numbers died from the resultant pneumonia.

But then, during my externship at Misericordia Hospital, a new weapon fell into our hands, a red textile dye called prontosil. How it worked was still a mystery, but a German scientist, Gerhard Domagk, discovered that by injecting the dye in patients, or by giving it to them orally, the deadly streptococcal infections could be controlled, and it became immediately apparent that the first cannon had been fired in what would prove to be the technological revolution against suffering and early death. It gave us the ability not only to treat pneumonia, but also deadly infections of the bloodstream.

Shortly after the introduction of prontosil, we found that the active ingredient was sulfanilamide. In due course various other sulfas were developed, and for the first time doctors had a number of agents capable of treating infections caused by gram positive organisms. With the ability to control infection we had the ability to perform safe surgical procedures.

My next good fortune came after my externship at Misericordia Hospital when I was accepted into a general rotating internship at Milwaukee County Hospital, then and now a great center for education. The infancy of modern medicine at the time is evidenced by an incident that occurred when I was walking past an orthopedic suite and Dr. "Boney" Smith called me in and said, "Here, I want you to put this patient to sleep." The patient had been prepared for the insertion of a nail to secure a broken hip. I told Dr. Smith I had never administered an anesthetic before, but he said he would guide me. Dr. Smith handed me a mask and a bottle of ether and told me to place the mask on the patient and start dripping ether on it; he would tell me when to slow down. It worked, but what a far cry from today's well-trained anesthesiologists, who account for our remarkably low mortality rates for surgery.

My time at Milwaukee County Hospital was a wonderful period for learning. As interns we lived in the hospital and were on call 24 hours a day. We were allowed one night off a week, and a whole day off once a month. For this we were paid $10 per month. I recall specifically that my check was $8.67 after withholding.

In recognition of the new skills being developed as a result of the new sulfa drugs, special studies were instituted requiring additional years of concentrated study and supervised practice to earn certification from any one of several newly founded speciality boards. Dr. Francis Murphy, head of the Department of Medicine, told me that he felt he could obtain a fellowship for me at the great Mayo Clinic. Though I was sorely tempted, I had to face economic reality; there were still four girls and another boy to be educated in my family. At the conclusion of my internship in 1938, I elected to go into general practice.

Following my graduation from high school I had visited my grandmother and an aunt and uncle living in Deland, a beautiful and serene town of central Florida. I made up my mind then that I would ultimately come back to Florida to practice medicine. Nine years later I returned, and though at the depth of the Depression I had managed to save a hundred dollars and to buy a second-hand car. But my resources were far shy of being able to open a practice. I took employment at the state mental hospital at Chattahoochee, Florida, which provided many valuable experiences in dealing with victims of the most tragic of human illnesses. Eventually, I moved in with an uncle at Tallahassee, the state capital, and borrowed enough money to open an office.

POWER, MONEY, AND CATFISH ·

Being single and a newcomer, I thought it a good idea to join the Junior Chamber of Commerce (the Jaycees) shortly after my arrival at Tallahassee. As it turned out, several of my new friends in the Jaycees became political leaders of my adopted state, four of them governors. I was also taken in by a small informal group of fellow Jaycees who were affectionately referred to around town as the Catfish Club. Franklin Delano Roosevelt was president, and we, the Catfish, were eleven enterprising young Democrats doing what we could to prod our community out of the Depression and back to progress.

I am always entertained by depictions of rich and powerful capitalists who join exclusive clubs where they conspire to exploit the lower classes and control the political strings of government to their selfish benefit. The Catfish did include some wealthy and politically influential people, and we did gather in the evening at a member's home on irregular intervals. One such gathering was held at the home of Al and Evelyn Block.

Al was a remarkable businessman, head of one of the largest printing plants in the southeastern United States. Everybody who was anybody in Florida knew Al and Evelyn Block. On this particular evening Al called me aside and said, "Ed, there has been talk about you in the congregation, and we're concerned about your business practices." (I was the doctor for Rabbi Kravitz and almost all forty families of his congregation.) Al continued, "You've been charging my family and some of the others two dollars for a visit." (That was about the norm at that time for a simple doctor's visit;

among the more expensive services was delivering a baby, for which
the going rate was $35, including prenatal care.) "We also hear that
you have been treating some of the other families for nothing."
(That was true too; it was a tradition among doctors not to bill
people you knew could not pay, or to give a reduced bill to those you
knew could not handle the going rate.) "How can you expect to stay
in practice unless you get more from me and the others who can
afford it?" The only conspiring Al and Evelyn Block ever did was to
make sure everybody had the chance to enjoy the blessings of life
that they enjoyed, especially good health care.

SOUR MILK AND SYPHILIS

It was rare for a doctor to join the Jaycees in those days, so perhaps
by default they made me chairman of the public health committee.
I recognized that there was a bacterial problem in the local milk
supply, and Al Block even brought a fresh bottle to a Jaycee meeting
to show debris accumulating on the bottom. I set out to investigate. I
found exactly what I had suspected: the milk wasn't pasteurized
before being sent out for home delivery, and at one dairy the pump
used to wash the returned bottles had been broken for several
weeks; the fellow was simply refilling the dirty empties.

Backed up by Al Block, LeRoy Collins (later our governor), and
several other Jaycees, I made quite a stir getting the dairies in-
spected regularly. Then a fellow named E. A. Gilbert opened a
dairy where everything was handled exactly as it should be. It was
spick-and-span, and I reported that all dairies should be required to
maintain those standards. Every Sunday after church many of the
townspeople would congregate at the corner pharmacy, Fain's Drug
Store, to solve the problems of the world. One Sunday LeRoy Collins
was there, and he told me that a dairyman by the name of Perkins
showed up so angry you could almost see smoke coming out of his
ears. Mr. Perkins stormed at the crowd, "There ain't no difference
between my milk and Gilbert's milk; we've got the same kind of
cows. The only difference is that he keeps the manure out of his and
I strain it out of mine!" That settled that; the county started regular
inspections.

I was quickly made chairman of the Jaycees' statewide public health committee, on which I served for some eight years, was later elected national director for the Jaycees, and for two years served as chairman of its national public health committee. I also became chairman of the State of Florida Public Health Committee and special emissary on matters of public health for my friend, Florida Governor Spessard Holland, who was later elected to the United States Senate.

On one occasion I was taken by police escort to see Georgia Governor Ellis Arnall. We had a problem with an outbreak of syphilis, a sexually transmitted disease with which I had had experience during my tenure at the state mental hospital; it attacks the brain long before it kills the victim. Georgia and Florida both had a policy of requiring blood tests before a marriage license would be granted to residents of each state, but nonresidents were exempt. The justices of the peace on both sides of the Florida-Georgia border had quite a business going by issuing marriage licenses to residents of the other state without the need of a blood test, and my mission was to get the loophole in the law plugged.

At his office Governor Arnall had just apologized, saying I was too late—the legislative committees had already met—when I noticed a photograph of his beautiful bride on his desk. She was a former Miss Florida from Orlando, and I pointed out that under the law she was exempt from having the blood check in Georgia, and he was exempt in Florida. I told him about the several cases I had seen in my office where people had contracted the disease unknowingly and had passed it on to their new spouses. The governor thought a minute, then picked up the phone to call the legislative committee on public health back to order; the loophole was plugged in both states. I was reminded of this story when working on the issue of AIDS, which is covered in a later chapter. As you will see, it is tragic that initial AIDS policies were established according to the dictates of gay and lesbian activists in defiance of common sense and sound public health standards, to the detriment of the very people the activists claim to represent.

Of all the medical efforts to save lives and keep people healthy, none can be more fruitful and cost effective than stringent public health standards. We know from experience with Third World nations that public health standards are only effective in industrialized nations, but industrialization has only occurred under laissez-faire governments, which creates a dilemma. Government is necessary to protect the public, but society must be mindful not to impose too much government or it will, by its very nature, strangle the same producers that make the high standards of public health possible.

THE GOLDEN YEARS OF MEDICINE

As war clouds loomed over Europe, I volunteered for the Army Air Corp, but I was turned down because of deafness in my left ear as a result of an infection during childhood. When the United States entered the war I was again turned down. It made no sense to me or anyone else that I was perfectly able to serve my community effectively as a medical doctor, but could not serve the military in that same capacity. That demonstrates how rigidity and inefficiency characterize government bureaucracy, even in a time of national crisis.

Before the war I had teamed up with Dr. Edson Andrews, an old friend from hospital training years. But Andy was called for military duty about the time another friend and associate from my days in Milwaukee, Dr. Harold Hallstrand, set up practice in Tallahassee.

In order to keep up with rapid changes in our profession, Harold and I alternated attendance at the Cook County Postgraduate School of Surgery in Chicago, each covering the other's practice during periods of absence. In each session at the school we would learn the latest techniques in a different procedure. But as we acquired these advanced skills, we were limited in their application because the local hospital was inadequate. As a consequence, and with much sorrow, in 1946 I moved my practice to Miami where I would specialize in surgery and gynecology.

It was during my early years of practice at Tallahassee that the medical and surgical revolution, led by pharmaceutical discoveries and developments, escalated. The success of the sulfas was followed by the manufacture of penicillin. (Although Alexander Fleming discovered penicillin in 1928 in England, it sat on the shelf until

American drug companies developed methods of production in 1943.) The success of penicillin in combating gram positive bacteria led to a search for a similar mold to treat gram negatives, resulting in the discovery of streptomycin. These great advances began the development of one new therapeutic tool after another. Because of these advances, World War II was the first war in history in which the implements of war directly caused more fatalities than infection as a result of wounds. And to this, in the early 1950s, was added the amazingly successful development of the American pharmaceutical industry which led the way to production of broad-spectrum antibiotics and immunizations. The introduction of these into the armamentarium of medicine set the stage for a veritable explosion of technology and new knowledge for both the medical and surgical approaches to illness and accidents.

Also during that era the physicians of America established Blue Shield in their respective states—founded upon actuarial principles—to provide a mechanism for people of modest means to afford the new lifesaving technologies. After the war, when my friend LeRoy Collins became governor of Florida and I was appointed chairman of the Citizens Medical Committee on Health, we got legislation passed for the state to reimburse hospitals for the costs of making their facilities, nursing care, and expensive medical apparatus available to the poor, while doctors provided services without charge.

My years in Tallahassee are also remembered through another marvelous and momentous event: my marriage in 1941 to the beautiful Florida State University coed, Betty McCue Stark. Betty and I have now celebrated over fifty anniversaries together, and we have raised eight wonderful children. Thinking back to that oratory prize I won in college for my speech about the importance and rewards of devotion to family, Betty and I can attest today to the fulfillment of those expectations many times over.

Upon establishing a practice in Miami, I was again fortunate to locate Wayne Martin, a brilliant and remarkably skillful young doctor, and to persuade him to move to Miami and become my associate. I also converged with Dr. Maurice Cooper who was a member of a group of outstanding anesthesiologists. With his help we were able to provide fine surgical care, and our practice grew quickly. We operated chiefly at Mercy Hospital, a modern Catholic hospital overlooking Miami's beautiful Biscayne Bay. I became head of the department of general surgery at Mercy Hospital, a position I enjoyed for ten years.

The United States had emerged from World War II as the leader among nations, and from my perspective, nowhere was that leadership more evident than in the field of medicine. By the 1950s, America had the world's most advanced medical schools and research centers, our hospitals were the most modern and best equipped, and most dramatically, our pharmaceutical industry was developing and producing more drugs to cure more diseases and ailments than I would have thought possible in a century of development. Health care in America was second to none.

The legal environment was ideal for the practice of good medicine. Tort laws had not yet been gerrymandered by self-serving lawyers in the legislatures; malpractice suits were rare, and when they did arise, they were handled efficiently and fairly by the courts. Hospitals required physicians with staff privileges to maintain membership in the local medical society. At any time it became evident that a fellow physician was dealing unethically or gouging the public, his or her membership in the local society could be terminated, and thus hospital privileges as well.

Unfortunately, in a few years the legislatures and courts put an end to those practices. The medical society's right to oversee billing practices was said to constitute price fixing, and hospitals could no longer deny a doctor his or her livelihood based on membership in a medical society. It's curious to note, but in all the years that I practiced medicine, my local medical society only censured member doctors for incompetence or overcharging, never for undercharging. In fact, undercharging those who could not afford the going rate was encouraged and almost universally practiced.

A typical example of how well the system worked occurred the day I was sent a little girl who had fallen from a tree breaking both bones in one arm. Her dad had just arrived in town and had not found a job yet. Due to the seriousness of the fractures, I called one of the best orthopedic doctors in town, Herbert Virgin, who willingly treated the girl without charge. Years later, when professional football came to town, the Miami Dolphins sought out a top-notch orthopedic physician to serve as the team doctor; the doctor selected to serve was Herbert Virgin, the same man who so diligently served the indigent when asked. During my tenure as surgical chief at Mercy Hospital, I was sent countless cases of indigent patients who required treatment outside my specialty, and not once did my fellow doctors fail to provide the care needed—without charge.

In those days there was no bureaucratic regimentation, there were few forms to fill out, malpractice premiums were affordable, and the overhead costs of running a practice were reasonable. Our bills were simple, spelled out so anybody could understand them without the use of codes. Patients usually paid their own bills, promptly too, for which an ordinary receipt was given. Hospital charges were set by the day, not by the aspirin. Medical care was affordable to the average person with rates set by the laws of the marketplace, and care was made available to all who requested it regardless of ability to pay. Doctors were well respected; rarely were we denigrated by a hostile press for political reasons. Yes, in the days before government intervention into the practice of medicine, doctors' fees were low, but the rewards were rich; those were truly "golden years" for medicine.

———————/\/\———————

CHAPTER 2

From Sick England to Healthy America: Following the Path of Decline

In stark contrast to the marvelous emergence of the United States following World War II, Britain fell to the melancholy of decline under socialist doctrine. Actually, socialist doctrine had found its way into the mainstream of British politics long before the war. But we commonly associate its initiation with the landslide election victory of the Labour party in 1945.

Despite its name, the British Labour party received political direction from a small band of socialist doctrinaires, the Fabian Society. The Fabians provided the political stimulus of the British trade union movement; they represented the political interests of miners, although few Fabians had ever been in a mine; and they represented fitters, although few had ever fit a pipe. Fabians were mostly wealthy heirs, writers, and intellectuals who extended their influence far beyond the confines of their elite group.

Among the most influential of the early Fabians were playwright George Bernard Shaw and his close friend, Sidney Webb, a lawyer and civil servant. Webb, the son of an accountant who had never been a laborer himself, found great political success in the trade union movement representing the Miners' Federation on the Sankey Commission; in 1924, as a Labour party official, he became president of the Board of Trade. An executive director of the Fabian Society since before the turn of the century, he wrote the organization's first and most enduring propaganda tract, *Facts for Socialists*. Upon marrying Beatrice, the daughter of a wealthy businessman, he quit work; living off her inheritance, the couple devoted themselves to the Fabian goal of transforming Great Britain into a socialist society.

Neither an historian nor an economist, Webb wrote a socialist's version of "history" and "economics" in two highly influential volumes: *The History of Trade Unionism*, and *Industrial Democracy*. In order to establish socialistic theories as "social science," Webb founded the London School of Economics to educate future world leaders. (The school's roster of former students includes the name of John F. Kennedy.) Webb also initiated the Fabian program called "permeation"—the infiltration of all major political parties to make certain socialist programs would be enacted no matter which party was in power. Sidney and Beatrice Webb wrote their final work in 1935, *Soviet Communism: A New Civilization*, extolling the virtues of what they asserted was the model socialist society in the Soviet Union.

George Bernard Shaw explained the tactic of "permeation" as "accepting, instead of trying to supersede, the existing political organizations which it intended to permeate with the Socialist conception of human society."[1] The success of Fabian permeation is apparent when one considers that during the first Labour party government under Prime Minister Ramsey MacDonald (secretary of the British Bureau of Socialist International, also a Fabian member) in 1923–1924, the only stated socialist objective achieved was recognition and trade support of the Soviet Union. Yet, under the coalition and conservative governments that followed, a great deal of the socialist agenda was realized in national health insurance, welfare, centralized economic planning, monopolization of broadcasting under the British Broadcasting Corporation (BBC), and even a push for nationalization of some industry. There was little significant rollback of the socialist state—not even under the popular leadership of Winston Churchill—until the Thatcher government of the 1980s.

Churchill had led his countrymen successfully through the difficult war years. After the war he warned voters not to believe the unrealistic promises of the radical socialists in the Labour party, but in vain. The Labour party took power and immediately embarked on wholesale nationalization of industry—and, most tragically, the socialization of the health care system. The socialization process was expected to bring an end to labor unrest; instead, it brought more strikes. Socialization promised to bring postwar prosperity; instead it brought decline and despair. By 1949 the country was in an economic crisis and the Labour government imposed an "austerity" program; productivity had declined to the point where rationing had to be instituted. The British socialists turned to the American taxpayer for relief and for forgiveness of war debts under Lend-Lease, which was, of course, granted.

Shortly after the turn of the century, a sister organization to the British Fabian Society was founded in New York called the Intercollegiate Socialist Society (ISS). It later became the League for Industrial Democracy (LID), drawing from the title of the socialist treatise, *Industrial Democracy*, by Sidney Webb.[2] In years past, LID was described as a "Provincial Society" in the annual reports of the British Fabian Society.[3] Like the Fabians, the founders of the League for Industrial Democracy (then the ISS) were mostly intellectuals, including author Jack London and criminal lawyer Clarence Darrow.[4] Also among those associated with the LID were several who would exert control over the Socialist party of America—similar to the relationship between the British Fabians and the Labour party—including Morris Hillquit and Norman Thomas.

But the original "live wire" of the Socialist party was Eugene Debs, president of the American Railway Union, who became interested in socialism through reading Marx and Engels' *Communist*

Manifesto while serving a prison term for violating a court injunction. Debs ran for president five times on the Socialist party ticket. He received the most votes in 1920, although at the time he was again serving a prison term, this time for interfering with the prosecution of defendants under the Espionage Act.

Norman Thomas was probably the best known Socialist candidate in America, having run six presidential campaigns by 1948. He was active on the college lecture circuit, served as associate editor of *The Nation*, and was associated with the Marxist-oriented *New Leader* until 1935. Thomas was also a founder of the American Civil Liberties Union and a codirector of the LID.

From this curious fringe element—barely noticeable by most Americans because it sat on the far left edge of the political spectrum—events would occur to change the political landscape in the U.S., perhaps forever. Prior to World War II, socialists in America, even the do-gooders and the clergy, commonly rallied behind causes to benefit what they perceived to be the consummate utopian society, the Soviet Union. These subversive causes with innocuous-sounding names—American Youth Congress, National Student League, National Negro Congress, American Writers Congress, American Artists Congress—became known as Communist-front organizations. No matter how good the intentions of some naive members, the strings were always pulled from within the Kremlin.

This cozy alliance with the Kremlin was easy to prove, and in the decade of the 1950s, contributed to the investigative excesses and blacklisting of the McCarthy era in Congress; the reputation of some gullible people suffered by association with Communist subversives. But by that time the American public had become aware of the totalitarian nature and expansionist drive of the Soviet Union and were alarmed at the extent of subversive activity by socialist elements in the United States.

But prior to this, the Socialists, frustrated by the exposure of subversive activities and by rejection at the polls, had fashioned a scheme of "permeation" after the example set by the British Fabian Society. The Union for Democratic Action (UDA), named after a similar Fabian "permeation" group in London, was formed in 1941 by members of the Socialist party, including prominent party leader Alfred B. Lewis, and members of the LID.

Although by 1919 Communists had established a party in addition to the Socialist party, dual memberships were common and political activity continued under a united front. This was the first time in the leftist movement of America that a socialist group would distinguish itself from those socialist groups that included Communists (Party members as well as other socialists with allegiance to the Soviet Union) in order to gain respectability and acceptance in the major political parties. Drawing from a liberal account of this movement, James Loeb, a former Socialist and national director of the new organization, was quoted as saying: "We were sometimes called 'the hang-back boys' because we refused to participate in so many 'worthy causes' that we knew were run by Communists."[5]

But this repudiation of Communists was more symbolic than substantive at that point. The primary focus of the organization was to pressure Congress and the administration to assure the security of the Soviet Union. The principal ideologue of the group was its research director, Louis Fraina, who served on the executive committee of the Communist International and who had in 1919 chaired the first Communist convention at Chicago.[6]

Then, in 1947, reeling from election losses in both houses of Congress to the conservative Republicans, the Union for Democratic Action underwent an incredible metamorphosis. Not only would the group be anticommunist, it would no longer be recognizable as socialist. This sudden feat was not accomplished through any mind alterations on the part of the membership, but through a name change, or more descriptively, through a rebirth. The old organization would be dissolved overnight and a new organization formed, retaining the same membership, but called Americans for Democratic Action.

A special meeting was called to reorganize the Union for Democratic Action on January 3, 1947, and the following day labor leader Walter Reuther of the United Auto Workers met with a small group to prepare a policy statement for the reborn organization. James Loeb, the administrator of the old group, was given the same administrative duties for the new organization along with the titles of executive-secretary and treasurer. Reinhold Niebuhr, chairman of the old group, became vice chairmen of the new group. Barry Bingham, editor of the *Louisville Courier-Journal*, was picked to issue a press statement announcing the formation of the Americans for Democratic Action (ADA), and to outline the group's principles and policies.

Written with glib professionalism, parts of that press statement came out sounding more like a coalition platform of the two major parties than the product of a group carrying forward the socialist traditions of the past half century. "These policies are in the great democratic tradition of Jefferson, Jackson, Lincoln . . ." And: "We reject any association with Communists or sympathizers with communism . . ." With the stroke of a pen, the organized socialists of America had exorcised their immediate past and were "born-again" as patriotic "liberals."

This cleansing of the political soul was dramatically illuminated by Max Lerner in his description of the Americans for Democratic Action: "Although it was itself, in the political spectrum, to the left of center, it helped provide a dynamic center between the totalitarian positions, to which men of diverse democratic beliefs could repair."[7] All was set for permeation. Lerner again: "It also undertook to provide some affirmative direction to creative energies in both major parties, especially the Democratic." Lerner also described the ADA as a "liberal organization" and himself as "working in the same direction" as the ADA. The Russian-born Max Lerner, former *New York Post* syndicated columnist and later national board member of the ADA, had previously served on the National Executive Committee of the Young Workers League, an affiliate of the Young Communist International,[8] and was active in over twenty-five Communist and Communist-front organizations—everything from the American Committee for the Protection of Foreign Born (an auxiliary of the Communist party) to the American Council on Soviet Relations (another creation of the Communist party).[9] He also became a leader of the League for Industrial Democracy.[10]

By the time Americans had read the morning paper the political spectrum had been moved, not by public sentiment, but by media semantics. Once, "right wing" and "reactionary" staked the ground upon which Adolf Hitler stood, and "liberal" described America's Founding Fathers. Then, suddenly, Max Lerner was a born-again "liberal" patriot, and I, a lifelong Democrat, was mysteriously permuted to "right-wing reactionary."

Americans for Democratic Action, in the interest of permeation, also tried to shake the stigma of socialism by carefully wording policy statements so as not to appear to advocate nationalization or expropriation of private property in accord with the Soviet model, as the British Labour government had done with major industries. A basic tenet of socialism is that the means of production must be in the hands of the state; therefore, policies must be developed to accomplish this without nationalization or expropriation, at least not in so many words. Thus, what the ADA promoted over the years were policies under which private citizens could, at least symbolically, conduct private enterprise, but government would be empowered to regulate that enterprise through infinite federal and state bureaucratic controls. Unlike Soviet socialism, the means of production would not be directly owned by government, but instead be regulated by government; the right to set prices, retain earnings, and direct capital—rights ordinarily associated with private ownership—would become the province of government. Producers would become the servants of government, exactly what our Constitution was designed to protect against, until even this obstacle would be "permeated" by the "liberal" interpretations of sympathetic Supreme Court justices, such as William O. Douglas.

Above all, this cunning twist of semantics would make it difficult to debate the ADA's collectivist policies on ideological grounds because the ADA would profess to be nonsocialist and in favor of private property and free enterprise, and thereby repel any attack as "reactionary."

Permeation had still, however, to overcome some early obstacles; dissolution of a fifty-year alliance was not easy. For one, the purse strings to leftist causes were held by labor union bosses with access to membership dues, and many of them retained procommunist, pro-Soviet sentiments. These moneyed forces felt more comfortable operating under the old order of the united front, originally established by the worldwide socialist alliance of the Second International.

The fission of the old united socialist front and the new order of permeation is best understood through a quick review of the events surrounding the third party presidential bid of former Vice President Henry Wallace. Wallace, originally Agriculture secretary in the administration of Franklin D. Roosevelt, subsequently served as Roosevelt's vice president until replaced with Harry Truman at the 1944 Democratic party convention. Roosevelt then reassigned Wallace as Commerce secretary. When Truman assumed the presidency upon the death of Roosevelt in 1945, Wallace continued at his post in the Commerce Department.

Truman's early days after taking the oath were tumultuous. Upon bringing World War II to an abrupt conclusion with two blasts of the atomic bomb, he attempted to reign over the peacetime economy using the ultimate weapon of economic intervention: government price controls. Failing to fathom the market system, he overreacted to peacetime demands for consumer goods with strict price controls only to create severe shortages. When legislative authority for the controls ended, prices skyrocketed—for most goods prices rose 25 percent in sixteen days. Congress renewed his authority and workers' real earnings plummeted 12 percent. Labor strikes became rampant, and Truman threatened to draft the strikers. Republicans took control of both houses of Congress in the midterm election of 1946, and Harry Truman, who had never been to college, got his first lesson of Economics 101: market equilibrium and the law of supply and demand.

Concurrent to these domestic events, the Soviet Union was showing its color with a murderous march into Eastern Europe, and the Truman Doctrine was devised to hold the communists in check. High-level left-wing holdovers from the previous administration were not pleased with Truman's hard line on the Soviets, and Truman ended up purging his administration. The most politically influential to be ousted was Henry Wallace, who openly criticized Truman's policy against communist expansion and demanded massive American aid for the Stalin regime. Other fired officials lined up behind Wallace, some taking positions with political action committees to facilitate a presidential bid by Wallace while Wallace himself became editor of the influential *New Republic*.

In September of 1946, the three largest left-wing political action committees gathered at Chicago for the "Conference of Progressives" at which Henry Wallace was the center of attention. These three committees included: (1) the Congress of Industrial Organizations (CIO-PAC), the giant labor confederation; (2) the National Citizens Political Action Committee (NCPAC), an emanation of CIO-PAC which collected money from nonlabor sources; and (3) the Independent Citizens Committee of the Arts, Sciences and Professions (ICCASP). A few months later NCPAC and ICCASP merged to form the Progressive Citizens of America with Henry Wallace at the center.

CIO President Philip Murray became vice chairman of Progressive Citizens of America, and his closest adviser, Lee Pressman, general counsel of the CIO, later worked full time on the Wallace campaign. Progressive Citizens of America provided the structure for the Progressive party under which Henry Wallace ran for the presidency when he bolted the Democratic party in the 1948 election.

There had been many rumbles in the press about Communist domination of Wallace's Progressive party, and although the charges were shrugged off by his campaign officials, Pressman himself later admitted to two decades of membership in the Communist party. (Pressman found the "new religion" and parted with Communist sympathies after the Wallace campaign failed, as did most Communists of that era.)

Union leaders attempted to reunite the old socialist front behind the new party, as evidenced by the president of the Brotherhood of Sleeping Car Porters, when he urged the ADA to support this "progressive political party similar to the British Labour Party."[11] But the ADA itself was a descendant of just such a (failed) attempt, the Socialist party of America, and its new mission was to permeate the major political parties. The ADA leadership knew that further collusion with Communists would ring the death knell for socialism in the mainstream of America, and they needed no hearings to discover who was or wasn't Communist; they had lived with Communists under the old front for decades, and among their own ranks were those who shed their Communist affiliations in order to follow the new religion into the mainstream of American politics. At the ADA annual convention the second resolution passed stated: "It is an established fact that it [the Wallace candidacy] owes its origin and principal organizational support to the Communist Party of America."

Henry Wallace, in an attempt to soothe differences with the Americans for Democratic Action, made a plea for reconciliation: "The fundamental progressive faith is so broad that we should not allow ourselves to be divided on any minor issues." But when communist forces marched into democratic Czechoslovakia and murdered several leading socialist politicians, Wallace irritated the festering wound by commenting, "One must not discount the degree to which American deeds ha[ve] provoked the Russians."

The Democratic party was further split when Strom Thurmond of South Carolina, upset at Truman's stance on civil rights issues, bolted to run as a "Dixiecrat" (the States' Rights party), and it looked as though he would carry several conservative Southern states. Harry "Give-em-Hell" Truman had given hell to just about everybody and in so doing had alienated the powers behind the Democratic party. The leadership of the Americans for Democratic Action felt Truman was too conservative and searched desperately for an alternative Democratic candidate. But the effort failed.

Truman was in deep political trouble and the tough-talking president soon turned to putty in the hands of ADA manipulators. As a veteran of the Pendergast political machine of Independence, Missouri, Harry Truman not only knew how to break a strike, he also knew how to strike a deal. Surely it was no coincidence that Truman, "the strike breaker," would turn around and veto the anti-union Taft-Hartley Act, and that the major labor unions, including certain Communist-influenced rail unions with whom he had had bitter conflicts, would abandon the ill-fated Wallace campaign in favor of the Americans for Democratic Action. (Surely Mr. Truman knew that his veto would be overridden anyway.) Surely it was no coincidence that Truman would address Congress with an eleven-item wish list, and that eight of those items would appear on the platform adopted at the ADA annual convention. And surely it was no coincidence that the most sweeping proposal on that wish list and on the

ADA platform was a renewed call for socialized medicine through national health insurance, and that the same proposal had first appeared two decades before on the platform of the Socialist party of America.[12] (A bill for national health insurance was originally sponsored in Congress in 1943 but it quickly fizzled in committee when President Roosevelt refused to endorse it because he said it would lead to socialized medicine.)

Truman's maneuvering worked wonders. The CIO executive board changed tack to support the Americans for Democratic Action, and at the first ADA convention at Philadelphia in 1948, the meeting was jointly run by William Green, president of the American Federation of Labor (AFL), and by founding ADA member Walter Reuther, who as head of the United Auto Workers represented the CIO. Even the Railway Brotherhoods had come on board.

Effective permeation was at hand. The Americans for Democratic Action had laid claim to the huge union war chests paid out of workers' paychecks—most of whom had never even heard of the ADA and knew little about the Socialist party from whence it descended—and the president of the United States was beholden to the born-again "liberals" of the ADA for his political survival in the general election of 1948. The ADA never did embrace the "reactionary" Truman, but it made him walk the chalk in the campaign while it set out to destroy what remained of the Wallace camp and to hand Truman a liberal Congress with which to enact ADA programs.

The whole nation had written off Harry Truman as hopeless and his opposition became overconfident. State by state across the nation, Americans for Democratic Action coordinated the efforts of local AFL and CIO unions. They created Students for Democratic Action to mobilize and radicalize college campuses, handed out propaganda pamphlets, bought radio time, and had ADA volunteers work the precincts and the wards. Voter turnout was low, but the fledgling zealots of the left wing got their vote out while the nation dozed, and the results were stupefying. Not only was Truman an upset victor, seventy-nine representatives to the U.S. Congress who had been endorsed by the ADA were elected, and nine new House members were actually ADA members. In addition, five ADA-backed U.S. senators and four ADA-backed governors were elected. In Chicago local elections, of the fourteen candidates endorsed by the ADA, twelve were elected. In Detroit, thirty-five were backed; thirty won.

The big prize for the ADA was the election of Hubert Humphrey to the U.S. Senate. The affable and articulate mayor of Minneapolis was a founding leader of the ADA who had worked miracles at the Democratic convention to control the party platform. He had been a tireless worker in the socialist movement, and had been honored at the "Reunion of Old Timers" by the League for Industrial Democracy.[13] Socialism had forced its way from that obscure little club of intellectuals into the mainstream of American politics, and Senator Humphrey would prove an effective preacher for the new religion of "liberalism." He would be so successful that masses of future "liberals" would be unaware of the origin of the ideas they would come to embrace; they would never relate those ideas to failed socialistic policies in Britain, the Soviet Union, and elsewhere around the world.

Hubert Humphrey's actions at the Democratic convention had pushed President Truman's campaign far to the left of Franklin Roosevelt's New Deal policies, but when the dust cleared it was time for Harry Truman to "give-em-hell" and get the ADA's policies through Congress.

Although not noted for ideological perception, it seemed apparent, to me at least, that Harry Truman was a fast learner and did not need another economics lesson to realize that America would follow Britain's decline if the policies of the ADA were enacted. I cannot believe that the man who pulled off the most stunning upset victory in American electoral history—the same president who brought together the Marshall Plan, NATO, and the United Nations to stabilize a volatile postwar world—could neither coax nor cow a Democratic Congress to accept his own campaign platform unless he wasn't truly interested in seeing those left-wing ideas become law. Most of the ADA's proposals died in Congress, with the notorious exception of the federal housing fiasco. The ADA's socialized health care measure never made it out of committee, and for years to come

Americans would enjoy the finest health care mankind had ever achieved; delivered efficiently at affordable rates; available to all regardless of ability to pay.

Truman's bureaucrats did, however, draw swords to fight for the unprecedented power they would garner under socialization. Oscar Ewing, head of the Federal Security Agency, which encompassed the Public Health Service (later the Department of Health Education and Welfare and today the Department of Health and Human Services), issued a 186-page report, at taxpayers expense, in support of socialized medicine.

The report was so riddled with oversights and unsubstantiated charges that their exposure became the primary weapon of those who opposed the plan in Congress. Most interestingly, the report charged that there was a shortage of doctors in America and that 325,000 lives a year would be saved by letting government reign over the system. (Today, those arguing for socialized medicine claim there is an overabundance of doctors in America!) As was brought out in congressional hearings, the report offered no documentation for these claims, and it failed to observe the amazing progress by means of which America was leading the world in medical care; in just two years, from 1945 to 1947, deaths from communicable diseases had dropped by forty thousand. Frank G. Dickinson, PhD, a veteran economics professor at the University of Illinois, wrote, "In all my twenty-five years of teaching, I have never had a sophomore student make a poorer case than did Mr. Ewing on the question of the shortage of physicians."[14]

Clem Whitaker, a consultant for the American Medical Association at the time, commented with regard to the bureaucrat's initiative, "Oscar Ewing . . . is grimly determined to bring socialized medicine from sick England to healthy America."[15] Testifying before Congress, a former employee at the Public Health Service charged that administration bureaucrats had conspired to nationalize medicine. Upon publication of an editorial in the *Journal of the American Medical Association* charging that Ewing's agency favored socialism, Ewing, in accord with the doctrine of the new religion of "liberalism," denied the charge on the grounds that to place an industry under government control through the financing mechanism of Social Security does not constitute government ownership or nationalization of that industry. Mr. Ewing then challenged his critics to prove their charges that he was promoting socialism. Proof was bounced back immediately in the form of an official government pamphlet bearing Oscar Ewing's moniker which stated, "Social Security and public assistance programs are a basic essential for attainment of the socialized state envisaged in a democratic ideology, a way of life which so far has been realized only in slight measure."[16] The embarrassed bureaucrat withdrew the pamphlet and his cause was lost—for the time being.

The Americans for Democratic Action did not wither during the years of prosperous stability during which they were out of power in Washington. This relatively small group, which received its intellectual guidance from the tiny but elite League for Industrial Democracy, worked diligently to secure a favorable Congress and another president to carry out its agenda. In 1948, the permeation of radical ideas had been shown to be workable. Within a year of its rebirth, the ADA had become the Washington power broker of socialist ideas under the guise of "liberalism."

George Bernard Shaw, the Fabian playwright, once described permeation as "wire-pulling the government in order to get socialist measures passed." Those who pulled the wires at the Americans for Democratic Action learned something else from their Fabian mentors: the doctrine of gradualness. The *Encyclopaedia Britannica* explains that according to the Fabian doctrine of permeation, as opposed to the communist doctrine of sudden revolution, socialism would be achieved "without breach of continuity or abrupt change of the entire social tissue."[17] The next attempt to socialize medicine would not be to socialize the entire system at once, but first to socialize the minority of the population that utilized the medical system most often—the elderly. Few would suspect that by offering government financed medical care to the aged, the government would be assuming the medical bills for those who consume one-third of the nation's total expenditure on health care, and that that total would soon grow to over 40 percent. Few would suspect that by this arrangement the federal bureaucracy, which would govern the health care providers of that minority population, would in reality be regulating the entire industry—every hospital and every doctor—because no provider could survive without serving a population that consumes a third of the industry's production. It was against the articulate spokesmen for that proposal, Senator Hubert Humphrey and labor leader Walter Ruether, that I would find myself debating on national television. The debate still rages today because the goal of complete socialization has not yet been achieved. But few realize that the economics lesson learned by President Truman when he attempted to regulate the consumer markets following World War II is the same lesson that begs to be learned in the medical marketplace today. As will be detailed in later chapters, government controls under Medicare have caused the very dislocations within the medical marketplace that now stir demands for a government solution to the health care crisis.

The debate no longer centers on whether socialism can work or not because the word "socialism" has been dropped in favor of "liberalism." John Dewey, who headed the League for Industrial Democracy until his death in 1952, expressed the determination of those who believe in the goal of socialism religiously—but have determined to call it something else—when he prophesized: "We are in for some kind of socialism, call it by whatever name we please, and no matter what it will be called when it is realized."[18]

————————/\————————

CHAPTER 3

Fighting for Noble Traditions

I knew Claude Pepper before moving to Miami, having taken care of members of his family in Tallahassee. He was a Harvard-educated lawyer from Alabama practicing in Tallahassee, and a fascinating individual. In 1920, long before I came to Florida, he had served in the Florida state senate representing a backwoods panhandle district, but failed to get reelected, so they said, because he voted against a resolution to condemn the First Lady of the United States, Mrs. Herbert Hoover, for inviting a black man to a White House tea.

The Jesuit fathers responsible for my education at Detroit and Milwaukee made it clear from the beginning that we are all God's children, but no matter where a physician is educated or reared, he or she soon learns for himself or herself the precious nature of human life, regardless of race. At Tallahassee all of the private doctors volunteered for rotating shifts at the county's free clinic where we cared for great numbers of poor blacks (as well as poor whites) who lived under the lingering encumbrance of the Old South. I thought Mr. Pepper's motives commendable and I genuinely admired the gentleman when he asked for my support, which I gave without reservation, in his quest for a seat in the United States Senate in 1938.

I would later become dismayed at the actions of Senator Pepper when he led a fight for passage of the bill to socialize medical care put forth by the newly reborn Americans for Democratic Action. Claude Pepper was fully aware of the long hours we doctors devoted without pay to make certain that everybody got adequate medical care in his home town. He nevertheless argued as a member of the Senate Education and Labor Committee (which was debating the bill) that Americans were in poor health because of economic barriers to adequate care, and made the even more outlandish charge, still used today, that the private system was "inefficient and wasteful" compared to a government-run system. At that time, before the federal bureaucracy intervened in medicine, the administrative cost of a doctor's office was negligible, especially when it came to serving the indigent because in such cases nobody even bothered to write out a bill.

The testimony that followed demonstrated just how wanton Pepper's charges were. The cost of health insurance through Blue Cross-Blue Shield at that time was about the same per day as a pack of cigarettes or a bottle of beer. And in those days, before the welfare state brought about our horrendous crime explosion and drug abuse, it was easy to demonstrate how remarkably well our medical system was working, especially when compared to the socialist systems of Europe. Life expectancy had risen from forty-nine years at the turn of the century to sixty-eight years by 1949, and the United States enjoyed lower death rates than England, Germany, and Sweden. Furthermore, since diphtheria was a deadly disease for which there was a known cure and means for prevention, it was used to compare the efficiency of medical care delivery directly: The American death rate was half that of England and Germany. A noteworthy incident at those hearings was the jubilation demonstrated by Senator Pepper on July 3, 1947, at the appearance of one witness whose testimony parroted Pepper's own absurdities. As it turned out, the witness, Ernest N. Rymer, represented the Communist International Workers Order.

Senator Pepper also fought to make wartime price controls a permanent feature of a centrally planned peacetime economy, along with the public school systems, which at that time were locally controlled with an excellent reputation the world over. This occurred shortly after Senator Pepper announced he would support Henry Wallace's presidential bid and joined the chorus of Wallace supporters calling for massive U.S. aid to the Soviet Union. (When Wallace bolted the Democratic party, Pepper joined the desperate ADA search for an alternative Democratic candidate to oppose Truman.)

In another instance, Floridians looked on in shocked disbelief as their senator in Washington departed for Moscow despite the delicate postwar situation. By that time, it was fully evident that Joseph Stalin had perpetrated atrocities against humanity far in excess of even those committed by the monster we had just defeated, Adolf Hitler. Yet, Pepper proceeded to the Kremlin and met with Joseph Stalin. On his return, his comments were carried in the *New York Times*, among other newspapers. Meeting Stalin was a "great honor," Pepper claimed. ". . . I do not believe the Russians have any aggressive intentions." Pepper also opposed the Truman Doctrine which granted military aid to Greece and Turkey to defend against a threatened communist takeover by Russian troops; he argued that the communist threat to those countries was due to "legitimate grievances."

Subsequently, another of my Jaycee friends, Congressman George Smathers of Miami, announced that he would oppose Claude Pepper for the United States Senate. Congressman Smathers had once served on Senator Pepper's staff, and he too was distressed by the left turn Pepper had taken. George Smathers and his supporters asked me if I would take an active role in his behalf, and this effort set the stage for the sequence of events that ultimately led to my election as president of the American Medical Association.

The year was 1950, and the professional environment at that time forbade physicians from advertising or participating in events attracting media attention in a manner that could be construed as promotional—therefore, unethical. The feeling was that professional recognition would come to those who earned it by virtue of competence and achievement. Until the push to socialize medicine in the 1940s, the American Medical Association devoted itself solely to the education and ethics of physicians and avoided any participation in matters of a political nature; the only publicity in which the AMA engaged concerned the promotion of public health standards and public education on healthy lifestyles.

But the policy of the AMA was also to make certain that anybody who needed medical care could get it whether or not he or she could pay for it. The AMA therefore encouraged voluntary health insurance for those able to pay, and worked with government to assure that the finest facilities would be available to treat those who could not. Then, when programs were being promoted in Washington to make government responsible for the care of self-sufficient people as well as the indigent, programs that would disrupt the market equilibrium in delivering health care, programs that would inflate administrative costs and disrupt the practice of medicine with obtrusive federal bureaucracies, the AMA bowed to the political realities of the day and opened a Washington office to lobby in Congress.

I was living in Miami when Congressman Smathers asked me to campaign for him, and given the tradition of avoiding publicity, I requested a meeting with the executive committee of the Dade County Medical Association. In a nutshell, I told them that Senator Pepper had become closely associated with left-wing factions of the labor movement and their demands for socialized medicine, and that if it were possible, Senator Pepper should be replaced. I explained that I had been called upon to use the radio as well as to make public appearances in behalf of Congressman Smathers and I did not want to do so without their approval. After long discussion I was called in and told they agreed, because I would, in fact, be rendering a public service by calling attention to a genuine threat to American freedom. This was an unprecedented decision on the part of the medical profession.

I spoke before civic clubs all over the state, and my radio presentations in behalf of Congressman Smathers were repeated time and time again. This activity having once been approved, the idea spread throughout the Florida Medical Association. It led others to establish the Florida Medical Committee for Better Government, and from that day on, doctors were silent no longer. I even got a call from some friends in Wisconsin who had become increasingly concerned about the activities of their own congressman, Representative Andrew Biemiller, a man with whom Senator Pepper had collaborated closely in the effort to socialize medicine. I flew up to Milwaukee to share my findings about the two men so that my friends could organize a campaign to replace Biemiller, which they did. (Walter Reuther was close to Biemiller, and after the election Reuther set him up as the chief Washington lobbyist for the AFL-CIO; with a staff of almost two hundred, it was the most powerful lobby in the nation.)

We were also successful in our Florida campaign; George Smathers defeated Senator Pepper in the Democratic primary by a landslide and won the Senate seat in the general election that followed (Florida had few Republicans in those days). Of the many events during that campaign, one stands out prominently in my mind.

One evening, accompanied by my wife Betty, I drove to a hotel in downtown Miami that housed a radio station where I had been scheduled to speak. As Betty and I approached the hotel we encountered Claude Pepper who was just leaving, having made his own presentation. In the truly magnanimous manner that characterized our relationship, Claude greeted me, gave his best wishes to Betty, and said he knew I was going in there to make a speech in behalf of his opponent, but he believed differences of opinion made this country great and he strongly supported my right to oppose him and his ideas.

I cannot explain why a man who so loved our constitutional freedoms did not feel the same freedoms should be allowed the citizens of democratic Czechoslovakia and the rest of Eastern Europe, which lay in the path of Stalin's murderous march, which march Senator Pepper would have had the American taxpayer finance. Nor can I explain why Claude Pepper wanted to alter our way of life so radically as to have it correspond with those societies where no such freedoms existed. I believe that Claude had good intentions but that a prejudicial mindset based upon a false premise had impaired his judgment. Owing to our rights, the people of Florida were able to deny him another term in office.

In 1962, congressional reapportionment created a new House seat that encompassed Miami Beach, with a large population of retired senior citizens, and the inner-city area of Miami, with a large black population. This constituted the most liberal congressional district in the state, and it was here, with the backing of an extremely liberal daily newspaper, that Claude Pepper made his political comeback. He kept the seat for decades, eventually becoming one of the most powerful House members as chairman of the Rules Committee.

As a freshman in 1962 he picked up right where he had left off in the Senate in the late 1940s: he championed the socialization of medicine, a fight which is carried on today by a commission named in his honor, the Pepper Commission, chaired by Senator Jay Rockefeller. Congressman Pepper fought for the "Great Society" programs of Lyndon Johnson and for federal involvement in public schools, which, as will be brought out in subsequent chapters, have created unbearable stress and inflation for our health care system that will last for generations to come. About the only difference between the old Pepper and the new was that the new Pepper had converted to the religion of anticommunist "liberalism": to bury his history of Marxist flirtations, he was placed on the House Select Committee on Un-American Activities. Pepper also became chairman of the House Select Committee on Aging, in which capacity he championed the expansion of Medicare to provide free eyeglasses, free hearing aids, and free dentures—even for millionaires.

On those many occasions when I would encounter Congressman Pepper socially, I would rib him about his voting record: "Claude, you vote for every federal program to give something away for nothing, then you vote against every measure to pay for it." He took it in good humor, but in fact more and more able-bodied Americans look to the federal government to take care of their needs, while we mount greater and greater deficits for future generations to pay.

THE CIRCUS COMES TO TOWN

With the specter of socialism in America on the wane, the decade of the 1950s was indeed a golden time to practice medicine and for our prosperous American society in general. Florida Governor LeRoy Collins had appointed me to the budget committee of Dade County; I also worked on the Senior Citizens Division of the Welfare Planning Council of Dade County and served on the county's Hospital Advisory Board. During this period, I was honored with the Brotherhood Award of the National Conference of Christians and Jews.

But it soon became apparent that the Americans for Democratic Action had been hard at work. During those golden years the ADA had recouped lost ground in Congress, and although it endeavored to permeate both major political parties, it succeeded overwhelmingly only in the Democratic party which had taken control of both houses of Congress by 1956. During the Eisenhower years the ADA sought legitimacy and support from the public with innocent-looking flyers belying the socialist nature of its programs and its radical origins. These flyers heralded the new anticommunist "liberalism" with statements indicating that the ADA "welcomes as members only those whose devotion to democracy is genuine. That means no Communists or fascists." Even Hubert Humphrey sponsored legislation to outlaw the Communist party in America. The same flyer claimed that the ADA sought "free enterprise coupled with government responsibility for full employment and rising standards of living." Who could argue with that? "Socialists" had become passe; there were only conservatives, "liberals," and diminishing numbers of Communists in America.

The issue of socialized medicine would, I knew, reappear, although the "socialist" label would be scrubbed. When it resurfaced it had taken form under the Fabian doctrine of gradualness; only those over the age of sixty-five would be covered. Although attempts were made to conceal its socialist tracks through the Social Security mechanism, it was clear the federal government would end up the sole financier of medical coverage for all eligible to enroll, and it was clear that government would end up regulating all providers of health care services.

By the late 1950s, we had had ample opportunity to observe socialized medicine in other countries, and while doctors fared quite well with good pay and shorter hours, patients didn't fare nearly so well. As the British like to point out, Americans are separated from the British by a common language, and through that jovial bond, the respective medical professions kept in close contact. American doctors knew of the increasing problems in Britain under socialized medicine—government-rationed health care, deteriorating facilities, and technological obsolescence—but, nevertheless, the American press increasingly touted the British system as a roll model for America. (Many years later, a study of the problems in Britain was commissioned by the Brookings Institution in conjunction with Tufts University School of Medicine.[1] The Brookings Institution is a think tank that cannot be accused of conservatism, and this work clearly demonstrated the pains taken by the authors to be accurate and fair, always giving the benefit of doubt to the British system. The findings shattered the argument for socialized health care in America, as will be detailed in a later chapter.)

Owing to my vocal reputation following the Smathers vs. Pepper campaign, I received calls from both the Florida Medical Association and the Dade County Medical Association asking that I represent the profession at a congressional hearing. Patrick McNamara, a chief of the pipe fitters' union in Detroit who had been elected to the U.S. Senate, was conducting hearings around the country to investigate alleged medical neglect of older Americans in support of a renewed socialization effort in Congress. The first hearing was scheduled for Boston; Miami was next. This promised to be a regular road-show with the unions orchestrating the acts. The charges were every bit as idiotic as those brought at the hearings of the 1940s by former Senator Pepper and his friend from the Communist International Workers Order. Before the federal government interceded, American medical societies from top to bottom always saw to it that anyone who sought care got it without regard to ability to pay.

About six weeks before the hearing I heard from a fellow Family Services board member that McNamara had sent a front man to town, Sidney Spector, to find witnesses who would testify to their neglect at the hands of the private medical profession. I thought at the time that this would prove interesting because I knew nobody of that description. I heard that Mr. Spector and crew were prepping the witnesses, telling them what to say and how to act. On the day this circus came to town, I was not the least bit surprised to find that former Senator Claude Pepper was on hand to help organize and testify, and that they had flown in Dr. Townsend, an Eastern academic socialist, one of few medical doctors in the entire nation who would testify in favor of socializing medicine. (In fact, he published the Townsend Plan, his own plan to socialize medicine.) The audience had been brought in by chartered buses from local nursing homes—all senior citizens on an outing, all well rehearsed by the front men who cued them when to applaud.

On the first day of the hearings McNamara called his star witness, a sweet, gentle, elderly lady who lived in a Protestant nursing home. She testified that her only source of income was Social Security, and that her only child was a daughter in Ohio who, with her husband and children, did not help in her support and care. In response to a carefully worded question by Senator McNamara, she said that if the need arose, she would not be able to pay for a hospital or a doctor.

I was permitted to make a statement at the hearing on behalf of the doctors of my area. When I was called, I asked if I could pose some questions to the lady who had testified, and the startled chairman acceded to my unusual request. First I asked her where she lived, and again she indicated a certain Protestant nursing home. I asked her if she had ever undergone surgery, and she confirmed that she had. I asked where, and she said at Mercy Hospital, a privately funded Catholic Hospital. I asked whether she had gotten a bill from the hospital, and she said that she had not. I asked if she remembered her heart doctor, and she said that she did and praised Dr. St. Mary who had come to see her every single day of her dozen days of hospitalization. I asked if Dr. St. Mary had sent a bill, and she said no. I asked if she remembered the doctor who put her to sleep for the operation, and she went on about what a wonderful man he was, and how he had checked on her every day too. And again, no, she had not gotten a bill from him. Before I could ask my next question she blurted out, "Dr. Annis, you and Dr. Martin never billed me for the surgery either!"

At that point I turned to Senator McNamara and told him that I objected, not only as a representative of the doctors of Florida, but also as a citizen, to the many false allegations he had put into the record the day before. I reminded the committee that I had been appointed by Governor LeRoy Collins to chair the statewide committee which ensured that nobody in Florida lack proper medical care when sought. I told them that under the program which we had devised—and similar programs that had been established in the other states—the state reimbursed hospitals, and the doctors of Florida provided their services without charge to anyone who could not afford to pay. This program had been in force for more than twelve years at the time and it worked well.

I learned from a friend later that the Washington office of the American Medical Association had sent an observer, a former newspaperman, to monitor the hearings. When he returned to headquarters he reported, "They've got a doctor down in Florida who doesn't care what he says, even to a United States senator, when he knows he's right."

A short time thereafter the AMA organized a speakers' bureau for the first time, and I was invited to join. I accepted and went to Chicago for a training session. They had a television studio set up to practice interviews, but at the session those in charge decided I needed no more training and I was asked if I would accept engagements to speak on behalf of the AMA, which I did.

I answered calls to appear on locally televised debates and programs all around the country. I debated Senator Jacob Javits of New York—one of the few Republicans involved in the Americans for Democratic Action—who had sponsored his own bill to socialize medical care. I also debated Wisconsin Senator William Proxmire and I met Senator McNamara in debate on the *Forum of the Air* in Washington D. C.

THE MOLDING OF A CANDIDATE

With the Republican presidential nomination going to Vice President Richard Nixon, it was apparent that John Kennedy, with his moderate record in the Senate and his Yankee origins, would be unable to attract much of the traditionally conservative vote in the general election of 1960. Since the soon-to-be nominee of the Democratic party needed the backing of the Left in order to win the general election, the ADA determined to make this a replay of 1948—they had their man at last and they would mold him like putty. John Kennedy would be beholden to the left-wing activists with their proven mobilization capabilities if he wanted the presidency—and he *wanted* the presidency. With John Kennedy's full backing, the ADA, an organization he had previously kept at a distance, was able to take control of the Democratic party's convention long before it met.

Several months after the hearings in Miami, another road show appeared with all the same acts. This one was hosted by New York's former governor Averell Harriman, longtime supporter of the Americans for Democratic Action, and it was under the auspices of the Democratic party's preplatform hearings. Again, the charter buses showed up filled with senior citizens on a field trip from their nursing homes. Claude Pepper testified that everyone sixty-five and over should receive a government check for $100 a month, whether they needed it or not, and he insisted that Social Security should provide health insurance for everybody, whether they needed it or not. I had to remind Claude that the Supreme Court had validated the Social Security Act as "welfare" supported by taxes, and that it was neither insurance nor actuarially sound, having wound up $1.7 billion in the red the year before. The taxpayers of America did not need to be burdened with paying welfare to the rich.

None of this made any difference to the orchestrators. In the past, platform hearings provided an opportunity for the many diverse elements within the party to work out their differences in a democratic forum. Although the official platform hearings were scheduled to begin July 5, 1960, Democratic National Chairman Paul Butler announced at the annual convention of the American Medical Association in Miami the month before that the platform would contain a "Forand-type" approach to federal health care financing, one of the several intermediate steps to full socialization under Social Security.

How did Chairman Butler know what the platform committee

was going to decide a month before it met? Leaders of the ADA had taken over the "democratic" process and had determined ahead of time what the outcome would be. With Kennedy's backing, a founding member and past vice chairman of the ADA, Representative Chester Bowles of Connecticut, was made chairman of the party's Resolutions and Platform Committee, and he alone appointed the subcommittee to draft the platform. Bowles made himself chairman and he appointed his close crony, former Solicitor General Philip Perlman, vice chairman of the subcommittee. He also appointed Joseph Rauh, founding father and national chairman of the ADA, to the subcommittee. The platform was written behind closed doors long before the convention in Los Angeles, and it contained many planks that had appeared and reappeared on the ADA's platforms for years. As Mr. Rauh later said: "We got everything we asked for, and it was so easy."[2] LeRoy Collins was permanent chairman of the Democratic convention, but the situation was well out of his control.

Dr. R. B. Robins, a trustee of the American Medical Association and a Democratic national committeeman from Arkansas, arranged for me to be allotted fifteen minutes to make a statement at the official hearing of the Democratic platform committee. Vice Chairman Perlman presided as I listened to witness after witness, each carefully selected by the committee, testify to the marvelous things the nation could expect from the federal programs they were touting; each witness was greeted warmly and listened to without interruption. At the previous hearings I had testified that the records indicated only 4 million of the nation's 16 million elderly would have difficulty meeting medical bills, if, that is, they ever received them. (I would again question the wisdom of creating a federal program to provide "free" health insurance to all the aged, and ask whether they would use the same logic to provide "free" food, housing, and clothing to all 16 million if it could be shown that only 4 million had difficulty paying for these necessities.)

At 4:15 P.M. when I was called, I could hardly get out a sentence without Mr. Perlman interrupting. At one point I read from the transcript of a speech given by Walter Reuther in which he stated that the legislation being supported was not an end in itself, but a step in the right direction (meaning that full socialization would come later).

At this point James B. Carey of the Electrical Workers union stood up from the audience to complain that the American Medical Association was not a member of the AFL-CIO and that I had no right to speak for them. Of course, Mr. Carey had no right to speak at all since he was neither testifying nor a member of the platform committee. But Perlman, for the first time since I was called, did not object. That satisfied me because it gave me the opportunity publicly to debate (the hearings were covered by radio and TV) one of the nation's foremost promoters of socialistic policies at that time.

When it was all over, my allotted fifteen minutes had become an hour and fifteen minutes. They would have been much wiser to have let me make a statement as originally agreed.

In order to keep the confidence of the left wing and secure their support in the presidential election, John Kennedy had to convince them that he would adhere to the platform handed him once elected. What those assurances were became apparent after he was elected—incidentally, by the slimmest margin in history. The cabinet post most sought after by the left wing, because it provided the greatest opportunity for "socializing" society, was head of the Department of Health, Education and Welfare (HEW). That coveted secretaryship went to ADA disciple Abraham Ribicoff, to whom the young president was deeply indebted for serving as his floor manager at the Democratic convention. At the president's right hand as his "special assistant" would be Harvard history professor Arthur Schlesinger, Jr., a founder of the ADA.

Schlesinger's words in *Partisan Review* in 1947 embodied the Fabian doctrine of gradualness that characterized the ADA platform thrust upon the new administration: "If socialism is to preserve democracy, it must be brought about step by step in a way which will not disrupt the fabric of custom . . . the transition must be piecemeal; it must be parliamentary; it must respect civil liberties and the due process of law." And from another passage: "Socialism, then, appears quite practicable within this frame of reference, as a long-term proposition. . . . The active agents in effecting the transition will probably be, not the working class, but some combination of lawyers, business and labor managers, politicians and intellectuals, in the manner of the first New Deal, or of the Labor government in Britain."

Other prominent ADA devotees who gained high office included HEW under secretary Ivan Nestingen, HEW assistant secretary Wilbur Cohen (an architect of socialized medicine since the initial push in the 1940s), Agriculture secretary Orville Freeman, Agriculture under secretary Charles Murphy, Labor secretary Arthur Goldberg (subsequently appointed to the Supreme Court), Labor assistant secretary George Weaver, Under Secretary of State Chester Bowles (who chaired the platform committee), Assistant Secretary of State Mennen Williams, Ambassador-at-Large Averell Harriman, India ambassador John Kenneth Galbraith, UN ambassador Eleanor Roosevelt, NATO ambassador Thomas Finletter, Peru ambassador James Loeb (whose leadership affiliation with the ADA went back through its predecessor organization, which began at the Socialist party), National Labor Relations Board chairman Frank McCulloch, UN Trusteeship Council representative Jonathan Bingham, Federal Power commissioner Howard Morgan, Export Import Bank director George Docking, and many more.

Some reports listed up to forty-five members of the Americans for Democratic Action in important posts of the new administration. That was quite a price our young president had to pay for their support, considering he was on record during his tenure in Congress as saying: "I never joined the Americans for Democratic Action . . . I'm not comfortable with those people."[3]

Before leaving office, President Eisenhower had signed into law a bill that was supported by the American Medical Association known as the Kerr-Mills legislation, named after its sponsors in Congress. It provided federal matching funds for state-administered programs helping the aged who could not afford costly medical care. It provided federal funds at a 50–50 ratio for wealthy states up to a split of 85–15 for poorer states like Mississippi, and it did not require beneficiaries to be destitute, only that they be unable to afford private health insurance.

This program galled the left-wing socializers because the beneficiaries had to demonstrate a need in order to qualify for government aid. They branded it "reactionary." And they claimed that since health care was a "right," nobody should have to demonstrate a need for it—no one needed to qualify for a right. This demonstrated just how radical the socializers were since surely an individual ought to show that he or she needs assistance before qualifying for care at taxpayer expense.

The only possible explanation for the vehement opposition to Kerr-Mills was that it would not lead to full socialism. Kerr-Mills drew the line at helping those who needed help and allowed states the flexibility to meet local needs. Since administration of Kerr-Mills was not centered at the federal level the bureaucracy would be unable to exert governmental control.

With the new administration came a new bill, or more correctly, a new version of the same old bill which had made its way from the Socialist party platform to the UDA, the ADA, the Democratic party platform, and then to Congress where it was defeated in the 1940s. The very same bureaucrats who had fought for the original plan collaborated to modify the bill to meet the Fabian doctrine of gradualism.

Wilbur Cohen and Isadore Falk, formally of the Federal Security Agency during the 1940s, worked with Robert Ball of the Social Security Administration and Nelson Cruikshank of the AFL-CIO to pare the original bill down. Wilbur Cohen, about whom Marjorie Shearon published the book *Wilbur Cohen: Pursuit of Power*, and against whom she testified at his confirmation hearing (to no avail), was one of the members of the ADA assigned to a high HEW post in the new Kennedy administration. Like Max Lerner and so many other disciples of liberalism as ministered by the ADA, Wilbur Cohen is listed in the *Biographical Dictionary of the Left* as having been previously active in several Communist-dominated organizations. The AFL-CIO's Cruikshank, in his earlier days, had been described in a Brookings Institution study thus: "A socialist in the 1930s with views so advanced that they were hard for the Methodist Church to tolerate in one of its ministers, Cruikshank was committed to the work of promoting social legislation, social insurance particularly."[4] Cruikshank was active in the Union for Democratic Action (the Socialist party breakaway), and continued with the group through its name change to the Americans for Democratic Action. Cruikshank, through the AFL-CIO's Washington lobbyist, former Wisconsin Representative Andrew Biemiller, had the bill sponsored in Congress by Rhode Island Representative Aime Forand, who later admitted he had not even read it when he complied.

The Forand bill died before the end of the Eisenhower administration, but when the new Congress convened, its body was resurrected under the sponsorship of Senator Clinton Anderson of New Mexico and Representative Cecil King of California. Known as the King-Anderson bill, it was officially supported by the new administration. King-Anderson was exactly described by Dr. Leonard Larson, president of the American Medical Association at the time of its introduction: "[T]he administration's medical care proposal, if enacted, would certainly represent the first major, irreversible step toward the complete socialization of medical care ... The King-Anderson program does not provide insurance or prepayment of any type, but compels one segment of our population to underwrite a socialized program of health care for another, regardless of need."[5]

It is interesting to note that King-Anderson, which became known as Medicare, required workers of that day to pay for the health care of 16 million senior citizens who had not paid a nickel into the system that would support them, the vast majority of whom were self-supporting and paying their own health bills (7.7 million already had their own private health insurance; health insurance was itself a relatively new concept).

Since it was impossible to argue that the proposed legislation would in some way benefit the workers of America, the union leadership embarked on a smear campaign against the American Medical Association to discredit its opposition to King-Anderson. Union bosses organized and financed the National Council of Senior Citizens, and labor's obedient lackey in Congress, Aime Forand, became its first chairman in 1961 after leaving office; Blue Carstenson from HEW, himself a former union executive, became its first executive director.

The press made it sound as if the 2 million members of the National Council of Senior Citizens favored King-Anderson, but in reality the "spontaneous" support was just a political campaign launched by the union bosses and paid for with union dues. If ever there was legislation *not* in the best interest of union workers, that legislation was King-Anderson; i.e., Medicare.

The AFL-CIO, through its massive political war chest financed by the dues of its members—and of nonmembers who worked for unionized firms and were obligated to pay dues under the law—also created the Committee on Political Education (COPE), which would serve as the labor bosses' weapon to promote political candidates and legislative proposals. It was commonly known that Walter Reuther ruled COPE, and its officers served at his pleasure. In 1960, COPE published and distributed a series of lies and misrepresentations about the American Medical Association, and the lies were aired by the mainstream press throughout the country without a trace of documentation.[6] According to COPE's smear campaign, the AMA's opposition to public health measures was driven by greed and its "reactionary" political posture. There were sixteen such distortions published. A small sampling follows:

COPE: "A generation ago, the AMA opposed the requirement that all cases of tuberculosis be reported to a public authority—the foundation for all T.B. control methods." (FACT: As early as 1899 the AMA commissioned a study on the nature of TB, the means of control, the extent of public education, and the advisability of establishing state sanitariums. Those efforts continued through the years, and in 1944 the AMA issued this resolution: "[I]t is necessary to extend procedures for careful, continuous supervision of TB by practicing physicians, who, in cooperation with duly constituted health authorities, federal, state and local, are in a position to deal with these problems by modern methods to prevent the spread of this communicable disease.")

COPE: "The AMA opposed the National Tuberculosis Act a week before Congress passed it unanimously." (FACT: The AMA was in sympathy with the purposes of the bill, but opposed the regulation of appropriations by the federal bureaucracy when direct aid to needy communities was available under the Lanham Act.)

COPE: "The AMA fought compulsory vaccination for smallpox." (FACT: As far back as 1899 the AMA resolved to urge the boards of health of every community to enact requirements for compulsory smallpox vaccinations and has supported that policy ever since.)

COPE: "The AMA opposed the Social Security Act, passed in 1935." (FACT: The AMA has never taken a stand on the Social Security Act; the AMA never takes positions on legislation unless it concerns the delivery of quality medical care to the people. The AMA only objected to using Social Security in order to socialize medicine in the mid-1940s.)

COPE: "The AMA fought the American Red Cross plan to set up a nation-wide reserve of civilian blood banks." (FACT: The AMA worked closely with the Red Cross to establish the national blood program, beginning in 1947 with official approval for the development of the Red Cross Plan and culminating in 1954 with the AMA's adoption of the program.

The union organizations set up road-shows across America— rallies orchestrated by front men with busloads of nursing home residents—and the speech makers referred to doctors opposed to King-Anderson as "liars" working in their own "self-interests," dubbing them "blackmailers" and "witch doctors" in the process.

Kerr-Mills was the law of the land, passed overwhelmingly by both houses of Congress, and it was the duty of the administration to carry out the law. Yet, under the new administration, Wilbur Cohen and Ivan Nestingen, together with other HEW bureaucrats, went all across the country at taxpayer expense to campaign for the partisan political issue of King-Anderson and to berate the Kerr-Mills law they were expected to uphold. Soon the press had the public believing that there was some sort of "health care crisis" in the land, although we had the finest and most cost effective health care the world had ever known. A health care crisis was exactly what we wanted to avoid.

CHAIRMAN WITHOUT A CHAIR

Shortly after the introduction of the King-Anderson bill, I got a call from the headquarters of the American Medical Association asking if I would care to go on national television to debate the proposal with Senator Hubert Humphrey, reputedly the most skillful debator on Capitol Hill. I jumped at the opportunity knowing that Senator Humphrey was a popular politician who would draw a sizable television audience, exactly the kind of exposure we needed to counter the beating we were taking in the press. We would appear on the NBC television show "The Nation's Future" with John Mc-Caffery moderating.

Soon after agreeing to the debate, I got another call from the AMA asking if I would accept the title of chairman of the Speakers' Bureau. Since the Speakers' Bureau did not hold meetings, I would be a chairman without a chair. But it seems that someone from NBC had said they couldn't ask Senator Humphrey to debate a nobody. Thus, upon hanging up, I had the satisfaction, for the first time, of being a *somebody*.

When I stood before the cameras next to Senator Humphrey on Saturday evening, January 14, 1961, I was well armed with facts and figures—the American Medical Association had engaged the most knowledgeable economists and analysts to examine the King-Anderson bill before deciding to oppose it. Today, some thirty-odd years later, I can attest that everything that I predicted would happen if the bill became law did happen. Among other predictions, the push to socialize the entire medical system is on, with a vengeance. Conversely, the exact opposite of what Senator Humphrey predicted came true.

In my assessment that night I pointed out that "the growth of insurance, private insurance funds, savings accounts, and investments is a testament of the recognition on the part of the American people that the prime responsibility for their financial security rests with the people and not with the government." And now, nearly thirty years after the enactment of the Great Society programs, our nation is in a savings crisis, industry is suffering a lack of capital commitment, our automobiles are built in plants over sixty years old, and able-bodied Americans increasingly look to government to take care of their everyday needs. Moreover, the socialistic politics of the union bosses have contributed more to the decline of union membership than any other factor; an undercapitalized economy cannot support union demands for better pay and benefits.

Senator Humphrey asserted that the exact costs of King-Anderson had been determined and would be budgeted precisely. He could not have been more wrong: by 1980 the program cost ten times the original estimate.

Senator Humphrey also contended that there would be no bureaucratic intrusion into the practice of medicine and that administrative costs would decrease under the Social Security system. He even claimed that contemporary Social Security administrative costs were low at 2 percent for managing retirement benefits compared to 5 percent for some private companies. Where those figures came from, I don't know. Most no-load mutual funds today manage the retirement savings of investors for under 1 percent, and considering Social Security was deep in the red at the time, there was no money in the so- called "trust fund" to manage. Even when there is a theoretical balance in the Social Security fund, there is still nothing to manage because the federal government simply spends the money and gives the trust fund an IOU. New York Senator Moynihan has an appropriate word for this process, he calls it "thievery."

One need only look at an actual hospital bill issued in the days before government-regulated health care to realize just how wrong Senator Humphrey was about bureaucratic intrusion and overall administrative costs. Guided by nothing other than common sense in management, hospitals kept administrative costs to a minimum by charging for room and board by the day, and private insurers, also guided by their own common sense, accepted these logical bills as proper evidence for reimbursement on claims.

Today, under federal bureaucratic micromanagement, hospitals must track and charge for every single aspirin and every single band-aid, and every physician's office is subjected to the same senseless intrusions that drive costs up astronomically. Former Surgeon General C. Everett Koop estimated on the MacNeil/Lehrer production "Hard Choices" that 26 percent of our current health bill is spent on administrative costs. That's more than is paid to all the doctors in the country combined, and that excessive wastefulness is due solely to the bureaucratic demands ushered in by passage of Medicare.

Senator Humphrey also said that once King-Anderson was enacted, health insurance for those under sixty-five would become cheaper. Health insurance did not become cheaper for anybody, of course; it increased dramatically. The huge federal handout of taxpayers' money not only created excessive demand and overuse, but also a tremendous opportunity for fraud by the unscrupulous few—like every massive federal program before it and since.

During the question-and-answer session of that debate, someone in the audience asked whether I was "concerned about the poor taxpayer that will pick up the tab or are you concerned about the doctors that probably will lose a fat morsel if the health program will be linked with Social Security." The notion that the greedy doctors were fighting King-Anderson because they would make less money became a recurring theme in the unions' campaign to smear the profession. But, in fact, doctors at that time were treating the needy without charge. After that I made it a point to predict that if King-Anderson became law, doctors' incomes would rise—and that is exactly what happened.

What concerned the leaders of the American Medical Association was the potential "monitarization" of the profession. Once people were no longer responsible for their own bills and once the federal government held out billions of dollars for the taking, our caring medical profession would become an insensitive business. They feared the consequences of the way patients might be treated in the future, they feared the type of entrepreneurs that might be drawn to the business, they feared that people would become numbers in a game of beat-the-system, and they feared that the one-on-one bond of trust between doctor and patient would be lost in a sea of financial scheming and tangled in bureaucratic red tape.

Doctors felt honored to be in a profession of noble traditions, and those traditions were worth a lot more to us than the taxpayers' money being held out for grabs. I never made a lot of money in the practice of medicine, but the rewards I derived from that practice were priceless. The value of those noble traditions were worth fighting to preserve.

I thought it somewhat ironic during that session that I would field a question from Nelson Cruikshank, one of the high lieutenants of the AFL-CIO's campaign to push King-Anderson. He asked if I believed that the people of this country had a right to choose the method whereby they would pay their medical bills. I told him yes, of course, but the people also had a right to know the facts before choosing.

The union manipulators, in fact, feared that their own membership might learn the facts. I had repeatedly requested to speak before union audiences only to be turned down or cancelled at the last minute. Then one day I got a break during a panel debate that was broadcast live with James Carey of the electrical workers as a fellow panelist. I asked him why I was never allowed to address the union membership, and in self-defense he said it would be fine with him if I spoke to his union; so we sealed the deal on the air.

On the day I addressed the union convention, I was scheduled to follow Walter Reuther at the podium. In his closing remarks he advised the assembly that a doctor would be addressing them and that they must be courteous, but not to pay too much attention because doctors don't tell the truth about some things. Fortunately, they were not paying much attention to him, for when I concluded I got an extended standing ovation, with the crowd chanting, "come back, come back." But the union bosses never allowed me to come back.

A few days after the debate with Senator Humphrey I stopped by the Washington office of my friend Senator George Smathers. George told me that Hubert had come by and asked, "George, why didn't you tell me about that friend of yours before the debate? The SOB knew more about that bill than I did!"

I developed a friendly relationship with Hubert Humphrey after that. On my frequent visits to Washington he always went out of his way to see me. I soon became convinced that unlike many people in the labor union movement and Congress, Hubert Humphrey honestly believed in what he was doing; he honestly believed that this country was so wealthy it could afford to provide the necessities of life as a "right" without requiring people to pay for them. He never questioned how America got to be so wealthy, he never appreciated the incentives of the free market system, nor the satisfaction that comes of self-sufficiency, causing people to work hard, and thus making this country great. He never understood that most self-sufficient people are willing to share their blessings to help those who cannot help themselves, but that when they become overburdened with taxation to support people who don't need help, it is the needy who suffer.

Walter Reuther, on the other hand, was basically motivated by power. Frankly, I was fascinated by the man; he was an intriguing study. He needed to be in control and he used radical political philosophy as a means to gain power. Reuther was a stern-looking man with piercing eyes who always tried to intimidate people, and usually succeeded. He was a victorious veteran of many violent union power struggles, and everywhere he went he had two bodyguards, one on each side.

Reuther was at the forefront of the movement of American leftists to disavow Communists. Not only was he clever enough to realize that the affluent and patriotic American worker would not knowingly revolt against his own freedoms, he also knew that organizers of Communist fronts were expected to take marching orders from the Kremlin and execute them with military discipline. And Walter Reuther was clearly destined to give orders, not to take them. Arthur Schlesinger, Jr., who worked with Reuther in the ADA, once prophesied of him: "Walter Reuther, the extraordinary able and intelligent leader of the United Auto Workers, may well become . . . the most powerful man in American politics."[7] That prophecy came true in the decade of the 1960s, and the people of America never even elected him to office.

Of all those involved in the struggle to pass King-Anderson, Walter Reuther wielded the most weight. He was the chief orchestrator of the campaign through his position in the Americans for Democratic Action and the AFL-CIO, and most importantly, through his domination of the federation's political battery, COPE. He never held public office, he never needed to; he just told the politicians what to do and they did it. Through his clout, he decided which politicians would get into (and out of) office, including the president himself, and which laws would be passed. He ruled the unions, he ruled the Congress, and he wanted to rule the people. But one cannot rule a society where the rights and responsibilities of individuals are respected. To afford the kind of power Walter Reuther craved, the people would have to depend upon government for the necessities of life, and to accomplish that end, the necessities of life would have to be dubbed "rights" which government would provide for "free." No longer would government's role be limited to aiding producers to care for those who could not care for themselves; government itself would become responsible for caring for everybody. Under such a system, those who produce the necessities of life become the servants of government, those who consume the necessities of life become dependents of government. Reuther wanted government to control and he wanted to control the government that controlled.

My debate with Hubert Humphrey had quite an impact on the nation. Television was still in its infancy with only three channels; about the only competition was wrestling and roller-derbying. Not long after my debate with Senator Humphrey I received a call from the AMA to say that Fred Friendly of CBS had called to set up a nationally televised debate between Walter Reuther and me on "Face the Nation"; the date was set for February 9, 1961. CBS was anxious to outdo the competition and Walter Reuther was anxious to put me in my place. (I believe that was a tactical error on his part, and although he promised to debate me again, he never would.) The debate became so heated that the moderator, Howard K. Smith, asked when the program had run its allotted time whether we would continue for another half hour so they could tape it to be shown on the next scheduled airing of "Face the Nation," which we did.

After the Reuther debate George Smathers told me that Senate Republican leader Everett Dirksen had asked to meet me. In my youthful naivete I walked right into Senator Dirksen's Washington office, not realizing what a busy man this stalwart of the Congress was. I opened the door to a long waiting room with two receptionists up front and perhaps forty or fifty people behind them waiting their turn to see the senator. Feeling a bit foolish I told the receptionist I would pay my respects the next time I was in town. She looked up and with a smile said, "Why Dr. Annis, do you want me to get fired?" With that she picked up the intercom and within a few moments Senator Dirksen emerged from his inner office, took me by the arm, and walked me out to the hallway.

Senator Dirksen was a tall man—at least from my perspective he was tall. Looking down at me he said with drawled but emphatic intonations, "You did good!" He explained that when a fellow gets to be a congressman, he starts feeling pretty important, and when he gets to be a senator with some seniority, he has some real influence. But when Walter Reuther comes to Washington, all those important senators and congressmen start bowing and scraping, "Yes sir Mr. Reuther . . . No sir Mr. Reuther . . . Whatever you say Mr. Reuther." He concluded by saying that I was the first person he ever saw shake a finger at Walter Reuther and say, "Mr. Reuther, that isn't true and you know it!" He told me he just wanted to meet me and encourage me to keep it up. I did.

THE MARTYRED PRESIDENT

During the following months I spoke in at least twenty-nine states. I spoke to anybody who would listen—women's clubs, Rotarian meetings, state legislatures. I did a lot of debating too, and I appeared on "Meet the Press" with Lawrence Spivack and on Ted Granick's "Theater of the Air." But, in truth, we at the AMA were amateurs at the political game. There were hundreds of doctors who pitched in, but we were just doctors, whereas the labor bosses were anything but laborers. Labor unions had been dominated by political extremists with powerful ambitions since before the turn of the century, and for the most part, the mainstream press was becoming sympathetic to their cause because college campuses had been radicalized and left-ist social theories had become the rage of journalism schools. The who, what, when, where, and how of news reporting was giving way to the new wave of advocacy journalism.

Dr. Larson, president of the American Medical Association, had tried repeatedly during those months to gain a private audience with the president of the United States, but to no avail. Nobody understood the White House refusal to meet with the opposition during a heated campaign over proposed legislation, so I asked Senator Smathers, who was on good terms with John Kennedy, to intercede. A meeting was set up for the Oval Office and I went with the delegation that included Drs. Larson and Blasingcame, the latter the executive vice president of the AMA, and Dr. Hussey, chairman of the AMA board of trustees and dean of the George-town University medical school. We decided that when the topic of Medicare, or King-Anderson as it was known then, came up, I would be the spokesman for the group.

The president greeted us in his magnanimous manner; in no way condescending, he was just as straightforward and likable as the guy next door. On his right side sat HEW Secretary Ribicoff and on his left another bureaucrat from HEW. President Kennedy told us his people had brought him a list detailing the many areas in which the AMA had been helpful to the administration. He turned page after page while expressing his appreciation for our assistance in providing physicians to the armed services, and in cooperating with the Food and Drug Administration, the Public Health Service, the Department of Agriculture, and on and on. Finally, when he had run out of pages to turn, he said, "Now we get to the problem of King-Anderson. I know there isn't anything I can say that will change your mind, and I'm sure there isn't anything you can say that will change mine."

I spoke up and said, "Well, Mr. President, why should we pass legislation to take care of everybody over sixty-five when only some of them need assistance?"

"But my people tell me we have the votes to pass it," the president replied.

"But, Mr. President, the question is not whether you have the votes, the question is whether it is a good policy for government to take care of everybody when only some need help."

With a grin on his face he leaned over his desk shaking his finger at me, just as I had done to Walter Reuther, and said, "Now, Dr. Annis, I know all about you from our friend Senator Smathers and I'm not about to debate you; you debate Secretary Ribicoff here." President Kennedy's humor was pertinent because I had been trying for a long time to debate Ribicoff, who kept backing out. A public debate had been scheduled to which he had agreed to appear with the official spokesman of the AMA, but when he learned that I was the appointed spokesman and not the current AMA president—a man with limited public speaking experience who had never debated in his life—Ribicoff cancelled, saying I was not the "official spokesman" of the AMA. Ribicoff, be it noted, refused to debate me even after I was elected president of the AMA.

I laughed with the president, then I continued, "There is a man in my hometown of Miami by the name of Arthur Vining Davis, allegedly a wealthy man." (Davis was an internationally known industrialist, head of ALCOA, and one of the world's wealthiest men.) "Mr. Davis is over ninety years old, and I'm sure if he got sick he would not mind paying his own hospital bill. Does it make good sense to force today's workers to pay his bills? Mr. President, I understand that there are members of your own family over the age of sixty-five who could afford to pay their own bills." (The president's multimillionaire father was in the hospital at the time.)

Quick as a wink, he shot back, "If he doesn't pay them I'll have to."

"So is it fair to tax workers trying to raise their own families to pay your father's bills?" I made my point as effectively as I could.

Without addressing my question and bearing the same grin as before, he said, "I told you I'm not going to debate you. You debate Secretary Ribicoff."

The meeting concluded, he followed us out of the study and gave me another warm handshake. He certainly harbored no animosities, and he gave no indication that he sincerely disagreed with our thinking. I was frankly baffled by his refusal to exchange ideas on King-Anderson. That is not the way a man who feels strongly about a subject responds, especially a president of the United States.

When I got to the airport I phoned Senator Smathers to thank him for the opportunity to meet the president. When he came on the line he told me he had already gotten a call from President Kennedy, and he relayed what the president had said, "George, how did you let that guy get out of the fold?"

Somebody in the Massachusetts Medical Society, apparently due to mistaken identity, received an invitation to attend a labor union political strategy meeting in March of 1962. From that meeting it was learned that King-Anderson had been given top priority— the union bosses wanted to force it to a vote in the Senate because they were losing ground in public opinion. All 150 Democrats in the Massachusetts legislature had already been contacted and committed to speaking out in favor of King-Anderson.

The same thing was taking place in every other state: Nationwide, five thousand public speeches had been scheduled over the following two months. Press coverage, radio, television, and the usual propaganda leaflets had all been arranged. An atmosphere of national crisis had been contrived, and the campaign would culminate with a nationally televised address by President John Kennedy at New York's Madison Square Garden on May 20, 1962; the arena would be packed with the unions' National Council of Senior Citizens. Similar rallies would be staged all across the nation in auditoriums where the president's message would be piped in, and in that way they would gain local news coverage showing local support all around the nation in addition to the national coverage of the main event. The president's address would also be carried live by all three television networks, free of charge as a "news event."

The American Medical Association requested equal time to deliver a rebuttal to the president's message, but all three television networks refused, saying that ours was a partisan political message. The AMA then decided to purchase the air time on a single network—a difficult decision because the AMA, contrary to popular belief, had only a small budget for lobbying and political campaigning. (At one point the AMA had to impose a special assessment of the membership just to combat the unions' campaign against it.)

In the meantime the AMA went to work on its own grass roots campaign to get our message out to everyday Americans, our patients. Ronald Reagan, before deciding to run for public office himself, was devoted to the fight against socialized medicine and he recorded his views for us which were played at coffee clutches organized through county medical societies nationwide. But in truth, no matter what we did our efforts were anemic in comparison to the other side. The ADA and union bosses had control of the majority party in Congress, the Democratic party, and even the presidency itself. The American Medical Association, by contrast, never desired to control anything except the delivery of first-class medical services.

Our only hope was that enough people would understand the logic in our message to overcome the hoop-la sponsored by union orchestrators. The problem was to overcome the drama of a presidential address, and that task went to the AMA's audio/visual director, Richard Reinauer. It was decided early on that I would deliver the rebuttal, but the question was how and where. Mr. Reinauer went to New York and came back with a freelance script writer and producer by the name of Harold Azine. Mr. Azine had vast experience, but I had never worked with a writer before; in fact, I rarely used a script. As it turned out Harold Azine was every bit as suspicious of me as I was of him: he was a liberal; he believed in socialized medicine; he supported John Kennedy.

Still, Harold Azine and I had a job to do, and I had to admire him; the man was a genius. He told us we were dead. There was simply no way we could out-hoopla the president, especially the charismatic John Kennedy. The best way to capture the imagination was not even to try to compete. He had a better idea. The drama of our message would arise from contrast—the insincerity of the professional political mobilizers vs. your trusted family doctor. Harold Azine told us to rent Madison Square Garden following the president's address, and leave everything just as it was—leave the presidential marquee in place, leave the banners and the balloons, and leave the tens of thousands of chairs empty. After all, who would come cheering your family doctor? I would be introduced as exactly what I was, a family doctor and surgeon. Alone on the empty stage in an empty auditorium I would tell my story, I would tell the American people the truth about King-Anderson, not a lot of political hyperbole, just the truth from the bottom of my heart.

Like all brilliant ideas, this one met some resistance at headquarters. Someone thought I should give the speech from the AMA headquarters in Chicago, someone else thought I should deliver it from my office in Miami. I thought the message would fizzle from either of those settings, and I told Mr. Azine I would call Chicago and help sell his idea, which I did. The plan had to be a complete surprise and the few who knew were sworn to secrecy. If word got out about our intended use of Madison Square Garden, we would be had; they would remove the banners and the president would say something to spoil it.

I wanted to get a feel for what the opposition was up to, so I arrived at Madison Square Garden early. The organization and the orchestration were magnificent. The place was professionally decorated—laden with banners made to look as if enthusiastic crowds had put them there. Thousands of balloons—red, white, and blue—were ready to be released. Then the chartered buses arrived, caravans of chartered buses, hundreds of them filled with retirees from the nursing homes of New York, Long Island, and New Jersey. Their union handlers gave each person a ticket as he or she got off the bus, then another was there ready with signs mounted on sticks, many of them designed to appear homemade, demanding Medicare—decent medical care for the elderly. I had seen it all before, the union handlers acting as cheerleaders, telling the people when to applaud, when to rise—as though overcome by the president's message.

I followed some inside and asked how they had heard about the rally, and they said the union people had told them. I asked them where they had gotten their tickets, and they said the union people had handed them out free. I asked what the rally was about, what Medicare was about, but no one knew much except that it had something to do with getting "free" medical care. I asked if any of them had trouble meeting their medical bills, but everyone I talked to already had medical insurance.

And so Madison Square Garden was filled with 18,000 boosters under the auspices of the National Council of Senior Citizens, as orchestrated by the AFL-CIO. (In the following days, the newspapers chided the AMA for using the wealth of its member doctors to rent the hall and buy television time to influence public opinion, whereas the hall for the president's speech had been funded by the senior citizens who paid a dollar each for tickets.)

I walked back to my hotel where I joined officers of the AMA to watch the president's speech on television. I listened intently, knowing that no matter how passionately I felt about the issue, cogent arguments could be made by the other side. There is always another viewpoint, and if anybody could deliver it effectively, it was President John F. Kennedy.

But I was bewildered again. The president's words fell flat, his speech was a flop. This is how it was reported later in *The New Yorker*: "President Kennedy stood before a capacity audience of 20,000 old people, smilingly accepted their long and enthusiastic welcome, and then put aside his prepared text to deliver one of the worst speeches of his career."[8] It confirmed my intuition gained at the Oval Office: this is a man who doesn't believe in his cause.

As I listened on I thought that his delivery would not really matter if those cunning people at the AFL-CIO and the ADA handed him something to trigger the compassion of the people, because Anericans are the most compassionate people in the world. The people would not tolerate even one legitimate example of neglect if told by the president that this was typical of what was happening under our system. But for years, Senator McNamara and bureaucrats of HEW had taken their road-shows all over the country, searching desperately for just such a case—unsuccessfully. When the president told his sorrowful tale, I thought I must have been listening with the wrong ear. For he told about the plight of a Massachusetts congressman whose father had been ill for the past two years, and the medical bills were so high that the congressman's daughter would be unable to attend her private boarding school in the fall.

Was the president joking? How could a U.S. congressman be so irresponsible as to allow his elderly father to go without medical insurance, whine about his inability to send his daughter to private boarding school, then demand that the working taxpayer foot the bill? Was this "horror story" really symptomatic of a "health care crisis"? As it turned out, our "health care crisis" was even less of a crisis than that silly-sounding hardship story made it appear: The story wasn't true! A newspaper reporter uncovered the facts a few days later. The congressman was Torbert Macdonald, a Harvard college buddy of the president; Congressman Macdonald's father had been sick for about four months, not two years; his father had full health insurance which paid the bills, no problem there; his daughter went off to boarding school as did her brother, just as planned. Yes, it appears the president *was* joking.

We were charged extra to rent Madison Square Garden without the cleanup crew coming through first. But the place was in perfect condition—perfect for our purposes, that is. Litter was everywhere, the banners were dangling, the balloons were still bobbing about, and many chairs were overturned. We taped my speech that night after the crowds had left, and I had the unique experience of seeing myself deliver it on prime time television the following night. It didn't seem to matter much that we were carried by only one network. For one thing, President Kennedy plugged our rebuttal when he mentioned in his final remarks that I would be speaking on television the next night. But I think the competition must have been wrestling and roller-derbying again, because the rating company said we had over 30 million viewers, one of the largest television audiences on record up to that time.

I spoke from the heart. I spoke about the noble traditions of my profession, about the many blessings of our free market system, about our American way of life and our sense of fair play. I spoke about how these noble traditions would change when government stepped in to assume responsibility for people who were already responsible for themselves, while ignoring those who really needed our help.

To those who questioned why doctors were so adamantly opposed to King-Anderson, I said, "Doctors will probably make more money, not less, under King-Anderson. Anyone knows there is more money in mass production." To those who believed that to qualify for government assistance was degrading, I asked, "When you apply for . . . public housing, don't you have to prove that your income is below a certain level? . . . Well, that's a means test, isn't it?" I then pointed out that King-Anderson would make government responsible for "everyone over sixty-five . . . That means everyone—the rich, the well-to-do and the comfortable . . . The American taxpayer, whose payroll tax would be hiked by as much as 17 percent to start with in order to pay for this program certainly has a right to question the free ride those who do not need these benefits would be taking at the expense of his children." Further, "This bill would put the government smack into your hospitals, defining services, setting standards, establishing committees, calling for reports, deciding who gets in and who gets out, what they get and what they don't, even getting into the teaching of medicine and all the time imposing a federally administered financial budget on our houses of mercy and healing."

And, finally, I predicted that it would "serve as the forerunner of a different system of medicine for all Americans . . . The King-Anderson crowd intends to take us all the way down the road to a new system of medicine for everybody . . . England's nationalized medical program is the kind of thing they have in mind for us eventually." As I read those words today I am not surprised, but appalled at how prophetic they were.

A day or two after delivering that speech to an empty auditorium, I still wondered whether anyone really heard it. At the time, I was at the Los Angeles airport waiting in line to board my airplane and I felt a tug on my coat. I looked down and an elderly lady in a wheelchair said, "Are you a doctor?"

"Yes," I replied.

"Are you from Florida?"

"Yes."

"I saw you talking to all those empty chairs, and I agree with you."

Then I got word from AMA headquarters. There had been an avalanche of mail; 42,000 letters had come in, over 90 percent of which were supportive of our position. I checked with my friends in Congress and they had the same report—more mail than they had ever seen before, and it was overwhelmingly in our favor. Lots of others were moved by the speech and the ensuing debates, and by all the other efforts doctors across the country had exerted to get our message out.

A year earlier a Gallop poll indicated 67 percent of Americans thought we should have King-Anderson. By March 1962, two months before the Madison Square Garden speech, at about the time the administration and the AFL-CIO began their go-for-broke media blitz, the polls indicated that favorable opinion had dropped to 55 percent; we were gaining ground. Another poll taken after the Madison Square Garden speech showed public support for King-Anderson had tumbled to 48 percent, while still another poll showed it had dwindled to 44 percent. Against seemingly insurmountable odds and with grossly inferior resources, we had turned the tide of public opinion.

A few years later, my eldest daughter entered college where she enrolled in a speech class. The professor announced he would show them a film of a speech with exemplary delivery. As my daughter tells it, when the film began she wanted to slide under her desk because it was her very own daddy on the screen talking to those empty chairs.

But the most moving accolade came almost three decades after the event. Harold Azine, the man without whom our rebuttal would have been "dead," had become a lifelong friend, and I quote from his letter of 1991: "At this point it is of somewhat diminished importance to me whether we made the right points with the right emphasis in all passages of the speech—and time has brought a whole new dimension of problems to the Medicare phenomenon—but all of that, as I said, is less meaningful to me now when I look back at the event of 29 years ago that changed *both* of our lives so importantly and permanently. I underline the word 'both' above because the changes in my life—while hardly as dramatic, noteworthy and newsworthy as those you experienced—were also tremendous in the scale of my own life. First, I came to the AMA's problem as a fully accredited and entrenched member of the 'Liberal Eastern Media Establishment'—and the total experience transformed me and my outlook on life to something better than the liberal shibboleths I had metabolized." It was Harold Azine, of course, who made the message a success and it was he who enriched our lives.

Many doctors had called me during the early months of 1962 to ask if I would consider running for president of the American Medical Association at the annual convention, and my answer had been a flat no. The presidency of the AMA was an honor reserved for doctors who had devoted many years to the organization—serving as trustees, or officers, or in the house of delegates. I had done none of that and most of those who had, and had become leaders, were twenty years my senior. But the AMA had become the object of a dirty media campaign, as witness Abraham Ribicoff's routine bullying of mild-mannered officers who tried to avoid political conflict. Ribicoff continued to refuse to debate with me, and I continued to refuse to run for the office of president of AMA.

Then the question changed in a manner that stumped me. Instead of asking "would you run," they asked, if nominated, "would you run from it." They had me. But I made it clear that I would neither campaign nor ask anyone to vote for me. At the annual meeting in June 1962, my name was placed in nomination from the floor, and the vote count on the first ballot was 142 to 65 in my favor. I had been swept into office with a landslide mandate to fight government bureaucrats from taking over medicine.

The crucial vote on King-Anderson (Medicare) in the United States Senate came the following month. Senator Anderson had attached King-Anderson as a rider on another bill which was sure to pass, so the vote was on a motion to separate the bills, thus killing King-Anderson for the session. I kept in touch with Senator Smathers who told me that Senator Kerr was leading our fight to stop King-Anderson. He said they had the votes to kill it, but it would be close, one or two votes would make the difference. If ever there was a time when presidential intervention could spoil it for us, this was it. The union lobbyists had done everything they could, but a little political

persuasion, a little deal making, a little arm twisting on the part of
the president could tip the scales. But by this point I had become so
convinced that John Kennedy did not want King-Anderson to pass,
that I wasn't surprised to learn that the telephones in the halls of
Congress had fallen silent; the president never called. On July 17,
1962, with all one hundred senators in attendance and Lyndon
Johnson presiding in case of a tie, the vote was 52 to 48; we had won,
King-Anderson was dead.

After that, President Kennedy never again seriously addressed
the issue, and public opinion continued to mount in our favor. But it
was not only King-Anderson that President Kennedy seemed to
shrug off, it was an entire array of welfare-state programs promoted
by the Americans for Democratic Action.

As president-elect of the American Medical Association, as president, and as past president, I worked hard to have the states implement the Kerr-Mills law. I worked closely with Congressman Wilbur
Mills and others to make the program more effective, and I met
with the governors and addressed the assemblies of several state
legislatures. We were successful in implementing the program in
forty-four states, and we had every reason to believe the remaining
six would come on board.

Working with the American Hospital Association, the American
Dental Association, and Blue Cross/Blue Shield, we devised a simple plan whereby states would use federal matching funds under
Kerr-Mills to supplement—on a sliding scale according to income—
private insurance premiums for those unable to purchase health
insurance on their own. The AMA also sought tax credits—again,
on a sliding scale according to income—to allow individuals who
earned too much to qualify for outright subsidies, but who were still
of modest means, to purchase health insurance without hardship.
These programs were designed to serve the needs of people who
were in need without expanding the role of government beyond its
intended purpose and without heaping an unnecessary tax burden
on working people. The programs encouraged people to be self-
sufficient to the best of their abilities, and beneficiaries could

choose their doctors, hospitals, and appropriate care. The programs also kept bureaucratic administration to an absolute minimum.

With ample public support, the future looked bright as medicine surged forward with new technologies, new medicines, and new methods. Then, suddenly, our nation was struck a blow from which we have not fully recovered. Lee Harvey Oswald, a strange and sullen American communist, whether working alone or in collaboration with others, assassinated President Kennedy on November 22, 1963.

Some time after the assassination, I was on an airplane when I came across an *Esquire* magazine, the cover of which featured a photograph of John Kennedy with tears on it, someone else's tears. Inside was a long and thoroughly engrossing article by Tom Wicker, a close friend of the fallen president. Near the end he told of some of the things Kennedy was politically obligated to do as president, but which he did not have in his heart to do. As an example he cited Kennedy's speech in favor of King-Anderson in Madison Square Garden.

Just three years before the assassination the ADA had berated Lyndon Johnson for bottling up their bills in committees. When Lyndon Johnson ascended to the presidency—to what he perceived as his throne—the new president and the ADA embraced. As the nation's heart bled, they forcefully expanded governmental power with the ADA platforms wrapped in the promise of a Great Society.

In the election of 1964, the media painted the Republican candidate, Senator Barry Goldwater, as a "reactionary" against all the wonderful things John Kennedy had stood for. Senator Goldwater tried to warn the nation that Johnson's welfare state would not work, and that the needy would be hurt the most. He also tried to warn the nation that Johnson was courting disaster in Southeast Asia—that no nation was strong enough to fight a war without the commitment to win. I was one of a few Democrats who spoke out in support of Barry Goldwater during that campaign. I did it because—just as I spoke out against King-Anderson and just as I spoke out for family values in college—in my heart, I knew he was right. I spoke from the heart. I only wish that John Kennedy had spoken from his heart when he had the opportunity; sometimes fate doesn't give us a second chance.

Through demagoguery and media distortion, Johnson won that election by historic proportions. Additionally, the AFL-CIO/ADA coalition succeeded in electing a new Congress which was overwhelming Democratic, including fifty-one "rubber stamps"—carefully selected candidates, who would give a rubber stamp vote for any legislation they were told to. And Wilbur Cohen, the ADA's faithful bureaucrat, was soon made secretary of the Department of Health, Education and Welfare in the Johnson administration.

I made several more important and seemingly effective speeches in opposition to King-Anderson, and in July 1964, a bipartisan congressional poll showed that popular support for King-Anderson had fallen to 32 percent with 61 percent in opposition. Through the efforts of doctors and supporters all over the country, another avalanche of mail descended on Capitol Hill—the postmaster at the House of Representatives told me he had never seen more mail on a single bill.

Wilbur Mills, chairman of the House Ways and Means Committee, invited me to Washington to meet with him. He explained that the new Congress had stacked his committee and that those loyal to their union sponsors could outvote him—and they were determined to enact King-Anderson.

I met with other members of the House Ways and Means Committee—Representatives Curtis of Missouri, Watts of Kentucky, and Hurlong of Florida—and they painted the same gloomy picture. I asked one of them if he had gotten any mail on the subject; he said he had gotten bushels of it, and that it was running about 25 to 1 against King-Anderson. Then he added that one of Andy Biemiller's boys (a lobbyist for the AFL-CIO) had come by, and when the congressman told him to go look at all the mail, the union man had responded, "Look, we elected this Congress, not your letter writers."

I also met with seven of the newly elected members, six of whom told me they were committed to voting for King-Anderson, even though they had never read it and had no intention of reading it. I then visited with a couple of old friends in Congress—longtime supporters in the fight to kill King-Anderson—and each told me he had gotten a call from the White House threatening to cut off appropriations for an important project in his home district and therefore both were forced to vote according to the president's wishes.

To overcome the public opposition to King-Anderson, President Johnson told his fellow Americans that of all the events in the short life of their sorely missed John Kennedy, the defeat of King-Anderson was the most disheartening. Riding a swell of mournful tears in the media, Johnson rubber-stamped the King-Anderson bill through Congress in the name of the "Martyred President." After the vote, the unions circulated a leaflet with a picture of a joint session of Congress on the cover. The caption read: "Fifty-one did it." It went on to praise the fifty-one union-sponsored members of Congress (the fifty-one rubber stamps) who made the Great Society programs possible, the crowning glory of which was passage of Medicare in honor of our "Martyred President."

Ironically, just one year after the opinion poll showed overwhelming opposition to King-Anderson, President Johnson flew to Independence, Missouri, with the King-Anderson bill in hand and signed it into law in the presence of former President Harry Truman, who so many years before had allowed the preceding bill to die in Congress, just as John Kennedy had done with King-Anderson. The Socialist party of America, where the plan for national health insurance was hatched, never garnered more than 6 percent of the popular vote for its specious programs. But through the cunning of the Americans for Democratic Action, aided by an assassin's bullet, King-Anderson became the law of the land known as Medicare.

During my debate with Walter Reuther, he emphatically denied that King-Anderson had anything to do with socialism, or that it was the first step to socialized health care for all Americans. But in accordance with the Fabian "doctrine of gradualness," it would only be a matter of time before America would be pushed toward the next step, and that was Reuther's intention all along.

Within just a few short years the cost of Medicare exploded, as predicted, and the cost of medical care in general accelerated, as predicted. In 1968 the Tax Foundation (a private citizens' organization) reported that in the two years since Medicare went into effect, medical costs for the nation had doubled.

Seemingly before Lyndon Johnson's signature had time to dry on the new legislation, Walter Reuther stood before the American Public Health Association in November of 1968 at Detroit and proclaimed a health care crisis in America, blaming private medicine for the escalating costs. He demanded complete federal financing of health care for all Americans to be administered by the federal bureaucracy, and announced the formation of the Committee of One Hundred for National Health Insurance, of which he would be chairman. He enlisted his most faithful rubber stamp in Congress, Senator Edward Kennedy, who professed to be deeply concerned for the health of Americans. And the renewed campaign for socialized medicine for all was on—with limitless support from a new generation of journalists, a generation indoctrinated with the new radicalism and besotted by "advocacy journalism."

Shortly thereafter NBC ran a television special report called "What Price Health?" featuring a four-year-old "blue baby" in need of surgery. According to the report, her father could not afford to pay for the operation, at which point a song was sung with these words: "If you can't afford to live, you die." Because the family lived in Cleveland, the Ohio Medical Association sought to intercede on the little girl's behalf, only to find that the child had been operated on five weeks before the program aired. Not only was the father covered by health insurance, the state of Ohio had a program to pick up the tab had he not been.

Walter Reuther died in a plane crash in 1970, but the smear campaign continues by those committed to permeation, all the while hiding the truth about the cause of our problems.

PART TWO

UNCOVERING THE HIDDEN TRUTH

CHAPTER 4

——————————— /\ ———————————

Hiding the Truth:
How the Press Does It

David Lawrence, Jr., publisher of the *Miami Herald*, was enraged. "Come on, Mr. Mas, be fair," cried the head of his half-page editorial. A newspaper's duty, the editorial instructed, is to "inform through its news columns and to serve as a 'marketplace of ideas' in its opinion pages."[1] Directly below came a second editorial, this one by the president of the *Miami Herald*, accusing Mr. Mas of "slander" for publicly criticizing the newspaper.

And what did Mr. Mas do to incite this attack by the publisher and the president of the *Herald*? Jorge Mas, chairman of the Cuban American National Foundation, charged in a radio broadcast that the *Herald* conducted a "continuous and systematic campaign against Cuban Americans, their institutions, values, ethics and ideals." And what do they have to do with health care? As you will see, the real issue was healthy babies. And one of the obstacles to a resolution of this problem has been the media, their bias, and their refusal to allow a point of view other than their own to be aired. For our purposes, I have used the *Miami Herald* as an example of the mindset that besets many of the most powerful newspapers in our country.

79

Nowhere in America has a single immigrant group settled in one place, at one time, and in such great numbers as Cubans have in Miami. The Cubans were driven to Miami by a vicious socialist dictator, Fidel Castro, whom the American media championed as the people's savior until he aimed Soviet missiles at the United States bringing the world to the brink of war in 1962.[2]

Cuban Americans believe in free enterprise and they believe in themselves. In America they found jobs, any job to start. In a remarkably short while, they had saved enough money to get educations and start businesses, many of which grew into sizeable businesses. Miami became a mecca for business and international banking. Today, the City of Miami stands as a living monument to the intelligence, diligence, resourcefulness, and self-sufficiency of Hispanic people.

From this background, Cuban Americans emerged in stark contrast to the indigenous Hispanic groups of other states. Most Hispanic Americans, like black Americans, endured social isolation and economic exclusion, followed by welfare dependency. This, to the media, was evidence of the failure of free enterprise and of the need forcibly to redistribute the wealth of the nation.

Quite the opposite, of course, is true. As Jack Kemp, former secretary of Housing and Urban Development, explains so lucidly: America has two distinct economies. In one economy we have a market system of incentives to be productive and self-sufficient: we work and save, maintain community pride, and have strong family values.

The other economy of America is where many of our indigenous minority groups live. Its participants, regardless of ability, rely on government for food, shelter, medical care, education, and income. Where the first economy is capitalistic, this second economy is socialistic.

Socialism here, as everywhere, restrains the human spirit, and discourages productivity, saving, and self-improvement. Should it surprise anyone that our inner cities, where the other economy is rampant, are plagued by malaise, despair, ignorance, filth, crime, drug abuse, and disrespect for authority and self?

*   *   *

Yet, our media would have us believe that capitalism, not socialism, has failed. How many times have you read editorials like this: "America's scandalous infant-mortality rate speaks volumes about how the nation regards its children, especially those of poor families."[3]

How many times have you read appalling statistics showing that the United States spends more per capita on health care than any other country, followed by an assertion such as: "And if you think we get more for our money, think again. Infant mortality and life expectancy statistics—indicators of just how good our medical system is—lag behind Japan, England, Canada, West Germany and Sweden."[4]

We are told by our news media that the reason for our scandalous infant mortality rate is the lack of "universal health care" (the latest euphemism for socialized medicine), and that if we had "free" medical care for all, poor women would seek the prenatal care they need.

But before you wire your congressman demanding that your taxes be raised, think about this: The high incidence of low birth weight babies and babies with congenital defects is what results in our high infant mortality rate. And what causes low birth weight and congenital defects? In the vast majority of cases, it is expectant mothers who neglect good nutrition, snort cocaine, shoot heroin, get drunk, smoke, and contract sexually transmitted diseases. The cause is not, that is, deficiencies in medical care, but in social behavior beyond the control and influence of any health care system. Many of these neglectful mothers-to-be qualify for free health care but they ignore it just as they ignore all warnings about drugs.

How does the medical community cope with this inundation of neglectful and abusive mothers-to-be and the resultant offspring? American medical professionals do exactly what they are trained to do: they do all they can to save lives without regard to the mothers' ability to pay. And their ability to save lives in this field is unsurpassed in the world. When infant mortality rates are adjusted for birth weight, America has the lowest infant mortality rate in the world. A low birth weight infant born in the United States stands a better chance for survival than in any other country. It is a very expensive exercise; good prenatal care is far cheaper and more effective.

We find that these neglectful pregnancies occur at an alarming rate among unwed teenagers of minority backgrounds. They are the products of our second, socialistic economy: a system lacking incentives for personal responsibility.

This phenomenon, however, is uncommon among Hispanics of Cuban origin. Young Cuban Americans, who cling to traditional family values and the doctrines of responsibility and self-sufficiency, are products of our capitalist economy. According to our National Center for Health Statistics, among America's indigenous Hispanic expectant mothers *not* of Cuban origin, only a few more than half obtain proper prenatal care, compared to over 80 percent for Cuban Americans. This includes not only the early 1960s' immigrants—mostly moral, industrious, law-abiding families—but also the "Marielitas" of the late 1970s, which included large numbers of Cuba's most hardened criminals and sociopaths.

A deep philosophical chasm lies between the *Miami Herald* and the Cuban American community it serves. But as suggested earlier, the *Miami Herald* is not alone in its liberal activism. As I travel around the country on speaking tours I find that the great majority of America's big city dailies, including the *Washington Post* and the *Los Angeles Times*, as well as the major television news networks, also engage in advocacy journalism and political bias, especially on health care issues. And when it comes to the treatment of doctors, the news media have conducted a continuous and systematic campaign against "their institutions, values, ethics, and ideals." As a result, most Americans believe that the greed of doctors, hospitals, and insurers has driven up health costs to the point where the less fortunate of our society are left to suffer and die without adequate medical treatment.[5] Even people who agree with the tenets of free enterprise come away from their newspapers believing that the medical marketplace must be an exception to the laws of economics, never realizing that the cause of medical problems is government intervention.

The situation with health care today closely parallels what happened in the 1970s with gasoline. Almost everybody remembers the monstrous lines we endured just to get to a pump that still had gas to sell. The media led us to believe that the oil companies were simply gouging us; they never mentioned that the shortages and inflation occurred because the government imposed price controls on domestic production and then rationed the wholesale distribution of gasoline. President Nixon even had ration stamps printed similar to those used during World War II: they were not implemented before his term ended.

In health care today, Congress has imposed strict price controls on the delivery of services, which have, of course, caused explosive inflation throughout the system. With costs out of control, many political leaders and media people are calling for a system of "national health care" or "universal health care"—their way of saying *rationed* health care. Should this occur, we can expect the same long lines waiting for vital surgeries as now exist in Britain and Canada. We are not being told this side of the story.

The news media ought to give us both sides of the story. When a news report quotes an opinion about public policy, a quote from a credible opposing view should be given as well. Advocacy journalism is, of course, acceptable in publications with a specified mission, but there is no place for it in daily newspapers professing fairness and objectivity. Nobody should have anything to fear from balanced reporting; truth will always shine brighter than sophistry.

THE VISION THING

To be fair, some in the news media are oblivious to the bias of the advocacy they practice. Sometimes it is simply ignorance: reporters often come across technical and scientific documents they do not understand, but they use them to make dramatic headline stories that draw false conclusions. But more often, journalists seem to be so set in their beliefs that they feel the opposing view lacks credibility. They may intend no harm in their handling of health issues, but that does not alleviate the danger it poses to the health of our nation.

The intellectual disdain and lack of tolerance for criticism boils down to what, in presidential parlance, was called "the vision thing." Many journalists in the mainstream of the American press view government as the great equalizer in a world rife with inequity.

They see disadvantage as the cause of social ills, and poverty as the cause of crime. To correct inequity between the classes, they believe government should tax the privileged and give to the disadvantaged, thus solving the nagging social ills. Forced income redistribution is justified because wealth under capitalism is earned by exploiting the workers. Society is to blame, not the individual; private property is not sacrosanct in face of social injustice.

But a growing number of Americans ascribe to a very different vision of government, a vision not adequately represented in the mainstream media. The vision I ascribe to, for example, is that of government as a cart. The cart has no engine of its own because government has no ability to create wealth on its own; government depends on taxes paid by working people for power. A self-sufficient and self-governing people, therefore, pull the cart down the road of prosperity. Those pulling the cart are working people, and the harder they pull the more progress the cart makes along the road of prosperity. Those who are unable to help pull the cart ride in it, and the able continue to pull—a taxing labor but not overly so because those who have only stumbled soon recover and rejoin the ranks of the productive pullers.

But when public policy corresponds with the media vision that government should redistribute wealth, more people end up in the cart, and pulling it becomes more difficult. Furthermore, without incentives for the able-bodied to get back out of the cart, more of the productive people become exhausted and they too climb in for the ride. As a consequence, Congress and the bureaucracy establish rules and regulations making it more and more taxing on those pulling the cart, while holding out the promise of a free ride for those willing to climb in. Soon the cart becomes too crowded and a few people get left behind—the weak and those who lack ability and political savvy—the very ones the cart was intended to help in the first place. And on and on.

When the weight of the cart becomes too heavy, it bogs down, backsliding of its own weight. By the time that happens, the people riding in the cart have become too dependent to get out and help pull, and they continue to vote for a free ride even though the cart is taking them nowhere.

This is exactly what has happened in the field of medicine. Instead of carrying only people who could not take care of their own medical bills, politicians and bureaucrats told people that they were "entitled" to ride in the cart if they had one thing and one thing only, a certain date of birth. As I pointed out in my speech at Madison Square Garden in 1962, of the millions of Americans who would eventually be covered by Medicare, about 80 percent required no government assistance; programs, moreover, were already in place to help those who did need it. Then, to make certain everybody eligible to ride in the cart did so, the politicians passed laws making it illegal for anyone to obtain private health insurance covering what Medicare covers; only supplemental policies could be purchased.

Once the government got all the millionaires, the middle class, and the paupers over sixty-five riding in the cart together, it began writing rules and regulations governing all doctors and hospitals that treated Medicare patients, meaning virtually all doctors and hospitals. The cost of this administrative burden today—paid for by the people still pulling the cart (the working people)—is greater than all the doctors' fees combined. To cure the rising costs, government added "cost controls," which caused distortions and misallocations in the medical marketplace, which in turn caused prices to rise even faster. At the same time, technological advancements have brought new and better treatments, but because the cart has become so overloaded, more and more working people (the press calls them the "uninsured working poor") are unable to save and pay for the new treatments. Now they too are clamoring to get in the cart. To solve these problems the press and the politicians are saying we need to expand the cart to carry everybody. But they don't tell us who is going to pull the cart.

NEWS OR OPINION?

Nationwide, the news media heralded the 1992 upset victory of Pennsylvania Senator Harris Wofford as proof that the public was ready for nationalized health care because that was his central campaign theme. Other factors that helped him win aside, and if the press is correct in its assessment of voter preference for a national health plan, my question is: did the press arm the voters with the "power which knowledge gives," as James Madison admonished would be requisite for a self-governing people? I think not.

Wofford's entire health care plan consisted of something like this: "If every criminal has the right to a lawyer, shouldn't every American have the right to a doctor?" What is so striking about this slogan is that it implies that we should solve the problem of universal access to health care the same way we handle a criminal's right to counsel: if the accused can afford an attorney, he must hire one; if he is indigent, the taxpayers provide one. Now, although I practiced medicine during an era when a doctor's care was universally accessible through just such a system, and although I embrace the senator's demand that we carry only those who cannot afford health insurance, what Mr. Wofford has in mind is something more taxing than his words would suggest. He has, in fact, joined Ted Kennedy and Jay Rockefeller in an effort to put all Americans in the cart under a socialized medical system. Just how taxing would his plan be? The press never asked him.

The same void is apparent with respect to press coverage of presidential candidates. I addressed a forum for presidential candidates that was hosted by Senator Jay Rockefeller, who chairs the Pepper Commission on Aging, Senator Bob Graham, and Florida Governor Lawton Chiles. During the morning session, as the physicians' representative, I was allowed exactly ten minutes to give our perspective before getting the "gong," as was Rick Pollack, executive vice president of the American Hospital Association. But the speakers who demanded some form of socialized medicine, including John Sweeney, chairman of the AFL-CIO Health Committee, and Gerald McEntee, international president of the American Federation of State, County and Municipal Employees—cheered on by the usual busloads of nursing home residents—were allowed well over twice the allotted time.

In the afternoon session we heard from the *Miami Herald*'s David Lawrence, Jr., and Senator Jay Rockefeller, followed by the three Democratic presidential candidates. (The Republican candidates declined to appear.) The candidates made passing mention that their plans for universal health coverage were "revenue neutral" and that "savings" would derive by eliminating the middle man as government took monopolistic charge of health care financing—but no candidate predicted what his plan would cost the taxpayer.

The headline story the next day reported how the candidates' plans would streamline the system and save us billions of dollars. But how creating a government enterprise with a budget nearly three times that of the Defense Department, which can't seem to figure out how to pay less than $30 for a toilet seat, would save these billions of dollars was never discussed. The most interesting aspect of the *Miami Herald* article, however, was Jerry Brown's admission: "The basis of this campaign is to put everybody in the same boat, to put the president and the homeless under the same health care system." Nobody questioned whether the boat would sink with so many people in it, just as it had in the former Soviet Union.[6]

And nowhere did the *Herald* article even whisper the "T" word. Could this newspaper have possibly thought that any questions about *taxes*—about how much it would cost and who would pay—were irrelevant to proposals that would socialize the nation's medical system, creating the largest government enterprise in the history of our republic? How, then, would these programs be financed? A clue is found in an editorial of October 2, 1991: "Only the federal government has the tax base to provide basic medical care for all." This implies that the federal government can somehow provide "free" medical care for all, without hinting that in doing so it would run up massive budget deficits and leave future generations to drown in our legacy of debt.

There is a common notion in the public mind that universal access to "free" medical care (and the solution to all social problems) can be financed by taxing the "rich," i.e., anyone who earns more than himself. But any such tax would have to cut deeply into the pay of middle-income workers, because there are simply not enough "rich" people for the purpose. Such a tax would also diminish the incentive of people to become "rich" and consequently would reduce tax revenue. When you starve capitalism of its capital, you kill the goose that laid the golden egg.

When President Bush gave his 1992 State of the Union address and released his budget plan to Congress, the front-page headline of the January 30 *Miami Herald* read: "Budget Called a Boon to Rich." And the lead story opened with: "President Bush's new tax proposal would pass over the poor, help the middle class and shower money on the rich."

News or opinion? Clearly, the piece was written to influence us and not to inform us in accordance with the publisher's proclaimed "duty." It described the source of the opinions it extolled as "respected liberal tax-reform advocacy groups," but offered no counterbalancing views.

Interestingly, the two pie-shaped graphs accompanying the front-page story demonstrated that Medicare and Social Security (so-called entitlement programs because all Americans over a certain age are entitled to them regardless of income) account for about half of all federal spending, while what was labeled "social insurance receipts" account for little more than a third of the federal government's revenue. In other words, we have more and more people riding in the cart and fewer and fewer left to pull it. To illustrate this trend, when Medicare was initially enacted almost thirty years ago, fifteen workers were paying taxes into the Medicare system for every Medicare beneficiary; today, there are only four tax-paying workers for each beneficiary.

Newspapers are great defenders of entitlement programs. It seems incredible how those who promote a program to tax the working class balk at the idea of a tax incentive for people to place a portion of their earnings in capital investments that would provide more and better-paying jobs for the workers. Does it make sense for government to deny a citizen the right to keep what he or she has rightfully earned from capital investments, while *entitling* the same person to tax-subsidized health coverage that was not earned?

We have the finest medical care available in the world, but too many of us lack the savings to pay for it. What we are really experiencing is a "savings crisis." Compare this to Singapore where each working citizen provides for his or her own medical care with a tax-free savings account earmarked for medical expenditure. Perhaps if we were allowed to save and provide for our own medical bills our government could afford to care for those who cannot provide for themselves.

We are often manipulated by the press with tear-jerking stories about those who have fallen through the cracks of our system. Below a full color photograph of a honey-blonde toddler the front-page headline declares: "System Failing 4-Year-Old Girl."[7] The little girl has spent a third of her life in hospitals suffering from a rare, little understood immune deficiency. She is subject to seizures and respiratory, urinary, intestinal, sinus, and blood infections, and she has endured numerous major surgeries. In her few years of life she has amassed nearly $2 million in medical bills, and with continued medical attention, she may survive to adulthood. Many of her bills were paid by insurance which has run out, and by state and federal taxpayers through programs to help the chronically ill who earn, or whose parents earn, too much to qualify for Medicaid. A community fund-raising drive is underway to provide more help. But after thirty-five column inches of text, the reader is still not aware that the girl's doctors receive little or no pay for tending her. Doctors and hospitals perform over $15 billion in uncompensated care each year, a fact few newspapers report.[8]

I doubt that a similar example to this child's plight can be found in any other nation, and that is *not* something we need be ashamed of. Over the years, since serving as president and council emissary of the World Medical Association, I have had occasion to visit innumerable hospitals and clinics the world over. And I can state without reservation my belief that in no other country would this child be alive today; she would have died long ago.

No other country has the facilities, the equipment, the expertise, the funding, and the will to cope with her tragic circumstance. With regard to the commitment of care, those countries which could deliver do not. To suggest that our system is failing her because totally free care has not been provided is a gross distortion of reality. In the United States, parents take a child like this to the doctor and say, "Doctor, do everything you can to save my baby." And the doctor does just that. In other countries, the doctor's abilities are severely restricted by government dictates to hold costs down. Under a system where government sponsors all medical care, this child would have been placed in a special corner of a hospital ward and the parents would have been informed that nothing could be done to save her. Medical care in America is not cheap, but it is the best the world has ever known.

The same tactic was used the following day with this front-page headline: "Impoverished Cancer Patients Fight Illness, System."9 This time the unfortunate not only suffered a medical ailment, but a social one: he had cancer and he was homeless. What is interesting to me is that this man clearly qualified for every welfare benefit on the books, including free medical care, but he lacked the ability or will to seek assistance in time. He was one of those pushed off the overcrowded cart and left behind. He simply could not cope with bureaucratic red tape. Eventually, he made his way to the free clinic run by Dr. Pedro Greer of Camillus House, a volunteer and church-supported charity.

Although the cart was designed to carry the needy, due to the impersonal and inefficient nature of bureaucracy, government cannot adequately aid the indigent without help and guidance from truly caring volunteers in the private sector. It is a tragedy of our time that the federal government "monetarized" the practice of medicine. When I entered the practice, almost all physicians devoted a portion of their time to free clinics for indigent patients: it was considered a privilege to serve our communities which, in turn, honored us in so many ways.

But times have changed. In the view of Washington's social engineers, charitable care is demeaning; medicine should be a civil right and charity should end. So successful have the media been in promoting this popular myth that 42 percent of the public think the U.S. Constitution guarantees a right to medical care.10 So unsuccessful has government been in fulfilling its promise to the poor that newspapers, ironically enough, hold up its failure as evidence that the federal government should now assume responsibility for the entire health care system.

What went wrong with Medicaid and what happened to the free

clinics of yesteryear? Over the two-and-a-half decades of bureau-cratic administration, the Medicaid program has picked up so much regulatory red tape that the cost of complying with the paperwork renders it unprofitable for many physicians to deal with Medicaid. Unlike free clinics, a doctor's office overhead must be paid out of revenue. Exactly as with federal housing programs, where government bureaucracies hold out billions of dollars to help the poor then dictate so much costly red tape that honest providers can't handle it, dishonest providers move in to help themselves. The massive fraud committed by the very few—the fraud that is shaking the system and tarnishing the profession—is used by the press to defame the entire medical profession for gouging the public.

One need only look at the swelling population of the homeless to see the extent of government's failure to care for the indigent. In the days when the United States government had few social welfare programs, few homeless people roamed the streets because there was plenty of room in the cart. The federal bureaucracy itself admits that over 40 percent of those eligible for Medicaid do not receive it. As those of us with experience in dealing with the indigent know, street dwellers are not suffering strictly for economic reasons. They are not just unemployed, they are unemployable. But there is nothing the medical establishment can do alone; their problems go beyond what medicine can remedy.

And there is nothing mindless bureaucracies can do alone. Over ten years the City of New York spent $2 billion to build shelters, yet an estimated fifty thousand homeless are still on the streets—the same number as before. A commission appointed by New York Mayor David Dinkins wisely advised the city to get out of the homeless business and leave it to private organizations that do the job more effectively and efficiently.

Often, alcohol and drug abuse play a big role in debilitating home-less people. But most of them have more basic problems than lack of medical care; they suffer from broken spirits, and it is critical that they be helped by someone who cares and knows how to nurture them back to spiritual wholeness. Organizations like the Salvation Army have done a remarkable job of bringing pride and purpose back to broken lives. The Salvation Army maintains well over a hundred rehabilitation programs across the nation. Here, for a period of three or four months, anyone seeking help is given medical care, a clean bed, fresh clothing, nourishing meals, counseling, pocket money, and a measure of self-respect; for example, by helping people unload donated articles from their cars at the loading dock. The only problem is capacity; the program needs to be expanded.

The federal government has never been able to replace this kind of volunteer care by truly concerned private citizens. Perhaps bureaucrats view such effective efforts as a threat to the continued expansion of government, for they persist in trying to eliminate private charity entirely. The business of government is welfare and it is a growth industry with a sinister marketing plan: The more the system denies help to the helpless, the more visible they become on the streets; the more visible the need for government assistance, the more compliant the public becomes or is to spending more tax money for more social programs—and the more staggering the contents of the cart.

If the bureaucrats get their way, the Salvation Army will be disarmed and forced to lose its private war on despair.[11] The government is claiming that the fifty thousand enrollees of this rehabilitation program are, in fact, employees of the Salvation Army by virtue of their help on the loading docks, and that they are underpaid because the pocket money they receive does not meet the requirements of the minimum wage.

Even Mother Teresa was stymied after spending $100,000 to renovate two New York City buildings to house the homeless.[12] Although the nuns physically carry the handicapped when necessary, city officials insisted on an elevator for the handicapped. The project had to be abandoned. Unfortunately, in a society in which government consumes 35 percent of Gross National Product in taxes—about three-and-a-half times what we spend on health care—government is effectively squelching charity for the needy.

OPINION OR PLOY

The other factor that has hindered care for the poor is the risk of malpractice litigation. Doctors are better trained and more capable than ever before, yet the risk of being sued is greater than ever before. A significant portion of a doctor's overhead, which Medicaid fails to cover, is malpractice insurance, and a doctor is as likely to be sued by a Medicaid patient as by any other. Free clinics are still around, but many private doctors in litigious states cannot afford the risk of being hit with multimillion dollar judgments while volunteering their services. As a consequence, the clinics are too few and most are understaffed.

In Florida, I have been fighting alongside my colleagues in the state medical association for legislative relief. The plan is called "Health Access Florida" and the object is to restore easy access to care for those currently being pushed out of the cart. Our request is to allow private doctors who donate their services to clinics of the state's Department of Health and Rehabilitative Services to come under the umbrella of the state's sovereign immunity which limits malpractice claims to $100,000, just as state-employed doctors are protected. The same protection would apply to private doctors when an HRS patient is referred to his or her office for specialized treatment. It is a simple and logical request by physicians who want to assure the best medical treatment for indigent patients at the least possible expense to taxpayers, but it is an uphill battle when legislative committees are dominated by lawyers seeking millions of dollars in contingency fees for malpractice litigation, and when some newspaper editors exploit the plight of the poor to promote their own political agenda of socializing medicine.

An example of the kind of heartless, mindless opposition encountered in our effort to rekindle volunteer care for the medically indigent is an opinion piece written by the president of the Florida Academy of Trial Lawyers and entitled "Proposed Law is Doctors' Ploy."[13] To support the outlandish assertion that malpractice liability is inconsequential to the delivery of physicians' services, this lawyer states that the American Medical Association's own data show that medical malpractice premiums make up only 1 percent of the cost of all health care. Even if this extrapolation of data were correct, what is the relevance? The total cost of health care includes every bottle of aspirin sold over-the-counter, every bottle of dandruff shampoo, and every other sundry that has nothing to do with doctors' malpractice premiums. To make such a percentage ratio valid one would have to add to the aggregate cost of physicians' malpractice premiums the cost of liability insurance paid by every health product manufacturer, every retailer of health care products, every pharmacist, every hospital, every nursing home, every medical testing lab, every physical therapist, every optician, and I spare you more. And once that had been done, the resulting percentage, which would be many times the 1 percent cited, would still have no relevance to the proposal of limiting liability to doctors providing charitable care for the needy.

If the state must provide this care at taxpayers' expense—which it cannot afford to do without increasing taxes dramatically or strictly rationing care—the liability of those doctors hired by the state would be limited to the same $100,000 under current law. Passage of this bill would do nothing to diminish the legal remedies of the patients of public clinics. Unfortunately for everybody who encounters a medical bill today, powerful lawyers fear that if any restraint of court awards should prove—as it most certainly would prove—that top quality medical care is far more affordable without the albatross of an unreasonable and inequitable tort system, the public would demand reasonable reforms to the system.

The lawyer continues his argument by saying that so-called "defensive medicine"—medical testing and procedures performed solely to protect doctors from law suits—"is less than 2 percent." Where on earth did he get this number? The AMA's most current data show that liability costs attributed to physician services are $20.7 billion, of which malpractice premiums account for $5.6 billion. With aggregate fees for physician services of $102.7 billion (about 20 percent of total health care expenditures), defensive medicine amounts to 15 percent and malpractice premiums come to 5.6 percent for a grand total of 20.6 percent. That is among the most conservative estimates I have come across.[14]

People impressed by what appears to be cost containment in countries with socialized health care systems might be surprised to learn that malpractice liability is negligible in those countries. For instance, a doctor pays ten dollars a year for malpractice insurance in Sweden compared to over $100,000 in many locales of the United States, including areas of Florida—ten thousand times more.[15] Even physicians who perform no invasive procedures and have limited their practices to low risk patient profiles frequently pay in excess of 10,000 dollars.

IGNORANCE OR PLOY?

When I think back to the days of my medical schooling I am awed by the technological progress we have made—the lives saved, the suffering eased. I am further dazzled by future prospects. We live in an era when the half-life of our accumulated medical knowledge is less than seven years. Just imagine, half of everything we know about medicine will be outmoded within the next seven years.

Of all the senseless and dangerous myths propagated by a hostile press, one of the most distressing is that we are paying an exorbitant price for technology that does little good. Among the most noxious examples I have come across is an article that appeared in *Financial World* magazine entitled: "How Doctors Have Ruined Health Care."[16] It is not surprising that this article was carried in a business publication. Because our tax laws discourage people from providing for their own medical care, while at the same time providing tax incentives for employers to purchase employee health insurance, most Americans are forced to rely on their employers to provide for them. Lee Iacocca and some other business leaders, therefore, are looking to unload this responsibility onto the government, or at least to reduce it.

Citing a bipartisan commission study, the article begins with what turns out to be data culled from a confidential memo of the staff—not the conclusions of the committee nor even of a dissident minority. The "incriminating" statistics indicate that between 15 and 30 percent of diagnostic tests are not needed, which, as discussed above, correlates exactly with the consequence of "defensive medicine," not something doctors have brought about willingly. The charge is also made that 35 to 50 percent of surgical deaths and postoperative complications are "probably preventable." Without even disputing the validity of this unsubstantiated claim, what the authors don't mention is that the death rate for most surgery today is minimal; even the most risky is below 4 or 5 percent.

The authors proceed to attack, in similar vein, some of the most remarkably successful lifesaving procedures, including cardiac by-pass surgeries and carotid endarterectomies. Obviously the early stages of most high-tech procedures involve high risk, high morbidity, and high mortality. Uninitiate journalists apparently believe that new treatments are devised by a lone scientist who, having mixed chemicals in a basement, suddenly emerges gripping a frothy flask and announces to the world that he has found a cure for heart disease; either it works or it doesn't.

In the real world, studies on promising treatments are published in scholarly journals and shared with doctors and researchers at other centers. Thus all doctors working in the same field can quickly devise theories, technologies, and methodologies to improve the outcome of the procedure. Progress is rapid today because we have built a tremendous network of knowledge and technology that works simultaneously with that of many medical centers around the country.

When we first began open heart surgery the mortality rate was 50 to 60 percent at many centers. The same was true with carotid endarterectomies, a procedure used to unclog obstructed arteries to avert an imminent stroke. Just a couple of years ago, many critics claimed it was too dangerous and that the benefits were minimal. Today, both procedures are universally recognized as highly successful, with mortality rates down to less than 5 percent—in a few clinics it is as low as 3 percent.

But when people without clinical knowledge and experience attempt to set policies and budgets for medical treatment, as is the practice under the socialized systems of other countries, the development of new lifesaving procedures is retarded. Today, new procedures are adapted under socialized systems only after they have been proven and perfected in the United States—albeit with severe rationing and long waiting lists for treatment. If U.S. treatment policies were set by the bureaucracy, as under any of the proposed plans for "universal health care," rapid progress would slow down the world over. At present the Canadian government must contract with American doctors and hospitals to perform high-tech heart procedures because their own facilities can no longer provide the volume of up-to-date care that is needed without long delays.

Detractors of high-tech advancement in medicine remind me of the story of Robert Fulton. As a young American he went to London and learned of early mechanical visionaries who foresaw using steam to power navigation. Back in America Fulton applied his own practical genius to the idea and built a boat, but it failed to work. Mercilessly ridiculed but undaunted, he tried again, and in New York in 1807 he launched the *Clermont*, dubbed "Fulton's Folly" by the press. In the end, Fulton's *Clermont* steamed up the Hudson River to break all previous speed records. The rest, as they say, is history.

In the field of medicine today, developments are far more revolutionary than Fulton's steam power. Fulton, moreover, had only to overcome the lack of encouragement; in that day government did not interfere in the enterprise of its citizens, and the welfare cart was not a drain on the capital of our emerging nation.

But back to the article. The writers continued their merciless attacks on doctors, displaying inexplicable viciousness with such unfounded statements as: "The incidence of operating room incompetence is chilling." Who of sound mind could concur? American medical schools accept only the best and brightest of abundant applicants and the curriculum involves the most rigorous training in postgraduate education. After medical school, competition for a limited number of residency slots is keen: again, only the most promising are accepted. In the years of residency, all but the most competent are weeded out. All surgeons are required to continue learning throughout their careers. Surgeons obtain training and are properly supervised before performing new techniques and procedures. As a result, incompetence is rare; our low surgical mortality rates prove that. Doctors from virtually every other country in the world come to America to advance their educations and learn the latest techniques under the guidance of our renowned surgical talent. And the same is true for our nonsurgical medical specialist.

Not satisfied, the authors proceed to propagate another media myth—the overuse of hysterectomies and cesarean sections—when in fact some of the largest jury awards are derived from malpractice suits against doctors who failed to perform C-sections before a normal delivery turned to misfortune. By court precedent, the law of the land says that physicians should use the cesarean procedure any time there is *any* doubt, no matter how remote, about the outcome of a normal delivery.

The article provides no source—once again—for the claim that by the time women reach the age of seventy, about two-thirds will have had their uterus removed. The press in general gives the impression that doctors can think of no better way to earn a living than to go around convincing women to let them remove their uterus, when the problem a surgeon faces is finding enough time to take care of all his or her patients.

But facts notwithstanding, the press has time and again created sensational headlines out of "scholarly" studies indicating overuse of hysterectomies. Most of these studies were conducted by "doctors" who were not medical doctors but doctors of philosophy, or doctors with no clinical experience. These investigations involved the review of pathology examinations of tissue removed during surgery. If they failed to indicate the presence of cancer or disease, they were tabulated as "medically unnecessary." What these studies did not reveal was the plight of the patient. Many of these women lived in misery one, two, or more weeks each month; many suffered chronic anemia which was unresponsive to other therapies due to excessive menstrual bleeding. Many more hysterectomies were performed on women who had given birth to several babies causing the tissues of the uterus to collapse leaving the uterus to hang like a lead weight down into the vagina causing extreme discomfort.

I once debated state Senator Jack Gordon of Miami Beach, a lawyer with no understanding of medicine but a lifelong advocate of socialized medicine. In the course of the debate he cited just such a study and asserted that putting a stop to these unnecessary hysterectomies was an example of how socialized medicine would save money. He was absolutely correct in one respect: where socialized medicine does save money is through rationing care, and only through rationing care. In my rebuttal I explained the fallacy of his report and the real-life facts. I also stated that in my years of surgical practice, no other procedure produced more satis⸜⸜ results and more satisfied patients than the hysterectomy. At the conclusion of the debate, I was detained by women who came forward from the audience to tell me how true my words were. For many of them, a hysterectomy had made life worth living again.

Without doubt the authors of this article had no intention of advocating the restriction of medical practices which, in effect, would be nothing less than sexist discrimination. This demonstrates how hazardous journalistic ignorance can be. The decision to undergo a hysterectomy is best left to the patient and her doctors: only they know *all* the facts.

IGNORANCE OR "MYTHINFORMATION"?

I have seen and heard many distortions and misunderstandings spread as a result of journalistic zeal to advocate public policies that conform to a misguided vision, but none better illustrates how the press hides the truth through "mythinformation" than this editorial statement that appeared in yet another issue of the *Miami Herald*: "While Washington waits, 31 million uninsured Americans—the conservative estimate—have no access to hospital care. . . . It is a national outrage that men, women and children suffer and die from untreated cancer, heart disease and preventable diseases."[17]

As anybody who knows anything about health care can attest, by federal law the emergency room of virtually every hospital in this country must treat any emergency patient that it can regardless of the patient's ability to pay. (There is nothing new in this; hospitals did it long before any law.) If the hospital has the requisite facilities, the patient cannot be transferred to any other hospital even though no provision for payment has been made. But if the hospital lacks the proper facilities, it must stabilize the patient to the best of its ability before transfer to another facility which can offer full treatment. Any doctor on call at the subject hospital must respond to the patient's needs as well.

The law further provides that the rights of patients to receive treatment regardless of ability to pay be conspicuously posted in every emergency room or outpatient clinic of every hospital.

According to the American Hospital Association, the amount of uncompensated care delivered exceeds $8 billion a year, and doctors perform close to another $7 billion worth of uncompensated care. In addition, local governments throughout the land fund and maintain a network of hospitals and clinics that accommodate the uninsured, as do a great number of churches, charities, and fraternal service associations.

This outrageous misstatement was not an isolated slip of the pen committed in ignorance of the laws and common medical practices of America; the occurrence of similar statements proves that it was not isolated at all. Just seven days later, in an editorial titled "A second opinion on doctor-dictated health-care costs," Martha Musgrove of the *Herald's* editorial board wrote that "31 million uninsured Americans will go without care."[18]

This is not to diminish the plight of the uninsured nor to say that the present situation is acceptable, but to state that "31 million uninsured Americans will go without care" is like saying that all of the unemployed in America will starve. Few of the unemployed will dine at a fancy steakhouse tonight, but they will not starve either, just as the medically uninsured will not go without care. At any given time, like any segment of society (except the elderly who are covered under Medicare), well over 90 percent of the uninsured are not currently in need of a doctor's care. Nor does the fact that they are currently uninsured indicate that they cannot obtain a doctor's care, with or without money, nor that other forms of insurance won't cover specific mishaps requiring medical attention, such as workers compensation insurance, automobile insurance, or the insurance of another liable party.

In stark contrast to what we are led to believe by the press, the majority of the uninsured receive free care or care at reduced rates (adjusted according to need) from private doctors. This has been the common practice of the medical profession throughout history, and although the legal establishment, the press, and the bureaucracy have done everything possible to deny and thwart the practice (shy of completely socializing the system), even today approximately 64 percent of doctors in this country provide this service to the uninsured.[19]

Many of the uninsured don't require the services of private doctors because they are veterans who obtain free medical treatment at Veterans Administration hospitals and clinics. Some of the uninsured are among the millions of college students whose campuses provide medical clinics paid for out of tuition money; many are schoolchildren whose school districts offer student health services; many others qualify for state and local programs that help those whose incomes are above the Medicaid threshold; many more obtain care through county health clinics and hospitals; a few can afford to pay medical bills without insurance; and then, unfortunately, there is a pocket of people who can afford health insurance but prefer to buy a new Japanese car. Many of the uninsured are people who are normally covered but have recently switched jobs and fall within the waiting period of their new employers' policies. Most in this category can afford incidental medical expenses, but would be exposed should catastrophic illness strike within the waiting period, although temporary policies and COBRA benefits are designed to cover just such gaps. For all the uninsured there is the safety net of Medicaid, but their net worth would have to dwindle to qualify (not a problem for college students of majority age who have few assets).

True, on rare occasions "men, women and children suffer and die from untreated cancer, heart disease and preventable diseases," but even then it is infrequently because care is not available; and in those instances where care was sought but denied, it is usually due to bureaucratic shuffling and bungling. On a population adjusted basis (as will be expanded upon later), many more people die of treatable and preventable diseases due to the rationing of care under the socialist systems of Canada and Britain than in the United States due to a lack of health insurance. But our newspapers do little, and in many cases nothing, to publicize this fact.

The ways the uninsured can seek care are complex—it is a cumbersome and confusing patchwork of care—but there are more logical solutions to assure adequate care to all than to subject everybody to government rationing under a socialist system. Many in the medical establishment have testified before Congress—to no avail—for government to supplement the purchase of health insurance by low income workers so that the incentive to work is maintained while making private insurance coverage available to them.

This approach correctly identifies the problem of the uninsured: between 12 and 15 percent of the population cannot afford proper medical insurance; therefore we should help make the coverage affordable to them. This is quite different from the false story the press is telling: 31 million Americans are denied hospital and medical care; therefore we must replace the present system with government-sponsored universal health care (a socialist model). It makes as much sense as saying that because some people need assistance purchasing enough food, we should place all food under government control to ration as it sees fit. My detractors in the press will allege that I am insensitive to the plight of the uninsured and the needs of the working poor. This is nothing new; the press to this day is distorting what I said thirty years ago. A case in point is a piece that ran in the *Miami Herald* claiming that: (1) the American Medical Association has always defended the existing system; (2) the AMA bitterly fought the creation of Medicaid thirty years ago; and (3) wonder upon wonders, the AMA today says the system is sick, and wants to expand Medicaid and make sweeping changes to guarantee access to all Americans.[20]

In truth, it has always been the creed of the medical profession that everyone should receive adequate care regardless of ability to pay, and throughout the history of the profession this has been achieved as much as humanly possible. Nobody denies that doctors earn a good living and that some entered the profession for that sole purpose (more, of course, since the "moneterization" of medicine by government). But the vast majority of doctors endured the rigors of training and the demands of practice for the satisfaction of healing sick people. That is precisely why, when scientific progress brought about new treatments that were prohibitively expensive for some patients, the AMA supported the Kerr-Mills legislation that later, through compromise, became Medicaid.

Not only is it false that the AMA fought creation of Medicaid, the AMA, in fact, sought to implement it, as noted in a previous chapter. Medicaid, as originally conceived (it has changed considerably), provided a cart for those who could not provide for themselves, but it did not burden the workers pulling the cart with unnecessary riders. The AMA fought the creation of Medicare precisely because it put everybody over a certain age in the cart regardless of ability to pay. In our objection, we correctly predicted the economic dislocations that currently plague the system, and noted that the dislocations would lead to a call by the political Left and the liberal media for more of the same; i.e., a completely socialist medical system.

The article continues to say that the AMA has a reform plan of its own, which the *Journal of the American Medical Association* introduced along with an impartial presentation of just about every other cohesive reform representing the entire political spectrum.[21] The newspaper article summarizes the AMA plan and points out that, although provisions are made for slowing the growth of medical spending, it offers "no assurance" that costs would not continue to spiral as they have.

But surely, in a humane society there can be no "assurance" that costs will not rise. When we develop a definitive cure for cancer, or as we continue to improve treatment of various cancers, and those treatments prove to be more expensive than the current crop, a cost assurance would inhibit us from implementing the new treatments. That is precisely what happens under socialist systems that dictate medical budgets.

But even this superficial questioning of a proposal is a step toward healthy journalism. A public policy proposal is much like the new medical procedures kicked around in the scholarly journals referred to earlier; available care is found through questioning the validity and experimenting with alternatives. Perhaps it is due to this kind of questioning that the AMA later refined its proposal to include more cost-saving and consumerism-type reforms.[22]

But before we nominate this article for a Pulitzer, note that the enlightened journalism ended right there. The article failed to discuss the free market proposal of the Heritage Foundation, or any other reform proposal except one—that of a small group led by left-wing Harvard academicians proposing a full-blown socialist system. The article repeated all the classical socialist utopian myths—the saved lives and dollars—and the reporter never questioned a word of it.

It is a pity this newspaper won't open its pages, as did the *Journal of the American Medical Association*, to let all sides be heard. Instead editorials abounded telling about the wonders of socialized medicine in Canada. (We used to hear about the wonders of socialized medicine in Britain, but since these have turned into horror stories, today's press avoids mention of Britain.)

It seems, however, that a break has occurred in the ranks of big city newspapers: the *New York Times* has let slip that medical care is rationed in Canada and that patients wait months for services, even for simple pap smears that are vital in exposing the presence of cancer.[23] Subsequently, President Bush, in a speech, citing the shortages and rationing of care in Canada, claimed that the Canadian system provided a "cure worse than the disease." Congressman Newt Gingrich took it from there and told of his own fact-finding foray into the Canadian system—among many other revelations, those over the age of sixty-five can no longer obtain elective knee surgery. For this and other medical reasons, Canadians flock to hospitals in Florida for care. (Of course, Canadians also seek care closer to the border, from Seattle to Boston.)

The dam had sprung a leak, the American public was beginning to find out what we in the medical profession have long known but have been unable to convince the liberal press to reveal. One would expect a legitimate news organization to jump at the *Time's* story and dispatch its most aggressive reporters to dig out the truth about what was really going on in Canada's socialized medical system. Unfortunately, the *Miami Herald*, like any political advocate reeling from the effects of embarrassing revelations, embarked on a program of damage control. It did not call a medical doctor to find out what really ailed the Canadian medical system; it called a "spin doctor" to deny it was true.

The expert who was contacted to say it wasn't so was a Canadian journalist who got top billing, replete with a cartoon and a lead headline that read: "Why are U.S. critics attacking Canada's lifesaving Medicare?"[24] To establish his credentials as an expert in Canadian medical affairs, the journalist said that, unlike Bush and Gingrich, "I live in Canada." Who, he wondered, had been feeding Gingrich, Bush, and the *New York Times* "all this stuff"? On orthopedic surgery he assured us that Canada had one of the finest facilities in the business: the Toronto Hospital for Sick Children. Which is all very fine, but was he unaware that seniors over sixty-five, whom Congressman Gingrich had referred to, cannot obtain knee surgery at a children's hospital? (As we will discuss when we take up the issue of rationing, the only thing "universal" about socialist medical systems is their discrimination against the elderly.)

The "expert" then told us that, contrary to the congressman's information, there "are only 400 Canadians being treated in U.S. hospitals." Where did he get this head count? God must have told him because only God knows how many Canadians are in U.S. hospitals. It is possible that four hundred Canadians at that moment had been sent to the U.S. for treatment under contract with Canadian health ministries, but this would in no way account for all the Canadian traffic to the U.S. seeking medical care. The reason is quite simple: Canadian facilities are unable to provide up-to-date treatment for heart disease and cancer, and the waiting lists for many surgeries are proving fatal to ever-growing numbers, as the American medical community well knows.

The writer also denied that Canadians were coming to Florida for treatment, which I found a particularly peculiar assertion to be made in a newspaper whose business section the year before disclosed the financial impact of Canadian patients leaving home from just one province, Ontario: $225 million per year. So many patients were fleeing the rationing of Canadian socialist health care that the province put limits on what would be paid out, sort of a Berlin Wall for sick people.[25] Was he also unaware that the waiting lists for pap smears, as disclosed by the *New York Times*, which he claimed was "simply not true," was in fact well documented in *Health Management Quarterly*? That the average wait in the province of Newfoundland was two and half months? That the same was true for mammography?[26]

Could it be that this journalist who lives in Canada was ignorant of what had been written in his own Canadian press about shortages and rationing and waiting lists for medical treatment in Canada? Had he never read reports of the forty children who needed heart surgery but were turned away by the Hospital for Sick Children?

Nor about the six people who died after waiting months for heart bypass surgery in a single Manitoba hospital in a single year? And what about the one thousand people waiting up to a year for heart bypass surgery at three Toronto hospitals? And the patients being kept in closets at the Moncton Hospital of New Brunswick despite three hundred empty beds because the wards were closed to save money?[27] These stories were published in *Maclean's*, the largest circulation weekly news magazine in Canada.

Was this Canadian journalist ignorant of the admission by the Manitoba Medical Association, as reported in the *Winnipeg Free Press*, that the waiting list for brain and spinal surgery was six months and longer in that province?[28] Had he never heard of the *Toronto Globe and Mail* report of a woman who was turned away by fourteen hospitals for lack of an intensive care bed and died without proper care?[29] Had he never read in that same Toronto newspaper that, due to an equipment shortage, seven hundred kidney stone patients per year were being sent to Buffalo, New York, for treatment, leaving about eight hundred patients on the waiting list for treatment in Toronto?[30]

Were the editors of the *Miami Herald*, with all of their fact-gathering resources, ignorant of these facts too? Several months prior to the publication of its testimonial to Canadian health care, the New York Times (wire) Service ran a news item, which I came across in the *Austin* (Texas) *American-Statesman*, noting that in the last two years the province of Ontario alone had taken 3,500 hospital beds out of service, Toronto had seen 2,900 acute-care beds closed, and British Columbia had lost 300 hospital beds, all to save money at a time when demand was going unmet.[31]

Granted, on occasion, unfortunate people in the United States don't get treatment when they should. We all know about those cases because each one makes front-page news for weeks. Anne Marie Lane, a maid who could not afford health insurance, went to Jackson Memorial Hospital in Miami, one of the world's largest and finest medical facilities which is funded by the taxpayer and charged with caring for those who cannot afford to pay. Although she had been diagnosed with a large but benign fibrous tumor on the uterus, a condition that afflicts 40 percent of women past menopause and is treated by hysterectomy, she was told that she needed a $200 deposit before she could get surgery because it was not a life-threatening condition. But because she was in too much discomfort to work, she could not raise the deposit money.

The case made headline news, and being so extraordinary, it was picked up by a Democratic presidential hopeful, U.S. Senator Bob Kerrey of Nebraska, who used it as his rallying cry to implement his plan to socialize medicine in America. "We've gotten to the point where people are dying before they get health care; that's not the kind of country I want," he told his supporters. Obviously Senator Kerrey was mixed up; he had fallen for the "mythinformation" provided by headlines and not bothered with the facts: People are dying in Canada without proper care because the socialist medical system cannot meet the demand. For every case similar to the plight of this woman, scores of patients die while waiting for surgery in Canada and Britain.

As for Anne Marie Lane, she underwent surgery in North Shore Hospital at Miami, a private hospital, under the kind and capable hands of Robert Fojo, a private doctor. Her total bill? Zero! Like so many others she received "free" care under private medicine. In addition, public donors gave the patient $2,000 to help her pay future medical bills. (This doesn't sound like such a bad country to me.)

Ira Clark, the judicious and capable president of Jackson Memorial Hospital's Public Trust, upon learning of this incident immediately implemented an admissions review system so that no future patient would be turned away for lack of deposit money, whether or not the patient's condition was life-threatening. It would make good sense if Medicaid funds were used to provide vouchers so that everybody, especially the working poor, could afford private health insurance and relieve the burden at public hospitals. But to rely on socialized medicine to correct such a situation would be suicide on the part of the American public.

It is heartening to find that lately the *New York Times* has been more forthcoming in its coverage of the failings of socialized medicine in other countries. But I am under no illusions that a climate of media fairness—where all the media air all sides—will soon be standard for the American people.

SEAS OF LEMONADE

Contemporary journalists attribute their independence from political coercion to Horace Greeley (1811–1872), the most influential newspaperman of his century. Horace Greeley has been called the father of the modern daily newspaper in America, which explains a lot about what we read today.

Early on, newspapers were commonly organs of the various political parties. But Greeley, according to his admirers, established a higher moral vision and introduced intellectually stimulating editorials at the *New York Tribune*, which he founded in 1841. Without question, Horace Greeley did much to raise public consciousness against slavery, but to what "moral vision" did he ascribe, and how does it explain contemporary journalism? What Horace Greeley in fact did to reform journalism was to establish the newspaper as the intimidator rather than the intimidatee; instead of allowing the political party to create the newspaper, Greeley used his newspaper to create the political party.

Horace Greeley was a devotee of François-Marie-Charles Fourier (1772–1837), a mad Frenchman who wrote about an imaginary utopian society based on "scientific" order. Fourier, like Greeley, knew nothing about science and conducted no scientific experiments to test his social theories held to be the result of "science," but Greeley promoted them anyway in his regular front-page column in the *Tribune*, titled "Social Science."

Fourier envisioned a society that would be more productive than capitalism because it would eliminate the waste of marketing and the duplication of effort involved in competing entities.[32] Instead, society would harmonize in a natural order in accord with Sir Isaac Newton's order of the physical universe. Dissatisfied with the spontaneous association of people in commerce, he envisioned mankind bonding in love at "phalansteries" where wealth would be distributed equitably according to need and human passions would be freely expressed. Public services would be free; men and women would plant in the morning and sing in the afternoon, if, that is, they were so inclined. In his more maddened state, Fourier taught that when man attained this level of noncompetitiveness, the physical world would ascend as well: the seas would turn to lemonade and wild beasts would serve mankind.

Due to the promotion of Fourier's ideas by Horace Greeley, Nathaniel Hawthorne, Ralph Waldo Emerson, and many others, an "intellectual" movement spread in America and several phalansteries were established, including Brook Farm at West Roxbury, Massachusetts, and the North American Phalanx at Red Bank, New Jersey, and Union Colony in Colorado.

Although the communes were short lived, the ideas did not, and have not, died. Editorial intolerance for any opinion or evidence at variance with the publisher's beliefs is exemplified by this quotation from Greeley's "Social Science" column:

"The plan of reform to which we refer is that of Charles Fourier. He has discovered and made known to the World the laws and mechanism of Social Order, based upon Association and combined Action Unity of Interests, attractive Industry and Moral Harmony of the Passions—in the place of the present Social Order, based upon isolated and Individual Action, Conflict of all Interests, Repugnant Industry, and Perversion and False Development of the Passions."[33] Critics who dared challenge the advocacy of these "laws" for social reform would be discredited for adhering to the "perversion and false development of the passions." Such intolerance would, of course, be carried out in the name of fairness and honesty.

But this was not all. In 1848, Greeley's managing editor and founding member of Brook Farm, Charles A. Dana, was dispatched to London accompanied by Albert Brisbane, a fellow Fourier disciple and *Tribune* columnist who wrote *General Introduction to Social Sciences* to promote the idea of socialism as an academic "science." Their mission was to recruit a man who had been a highly effective editor of *Rheinische Zeitung*, a leading newspaper of Cologne, Germany, which had been closed by Prussian authorities. The editor had written a pamphlet for a secret society in London called "League of the Just," for which he had borrowed much of the underlying philosophy of Fourier and of Fourier's contemporary, the comte de Saint-Simon. The editor in question was Karl Marx, and the pamphlet was *The Communist Manifesto*, which he coauthored with Friedrich Engels.

The following year Marx founded a new paper, the *Neue Rhein-ische Zeitung*, but again it was closed, and by 1851 Karl Marx was working as the European correspondent of the *New York Tribune*. Over the next decade Karl Marx is credited with contributing nearly five hundred "news" reports and editorials to the *New York Tribune*, but his work, it is said, was often published in the newspaper anonymously.

Through his writing, Marx took socialism from Fourier's agrarian perspective into the Industrial Age with his vision of history as a struggle between the bourgeoisie (the privileged) and the proletariat (the disadvantaged). He advocated ten reforms to create a just society, including the progressive income tax, the elimination of inheritances, and state-sponsored free education (what Greeley championed as "free common-school education for all"), all to be administered by a centralized state bureaucracy. And like Fourier, Karl Marx asserted that his formulations for society had been arrived at "scientifically," meaning that his word was above dispute.

Horace Greeley was so certain that what Fourier and Marx had put in his mind was valid "social science" that he determined to become president of the United States in order to spearhead the social reforms of this vision. When the Whig party did not nominate him, he helped organize the Republican party. Again passed over, he corroborated with fellow publisher and like-minded visionary Joseph Pulitzer of the *St. Louis Post-Dispatch* to organize the Liberal Republican party, which nominated Greeley for president in 1872, as did the Democratic party; but he lost the election to incumbent Ulysses S. Grant.

Greeley and Marx carried their vision to their graves and beyond. In America a limited version of that vision has helped lead to our current government by bureaucracy: the Great Society welfare state. In the former Soviet Union the absolute application of that vision led to human tragedy of proportions never before recorded in history.

Lacking incentive for individual initiative, the communes of Greeley's era failed: the water at the shores of Massachusetts and New Jersey did not turn to lemonade; the beasts of Colorado remained wild; and Hawthorn left Brook Farm after six months because he said he could get nothing done there. Union Colony became known as Greeley, Colorado, and today its economy is as capitalistic as the rest of America, although Greeley's legacy left the people with a very heavy cart to pull.

As for Charles A. Dana, Greeley's managing editor, after a falling-out with Greeley and upon observing the miraculous Industrial Revolution unfold in America—a phenomenon that took place through the spontaneous association of people in commerce with no central government planning, no federal regulatory code, no income tax—he became convinced that socialism was the "farce" that James Madison had warned would beset a people should information necessary for self-governance be withheld.

CHAPTER 5

A Slit of the Wrist or a Shot
in the Arm: Does Medicine
Really Bleed the Economy?

In a syndicated column, Paul Harvey related a story about Senator Tom Harkin of Iowa, campaigning in a Democratic presidential primary. Before entering a room where a public forum on health care was to take place, Senator Harkin announced to the waiting reporters: "There is but one issue in this election and that is jobs!" Once inside he reasserted: "There is but one issue in this election and that is jobs!" Upon hearing this an aide discretely informed him that the issue before the forum was health care. Harkin beamed back to the crowd: "There are two issues in this campaign—jobs and affordable health care."[1]

The irony here is that politicians like Harkin advocate lowering medical costs with government-imposed limits in face of the fact that the health care industry is the national leader in creating new jobs. Liberal politicians fail to grasp the link between the growth of an industry in response to increasing demand for its services and the public's ability to secure good jobs. The *Wall Street Journal* reported that during a six-month stretch of the economic recession—the recession that made jobs a campaign issue—828,000 jobs disappeared; but during that same six-month period, 241,000 new jobs were created by the health care industry.[2]

Oddly, the impression liberals give is that health care jobs are not beneficial. When Detroit sells another automobile, the event is looked upon as good for the economy because it keeps auto workers employed. And the fellows who repair your car at the body shop are viewed as productive members of society when they return your car to service as quickly as possible. But if you are injured in the same accident that put your car in the shop, the efforts of the doctors and nurses who work to repair your injuries and return you to good health are viewed as a drain on the economy!

Why—another instance—is it that when a family goes on a ski vacation, its expenditures are reported as good for the economy because they pump money into the ski resort business thus creating jobs, but if a member of that family falls on the slopes and requires hospitalization, the expenses incurred are considered a drain on the economy? Hospital workers, including janitors, cooks, nurses, doctors, technicians, and administrators, are productive workers just like all other workers in society. They shop at the same stores, eat at the same restaurants, bank at the same banks, pay taxes just like everybody else in the work force, and they *contribute* to the well-being of the economy along the way.

But instead of being thankful for the employment benefits of an advancing industry, the egalitarians perceive such an industry, in this case health care, as overwhelming others, and therefore in need of restraint. That mindset would have us believe that an advancing industry expands at the expense of other industries; therefore, if the advancing industry were turned back—shrunk to a lesser portion of the gross national product—society would benefit. Preposterous, of course.

Consider this reasoning when applied to the travel industry: Because Americans have spent almost three times as much on travel as Canadians on a per capita basis, the travel industry has absorbed too much of our gross national product (GNP). But unlike health care, the travel industry encountered turbulence en route: during a span of less than five years America's airlines sent 55,000 workers to the unemployment lines.[3] During that same period, eleven airlines declared bankruptcy and the industry lost more money than it had earned in all of its previous existence. Was this healthy for the economy?

Most people immediately recognize the fallacy of this reasoning. Most people understand that unemployment in one industry causes unemployment in other industries, and we all suffer. For, obviously, the more people travel, the more people are employed by airlines. And these in turn—through their spending and saving—create more employment in more industries. Moreover, if the industry is expanding, it will hire contractors to build new plants, purchase increasing quantities of supplies from vendors, and invest in capital equipment manufactured by other industries—all of which helps people secure employment. In short, more wealth for more people is created, not the other way around.

Yet, news reports continually tell us that health care *consumes* 12 to 13 percent of our GNP, or that our nation *spends* 12 to 13 percent of its GNP on health care. This bit of "mythinformation"—probably more than any other—is the basis upon which those proposing to socialize our health care system fully build their arguments. Again, this delusion is derived from the socialist vision of a static society of finite wealth that must be redistributed. The authors of this sophistry view the expansion of the health care industry as a drain on the economy; they believe industrial success must be challenged by government; they fail to comprehend that expansion and success are the result of industrial satisfaction of public demand. In a previous chapter we recalled the service station lines and soaring gas-pump prices that resulted when government disrupted the oil industry with well-head price controls and "windfall" profit taxes; those same conditions will occur in health care if government intervention increases.

This delusionary mindset was epitomized when—during a period of mounting unemployment—President Jimmy Carter twice implored Congress for approval to repress capital investments in health care facilities in the belief that he could hold the industry to a more "acceptable" percentage of GNP. Essentially, President Carter wanted to do for health care what he had done for the oil industry. Had he succeeded, he not only would have thrown untold numbers of construction and health care employees out of work, but Americans would have experienced their first shortages in health care capacity.

The fact that the news media have been able to advance the myth that the health care industry bleeds the economy is a further tribute to the media's success in advancing the socialist notion of "entitlement"—the notion that health care is a "right," just like life, liberty, and the pursuit of happiness, which are "free" and guaranteed under the Constitution. This recalls a quotation attributed to Ben Franklin. When asked what happened to all the happiness promised by the Constitution, Franklin replied: "The Constitution, my good lady, promises the pursuit of happiness, but you have to catch up with it yourself." Good health care is a worthy objective in an individual's pursuit of happiness, and for health care workers, the delivery of good care is a means to that pursuit. But if a person thinks that something should be free and guaranteed, then whatever amount he has to pay for it—for what is rightfully his—is unjust and wasteful. Inundated by the media's misleading campaign, the public has lost sight of the fact that health care is a viable and healthy participant in the economy, that it is not a "right," that it is not a drain or wasteful.

In reality, health care *contributes* to the GNP in a very positive way. Not only does it provide vast employment, which stimulates hiring in all sectors of the economy, but the products and services it provides are in great demand. The health care industry is the true bellwether of all service industries; it employs well over 10 million Americans with good paying jobs and ample opportunity for advancement.

In communities all across America, the world's most modern and best equipped hospitals employ highly trained nurses and some thirty categories of specially trained technicians ready to serve the needs of the public, 24 hours a day, 365 days a year. On those unfortunate occasions when we need hospitalization, we demand

(and deserve) prompt professional nursing care at the push of a button. The individual who responds to our needs when we are ill or injured must be well educated in medical matters and in the administration of care. But willingness is not enough; our hospitals report a severe shortage of qualified nurses to meet the demand, as evidenced by the reams of help wanted ads, even during economic recessions. Thousands of dollars in cash bonuses are offered to qualified nurses just to sign up at some hospitals, and many hospitals will repay student loans for new hires and offer tuition help for continuing education and advanced degrees. Nationwide, there are an estimated 300,000 unfilled nursing positions, and that figure is expected to double by the year 2000 despite that nursing school enrollments have been increasing at the rate of nearly 10 percent per year.[4]

Comparisons with other countries seem to belie our "shortage" in staffing: on a per capita basis, America employs almost two and-a-half times the number of nurses employed under the health care systems of Canada or Britain. Obviously, we demand, and are receiving, a different standard of service from those of other systems. Most Americans do not realize, when they check into a modern semiprivate hospital room covered under private insurance, that their British counterparts under national health care are likely to be crammed into wards containing eight or nine other patients with communal toilet facilities at hospitals built near the turn of the century. (Our Canadian neighbors enjoy more modern medical facilities because the system has been socialized barely twenty years; Canada, however, is already experiencing severe shortages of up-to-date equipment.)

According to the Bureau of Labor Statistics, moreover, health care services are projected to continue offering the strongest employment opportunities of any industry in America: job opportunities at private hospitals are expected to increase 27 percent by the year 2005. This is due not only to our growing population of the elderly (the fastest-growing segment of our population is eight-five years and older) and to the advancing frontier of new technologies that require newly trained technicians, but to the spawning of myriad new services demanded by the public. These include "wellness" information centers, nutrition and weight-loss clinics, osteoporosis diagnostic centers, home health care franchises, and birthing centers—all of which *contribute* to our GNP under the health care banner. And as the public shows greater interest in preventive health care—a phenomenon which I hope is not a passing fad—we will see continuing growth in the demand for medical services; and this because people with healthy lifestyles generally live longer, and the longer we live the greater our need for medical services.

The introduction of new technologies in some industries render certain manual employment redundant. But in health care, technological advancement brings new treatments for previously untreatable maladies, and better treatments for and earlier detection of other diseases, all of which translates into greater consumer demand for these services, more job opportunities, and an even greater *contribution* to the GNP.

Carol Kleinman, author of *The 100 Best Jobs for the 1990s and Beyond*, points out that as our economy becomes more service-sector oriented, the best job opportunities will lie in the growth industries of health care and computer services. She predicts that ten thousand openings will arise for paramedics by the year 2000 just to accommodate our aging population, and that positions for emergency medical technicians offer a clear path for advancement through continuing education; she also cites encouraging opportunities for radiology technologists. While doing all this, she drives home the message that we must adjust to the progress of new technologies: three out of four American workers will require retraining as we approach the next century. As a high-tech, service-oriented society, we cannot count on smokestack industries to provide employment any more than previous generations could rely on agriculture for employment after industrialization.

In many communities across America, health care is the primary employer and the economic good that draws patients from other areas—including foreign countries—adding to the industry's healthy *contribution* to the gross national product. Lest you think this only pertains to a small town where health care predominates—such as the world famous Mayo Clinic at Rochester, Minnesota—consider this: According to the Bureau of Labor Statistics, the largest private sector employer in New York City after business services is health care, which provides employment for a quarter of a million people.

My own community offers a typical example of how our superior level of care creates economic benefits. The Bascom Palmer Eye Institute—part of the University of Miami School of Medicine/ Jackson Memorial Hospital complex—reports that 40 percent of its patients come from out of state, half of these from foreign countries. This foreign influx is not unique to us. Subspecialty clinics like this are found all across America, most often associated with major medical schools and teaching hospitals.

Reflect upon the economic blessings bestowed on greater Houston by the success of the M. D. Anderson Cancer Center, a part of the University of Texas System and the Texas Medical Center comprising fourteen hospitals and twenty-six other nonprofit clinics and institutions. When Houston was hard hit by a double-barreled economic hardship—turmoil in the oil market and a depression in real estate development—M. D. Anderson proved to be the economic white knight that led the city back to prosperity. Despite bleak business prospects in other sectors, M. D. Anderson, already among the world's largest comprehensive cancer centers, embarked on a $250 million expansion project to meet the demand of patient admissions that had grown 60 percent during the decade. Scheduled for completion in 1996, the project included a 150,000 square-foot outpatient cancer screening center and a 726,000 square-foot inpatient care and research center. This expansion, coupled with another $626 million in new construction plans at the whole of the Texas Medical Center, spelled *jobs, jobs, jobs* for the people of Houston.

So outstanding is the medical care in America that the names of many of our comprehensive diagnostic clinics are as well known in Madrid, Hong Kong, and Buenos Aires as they are on Main Street America. No other country has facilities that can match the excellence of the Mayo Clinic (Rochester, MN; Scottsdale, AZ; Jacksonville, FL), the Cleveland Clinic (Cleveland, OH; Ft. Lauderdale, FL), the Lahey Clinic (Boston, MA), the Oschner Clinic (New Orleans, LA), the Scripps Clinic and Research Foundation (La Jolla, CA), and others too numerous to list.

Not only do these clinics and the great teaching hospitals of America draw patients from the far reaches of the earth, they also draw untold numbers of foreign doctors who come to advance their educations. It may be that Americans buy Japanese autos for their superior quality and that U.S. auto makers travel to Japan to learn how to build better cars, but when it comes to medicine, the whole world revolves around the United States, and that is one reason health care *contributes* 12 to 13 percent of the American GNP. While the news media berate our health care system for bleeding our GNP, our health care professionals have been busy earning world recognition for giving our economy a good shot in the arm when it needed it most.

Nothing in this discussion, of course, should be construed to mean that the American health care system is without waste. Clearly, the American public is not getting full value for the total sum spent, and I too call for "reform" of public policy. But as I have stated before, and will again, wasteful spending is induced through onerous regulation, an abusive tort system, "entitlement" programs providing welfare for the rich, and tax laws that put employers and third party administrators in charge of employees' health care, stripping the American worker of the right to control his or her own health care spending.

The health care industry has performed very well; it is government that has failed to deliver on its promises; it is government that must be curtailed. Unlike health care and all other productive industries, a large portion of government consists in a bureaucracy that produces nothing; on the contrary, it impedes production with regulations and takes money from working people who are producing and redistributes it to those who are not. The alarming fact about our GNP is not that health care contributes 12 to 13 percent, but that government takes over 35 percent of it in taxes— well over two and-a-half times the total production of the entire health care system![5]

Even if common sense reforms come to pass, the health care

portion of GNP would probably not be reduced; as medical technology closes in on cures for cancer and cardiovascular diseases, I believe that public demand for this technology will fuel continued expansion of the industry. The savings would be translated into more and better care, and because health care is labor intensive (75 percent of health spending goes to labor costs), we will have more employment, a healthier economy, and a healthier populace. A static view of society must be resisted, for it will lead government to penalize successful industries like health care while propping up failing industries; this would ultimately cause the wealth of our nation to diminish and leave more and more Americans unemployed.

Is the Grass Really Greener?

As though in "proof" that American health care consumes too much of the gross national product, the news media compare the GNP of the United States detrimentally with that of other industrialized countries, especially Canada. At first glance, these comparisons appear indisputable, even dramatic—so convincing, in fact, that most people ignore the red herrings in the numbers. How can it be—with what we know about the inefficient nature of government bureaucracy and the failure of socialism to provide even the basic necessities of life—that countries with socialized medicine spend less (as a percentage of GNP) than the United States where medicine is only partially socialized?

Obviously, the data are suspect; the distortion of government statistics for political purposes is not new; any journalist relying on these statistics should read Oskar Morgenstern's classic study, *On the Accuracy of Economic Observations*.[6] In it one learns how national income statistics are made to fit a bureaucratic "conceptual framework" and how data from government agencies are a by-product of administrative functions, giving rise to "a very strong reason to suspect the quality of data obtained in this manner." Exemplifying bureaucratic manipulation of statistics for political ends is the case of post-World War II Japan when national income statistics for that country, bearing no relationship to any objective criteria, were negotiated by the U.S. administration and Japan to reach a "suitable" figure upon which the U.S. Congress appropriated financial aid.

Of particular concern to Morgenstern, however, are the attempts to make international comparisons of national income statistics: "Such comparisons are freely made and far-reaching consequences are drawn, for example, when different degrees of welfare, economic development, etc., are being evaluated. Many uses are strictly of a political character."

What is most interesting—and almost always ignored by the popular press which uses these statistics to manipulate public opinion—is that the bureaucracies generating the reports continuously warn about the lack of reliability in the data and about the insuperable conceptual problems in making comparisons between nations. To underscore these warnings, once statistical reports have been released and reported in the popular press, they are invariably modified several times during the ensuing months by 20, 30, 50, and sometimes 100 percent. Added to those problems is the comparability of statistical reports between different bureaucracies within the U.S. government: "Things are complicated further by the fact that for the purposes of GNP segments, the Department of Commerce produces its own estimates of health expenditures—which have no direct relation to commonly used figures produced by the Health Care Financing Administration."[7]

Canadian bureaucrats, who, under socialized medicine, are in control of that nation's health care system, have a vested interest in devising methods of reporting data that reflect favorably on their performance and that justify further tax increases. Conversely, American bureaucrats have every incentive to demonstrate that the U.S. system performs poorly and therefore should be subject to increased regulation and a more powerful bureaucracy. The liberal media's fascination with comparing statistics reported by these bureaucrats leads to conclusions as fallacious as those drawn by John Kenneth Galbraith when he declared in 1984 that the socialist system of the Soviet Union was superior to Western capitalism.[8]

Setting aside the issue of the accuracy of the underlying data, studies in the scholarly press have attempted to adjust for differences in reporting techniques and other areas between American and Canadian health care statistics. One study published by the James Madison Institute and written by Jacques Krasny, a Canadian expert in health care policy, calculated the following adjustments.[9]

First, American accounting practices dictate that the cost of private sector health care working capital is reflected as an expense. Canadian health care facilities incur the same expense, but the cost is not reflected under the system of government-funded global budgeting for hospitals. Instead, the cost is hidden in Canada's national debt, which generally runs higher than the U.S. whether taken as a percentage of GNP or on a per capita basis. By applying Canadian money rates to capital employed by Canadian health care facilities, the studies indicated an adjusted increase of 3.15 percent in Canadian health care spending in 1987, the year upon which the studies were based.

Next, health care benefits of those employed in the American health care system are reported in operating costs of the respective health care facilities; whereas, in Canada these costs are over-whelmingly paid out of taxation and not reflected in health care costs. This adjustment raises total Canadian health cost by 6.3 percent. Although the Canadian statistics excluded the above expenses, included in the costs for both countries are expenditures on research and development. The only problem with this is that Canada relies on the U.S. for research and development, as does most of the rest of the world. If Canada were to invest a proportionally equal share in research and development, its total health bill would rise another 2.4 percent.

Finally, it is estimated that those 65 and over constitute 12 percent of the U.S. population, but they consume over half of the health care services. (Other studies estimate elderly consumption to be closer to 40 percent, but the difference would still be mitigated by the disproportionate number of Americans over age eighty-five.) By contrast, the Canadian "over 65" population as a percentage of total population is 1.2 percent less than the U.S. The adjustment for this demographic difference leads to an adjustment which increases the Canadian costs by 5.3 percent.

These four adjustments alone bring the Canadian percentage of GNP attributed to health care to within a half of a percent of the

United States. Even if the underlying data were reliable, the difference would be negligible, given the common margin for statistical error.

But this is not all. Many more factors affect comparisons between the two countries, some of which are incalculable, but none of which, as the following pages show, should escape our consideration.

Canadian government bureaucracies, both provincial and federal, administer that nation's health care finances and collect revenue for the health care system, but, unlike the United States, the costs of these functions are not reported as health care expenses. The true cost of administering the Canadian bureaucracy, which governs health care, is a guarded state secret—and almost always overlooked by journalists who compare the Canadian cost of administration with that of the United States. Because the paychecks of government bureaucrats are added to the GNP regardless of services performed, these Canadian administrative costs inflate the portion of GNP not attributed to health care while deflating the portion attributed to health care, thus grossly distorting the ratio when compared to the United States.

Another measure of comparison involves immigration. No other country in the world faces the same consistent onslaught of illegal immigration as does the United States. Our shores have been known to greet a thousand refugees from Haiti in a single day, not to mention the numbers that cross the border from Mexico, a nightly ritual. Most of these people are destitute, many are ill and in urgent need of medical attention. Many have never before been seen by a medical doctor, one reason they risk all to come to America. (Among Haitian refugees intercepted at sea and detained by U.S. authorities at the Guantanamo Naval Base, 10 percent tested positive for the AIDS virus—that is, 25 times the incidence of HIV infection in the U.S.) Since courts have ruled that all who have entered, illegally or not, are entitled to medical assistance, hospital emergency rooms are obligated to tend to their needs. And those costs—costs not incurred by Canada—are fully accounted for in America's percentage of GNP attributed to health care.

Another area of comparison has to do with veterans. Canada has not engaged in any military action of consequence since World War

II, whereas America has been involved in Korea and Vietnam. The continuing cost of caring for American casualties of these wars is substantial. The U.S. Veterans Administration reports that 20 percent of its patients are of the Vietnam era (although not all are war veterans); moreover, according to the Centers for Disease Control, Vietnam War veterans are far more prone to clinical depression, anxiety, and alcoholism than previous veterans. Whether these veterans are cared for by the Veterans Administration or privately, the additional treatment necessary for service-related maladies is often perpetual and costly.[12]

Age is another factor. Although an adjustment was made in the GNP comparison for America's disproportionate population over sixty-five in the above study, it should be noted that in the United States the population ratio for those over the age of eighty-five is one-third greater than in Canada. This compounds the difference between the countries because the medical needs of a typical eighty-five year old are substantially greater than those of a sixty-five year old. Studies have shown that about 50 percent of those over eighty-five suffer from Alzheimer's disease or some other form of dementia, often requiring round-the-clock care.

Another factor involves the legal environment of the United States, which is unique and bears heavily on medical costs. Consider the economic effects of these distinctions: Canadians have no right to sue government health officials or the ministries of health that run the medical system; as a practical matter, under Canadian law, there is no such thing as a class action suit against a manufacturer of drugs or medical devices; Canadian lawyers are prohibited from accepting contingency fees; in Canada, no punitive damages are awarded in cases of malpractice; in Canada, overutilization of medical testing for legal defense purposes is minimal; American doctors, whose education and practice procedures are quite similar to Canadian doctors, are fifty times more likely to be sued than their Canadian counterparts; American doctors, the U.S. General Accounting Office reports, pay malpractice insurance premiums that average ten times more than those paid by Canadian doctors.

Then there is violent crime. In America it is rampant. The male homicide rate in the U.S. is five times that of Canada. But it is the survivors of assault who run up expenses, and at a cost of about $75,000 per treatment of a single gunshot victim. The Canadian health care system does not begin to contend to the same degree.

AIDS is yet another drain on our health care system. It costs an estimated $100,000 to treat the average AIDS patient; and the incidence of AIDS, when adjusted for population, is over three times greater in the U.S. than in Canada. To some extent, the accelerated spread of AIDS in the U.S. compared to Canada is the result of intravenous drug abuse.

Drug use causes another slew of medical problems, as do neglected or handicaped babies. Highly intensive and expensive medical treatments are applied to low birth weight newborns and babies with congenital defects—cases which overwhelmingly result from unwed teenage pregnancies. The magnitude of this problem in the U.S. is evidenced by our teenage pregnancy rate which is two and-a-half times that of Canada. Added to that is the incidence of drug-exposed babies, what we call "cocaine babies," each one of which costs over $60,000 to treat. It is also estimated that hospital emergency rooms in America treat between 350,000 to 425,000 drug-related cases each year. Canadians should be very proud that their medical system is not called upon to deal with these problems to the extent that the U.S is, but this does not reflect on the efficiency of their health care system, as even a superficial comparison GNP ratios shows.

These are but a few of the cultural, legal, and demographic factors that differentiate the United States from Canada, greatly impacting the proportion of GNP allocated to health care. They do not reflect efficiency in the health care systems. So far as can be ascertained from the respective GNP ratios, the grass is not greener north of the border. The Canadian socialist system demonstrates no overall efficiencies or effective cost-containment features in comparison to the U.S., except for the ability of government bureaucrats to withhold care or delay treatment.

Beyond a direct comparison of national production statistics, it can be demonstrated that the U.S. health care system offers economic

benefits that cannot be analyzed by statistics alone. The American
health care industry, for example, is heavily criticized for the level of
aggressive and expensive care it provides, especially the expensive
prophylactic antibiotics after surgery, but few people consider the
economic and social benefits of returning sick, injured, and handicapped Americans back to productivity and self-sufficiency in the
minimum time possible. Compare the average length of hospitalization required in Canada and the U.S. for these common but often
serious maladies: In the U.S. the average hospital stay for heart
attack is less than 9 days; in Canada it is 14.7 days. In the U.S. the
average hospital stay for hernia is 3 days; in Canada it is 5.5 days.
Overall, Canadian hospital stays are 70 percent longer than in the
United States.[10]

The United States enjoys the best record in the world for efficient
postoperative ambulation. According to the Health Data File of the
Organization for Economic Cooperation and Development, the average hospital stay in the United States is less than six and-a-half
days compared to over forty days in Japan. Our expensive methods
pay for themselves many times over when patients return to work
that much sooner.

Even fewer people take into consideration the economic benefits
of treating patients promptly rather than leaving them to languish
unproductively while waiting for surgery or other treatments.
Think about this: In the Canadian province of British Columbia,
the average wait for heart bypass surgery is 5.5 months, the average
wait for hernia repair is 5.7 months and often more than a year.[11]
And it is not uncommon for British patients to wait a year for
cataract surgery, a procedure that does not even require hospitalization and is readily available in the United States.

And this does not include previously mentioned surgeries termed
"medically unnecessary" by socialists simply because the patient's life
is not in danger. Many women in America showing no signs of cancer
choose to undergo hysterectomies to remove fibroids and treat other
uterine problems that cause excessive menstruation, chronic anemia, debility, and disquieting mood swings. Again, the economic
benefits lie in productivity and quality of life.

Similarly, one should not discount the contribution of plastic surgery, an almost exclusive American specialty (many of Canada's most respected practitioners have moved to the U.S. due to a lack of government commitment to their field). Because we commonly associate this endeavor with the frivolous vanity of the wealthy, we neglect to consider the benefit received by thousands of burn victims, children born with deformities, and those disfigured in auto accidents and industrial mishaps.

All of these—and other—medical conditions are tended to without delay in the United States. This outstanding level of health care is one of the reasons we still have the most productive work force in the world, despite the heavy welfare cart government is making us pull.

CHAPTER 6

———————————/\\/—————————————

Apples to Oranges: Comparing Old and New Technologies

Contrary to conventional wisdom, modern technology has reduced the cost of medical treatment. We hear a great deal about how American health care is hooked on expensive technology, accelerating medical inflation faster than the general inflation rate, but this is more media "mythinformation" than objective observation.

In the days when I started surgical practice, one of the marvelous advantages of the new infection-fighting wonder drugs—the sulfa drugs and antibiotics—was that we were able safely to discover hidden medical problems by physically opening the patient and having a look, a procedure known as exploratory surgery. By today's standards, the idea of invading the body to search for the source of pain is primitive, almost barbaric. Besides, surgery is expensive. Nowadays, a patient is scheduled for a magnetic resonance imaging scan (MRI) at a cost of less than $1,000 compared to a surgical operation costing $30,000 and more—not to mention the economic loss of keeping the patient out of work for months to recuperate.

MRI scans came on the scene in the 1980s and made possible precision, multidimensional images wherein we can see soft tissue as well as bone; we can even spot the tiniest of capillaries almost anywhere in the body. The MRI uses an electromagnetic field to cause certain chemical molecules of the body to respond like gyroscopes, spinning and pointing in the same direction; when the electromagnetic field is released, the precessing molecules emit radio waves which are projected on planar maps of the organs under observation.

Few abnormalities can escape detection with the MRI; tumors, blood clots, and herniations, moreover, can be located much earlier in their development and with great precision. A very few years ago we lacked the ability to determine with ease when a spinal disk had ruptured, resulting in a great deal of unnecessary back surgery; this has now been eliminated due to the new technology. The procedure is fast, painless, noninvasive, and hazard-free, requiring no dyes, no radioactive fluids, no ingestions of foul, chalky substances, and no harrowing injections of air into the cranium. (All of these archaic alternatives produce relatively crude images of limited utility, but they are still used under health care systems where technological investment is restricted by government.)

So why is it that medical costs outstrip overall inflation, some years more than doubling the inflation rate? But the better question is: Why is it that the more regulatory price controls government places on the practice of medicine, the faster costs seem to rise?

What we read would have us believe that hospitals are fueling medical inflation by purchasing the latest equipment; price tags of several millions of dollars are often mentioned for a single imaging machine. But in truth this machinery saves money. All those new and ever-changing bureaucratic regulations to control costs actually create greater compliance costs—and administrative compliance represents one of the fastest growing components of health costs—while new technologies create new and better treatments for medical maladies.

With advanced imaging techniques, for instance, an aneurysm of a blood vessel of the brain can be pinpointed enabling a neurosurgeon to effect a repair. Fifteen years ago, the rupture of such an aneurysm spelled certain death or irreversible impairment; doctors were helpless without the ability to locate the offending vessel and without microscopic instrumentation to make the necessary repair. The estate of the patient fifteen years ago was likely to incur the cost only of a relatively inexpensive ambulance ride; today's patient incurs a $50,000 neurosurgical, hospital, and rehabilitative therapy bill. What the media are comparing is a healthy recovery to a fatality; new technology to old; an apple to an orange. Is that inflation?

The consumer price index (CPI), which government statisticians use to track inflation, is composed of commodities that the typical household consumes on a regular basis. Prices of bread, butter, and other staples of our existence are recorded and compared over time with the resultant increases reported as inflation. A stick of butter and a loaf of bread today are not much different from the bread and butter my mother served with dinner when I was a child. Medical treatment, on the other hand, advances so rapidly it cannot be compared over time. When I was a schoolboy, scarlet fever, whooping cough, diphtheria, and consumption were dreaded killers that attacked families and friends with regularity. Most schoolchildren today have never heard of these diseases with funny-sounding names because medical advances have overcome their ravages, just as future generations of schoolchildren will query the odd-sounding "cancer" diseases that inflict so much grief today.

Medical costs continue to climb because technological advances make possible more effective treatments which, in turn, create new demand. Those afflicted with ailments that can be helped with the use of advanced technology want the new treatments, of course, but that is hardly inflation, because the treatments did not previously exist.

What is difficult to grasp in the current technological revolution is the exponential rapidity by which advancements build upon prior achievements; the more scientific knowledge we accumulate, the faster we are able to acquire new knowledge.

Ether was first used to perform "painless surgery" in the 1840s, and although steady progress was made during the intervening years, ether was still the anesthetic of choice when I entered practice

nearly a century later. But with the use of newly developed anesthetics and accompanying instrumentation and methodology, skillful anesthesiologists now can effectively slow blood circulation to a
trickle for hours, safely bringing body temperature down to a mere
60 degrees, allowing surgeons using microscopic instrumentation
to repair heart defects, even on the tiniest of newborn infants. Such
a feat was the stuff of science fiction just a few years ago.

Think how slowly we progressed during the century before 1940
compared to the current pace. More than half of the diagnostic and
therapeutic tools of medicine in use today did not exist just seven
years ago, and the half-life of medical knowledge continues to grow
shorter.

If you were the parent of a child with a congenital heart defect,
would you demand the most modern anesthetic, instrumentation,
and methodology so surgeons could attempt a repair? Or would you
be satisfied with the cheaper dripping of ether on a mask, in which
case there would be no possibility of repairing your child's tiny
heart? Like most people, of course, you would demand the latest
and best for your child, and that translates into greater demand for
medical services. People have always demanded that doctors do
everything possible to cure their ailments and those of their loved
ones. The difference is that we can do much more than in the past.
And, once again, that is not inflation.

There is no question that new medical technology has not always
been acquired prudently; but, then again, it has not always been
acquired on favorable terms, as it would have been under a free
market system. For more than twenty years—in a fashion typical of
bureaucratic intervention in the marketplace—perverse incentives
that kindled wasteful disregard for economic considerations were
built into Medicare reimbursement rules. Hospitals were simply
provided a guaranteed return on capital outlays; the more they
spent on equipment, the more profit they were guaranteed to earn.
You can add to that the fact that most patients have little incentive to
compare the costs of using the equipment, and that no effective
methods have been provided for patients to make comparisons
because government and third party administrators have taken on
the responsibility for paying the bills.

But these disruptions of the marketplace aside, one would be hard pressed to find an example of new medical technology that tends to increase the cost of diagnosis or treatment without a corresponding increase in the quality of that diagnosis or treatment. Better quality health care means more efficient health care, and any time a patient is returned to health more efficiently and quickly, economic goods ensue.

These economic benefits are clearly demonstrated with new, minimally invasive techniques such as angioplasty—the insertion of a catheter with a tiny balloon on the end to unclog a blocked artery. Similarly, arthroscopic techniques in orthopedics and laproscopic techniques in gynecological and general surgery have shown cost reductions of up to 50 percent for those patients whose conditions allowed them to forgo traditional surgery, not including the economic benefits of returning to work in half the time. These feats are made possible by viewing instruments and surgical tools that require only tiny punctures rather than gaping incisions; and although the technology is in its infancy—under guarded utilization by doctors—instrument manufacturers predict that 80 percent of abdominal surgery will involve these techniques by the end of the decade.

Among the most dramatic technological success stories is the revolution in cataract treatment. Every year nearly a million and-a-half Americans have the blessing of unobstructed vision restored in their doctors' offices with remarkably few complications. What began as a very expensive procedure requiring hospitalization and months of healing before the effectiveness of the surgery was known, is now performed with the use of ultrasound to break up the cataract for removal through a microscopic incision. Still other technologies have made it possible for ophthalmologists to prevent blindness due to glaucoma and complications of diabetes mellitus, and even from a detached retina. The result of these advances is more and better eye care, not inflation.

Another popular myth about America's advanced medical technology is that it really doesn't work any better than old-fashion methods of care. The media, moreover, often criticize the medical establishment for not emphasizing preventive care over medical intervention. In truth, the American Medical Association—funded by its member doctors—has always devoted its resources to researching the causes of illness and educating the public on those findings. In spite of these efforts, the Center for Disease Control reported that too many Americans are overweight and that nearly 60 percent of us get little or no exercise. On the other hand, there has been modest improvement in smoking rates; tobacco creates such a potent miasma that any reduction in its use is bound to help dramatically in avoiding heart disease and strokes. A breakdown of the statistics on lifestyle risk factors is, nevertheless, still disheartening, as you will see in due course.

The bright side of this picture for those of us who have failed to follow the doctor's orders is the heroic roll medical technology plays in saving us from ourselves: the American Heart Association reports that the death rate from heart attack dropped 30 percent in just ten years between 1979 and 1989.

Even more dramatic is the reduction in the death rate from strokes: down 31.5 percent during the same decade. With the development of new pharmaceuticals, ultrasonography, and carotid endarterectomy, we can avoid strokes for those at risk through drug therapy and we can locate arterial obstructions and surgically remove them to preempt a stroke. Ultrasonography—an imaging technology similar to sonar—not only avoids the hazards and discomforts of radiation and physical intrusion, it significantly undercuts the cost of an MRI scan. (Unfortunately, it cannot be used to examine the brain, spine, or lungs like the MRI.)

America's commitment to medical technology pays off with big dividends in other ways too. Our investment in research and development for medical purposes from both public and private sources dwarfs that of any other country. While it may appear as though the rest of the world is getting a free ride, in reality, American manufacturers have captured 48 percent of the world market for medical devices, and the industry reels in an export trade surplus of over $2 billion a year.[1]

Add to that the Commerce Department's report of an export trade surplus of $1.4 billion produced by U.S. pharmaceutical manufacturers, and one can see that industries devoted to technological innovation hold the key to solving our country's persistent balance of trade deficits. Perhaps if our auto industry had invested in technology to the same degree as medical industries, we would still be a net exporter of cars. Interestingly, a study released by the Council on Competitiveness and the Harvard Business School indicates that American industry lags behind Japan and Germany *not* because of unproductive workers, but because of a lack of commitment to the long-term goals of research and development.

During the half-century that I have been in medicine, I have witnessed life-saving miracles arrive—one after another and more today than ever before—in the form of a simple and relatively inexpensive dose of medication. Nothing else that modern society has made can come close to the marvels produced by the ethical drug industry. And with the exception of public health measures that are themselves dependent on vaccines and other products of the industry, nothing is more cost effective than these medications in the fight to save lives, relieve suffering, and return the sick and injured to health and productivity.

Although a relatively small industry, private pharmaceutical manufacturers currently invest nearly $11 billion a year in research and development, a figure that has doubled every five years since 1970, making the industry the principal biomedical researcher in the world. This private commitment to biomedical research exceeds even the U.S. government-funded National Institutes of Health.

The United States leads the world in pharmaceutical production. Of new medications achieving worldwide acceptance over the past fifteen years, nearly half were developed in the United States; American firms introduced more than twice as many new drugs as Britain, their closest international competitor. Worldwide, U.S. manufacturers were awarded 83 percent of the biotechnology patents and 72 percent of the generic engineering patents, according to an industry survey taken in 1989. It is important to note that these achievements are primarily the result of private enterprise, as evidenced by the fact that of the hundred patented drugs most often prescribed in the United States, ninety-six were patented by private industry and individuals compared to only four by government and universities.[2]

Research-based pharmaceutical manufacturing in the United States is an intensely competitive business. To put the industry in perspective, consider that in terms of sales General Motors alone is two and-a-quarter times the size of the combined pharmaceutical industry worldwide, but unlike the auto industry with only three American manufacturers, there are about two hundred American pharmaceutical manufacturers, and no single firm holds more than 7.6 percent of market share. While General Motors reports that it reinvests only about 4 percent of sales revenue in research and development, member companies of the Pharmaceutical Manufacturers Association report that they reinvest 17 percent of sales in research and development, an imperative in such a competitive environment.

The economic and social benefits of the pharmaceutical industry are equally impressive. Reflecting on my early days as a resident physician at Milwaukee County Hospital, I recall that my first assignment was to a sequestered ward where I treated patients suffering from diphtheria, whooping cough, tetanus, measles, polio, erysipelas caused by the deadly streptococcus, and other infectious diseases that were, at the time, the number one killers in American society. During that era, too, the land was dotted with sanitaria devoted exclusively to victims of tuberculosis.

Due mainly to pharmaceuticals—drug therapies and vaccines—the incidents of infectious diseases have been brought under control; smallpox has been eradicated worldwide, and cases of diphtheria, polio, and whooping cough have been virtually eliminated in the United States. The incidence in the United States of typhoid fever has been reduced by 95.3 percent since 1940; measles by 93.8 percent; syphilis by 90.6 percent; and tuberculosis by 77.2 percent.[3] In the case of tuberculosis, the fatality rate has declined a remarkable 91 percent since 1953. More than any other single factor, pharmaceuticals, with their ability to control infectious diseases, have been responsible for our dramatic increase in life expectancy from fifty-four years in 1920 to over seventy-five years today. (Recent failures to vaccinate have caused a resurgence of measles, the result of parental neglect despite the vaccine's proven value.)

One truly remarkable aspect of some new drug therapies is their ability to eliminate the need for costly and painful surgery. Fifteen years ago the only cure for a stomach or duodenal ulcer— potentially fatal if left untreated—was corrective surgery at a current cost of about $30,000. Today, using the drug Tagamet at a cost of about $1,000 per year, ulcer surgery is only rarely required. Since the introduction of Tagamet in 1975 the savings in ulcer treatment worldwide are estimated to be nearly $6 billion. In another example, according to a Veterans Administration study, many coronary artery patients whose conditions are responsive to the drug therapy of beta blockers and nitroglycerin can be treated for about $500 a year compared to the alternative bypass surgery at a cost of $40,000 plus.

Two consecutive studies commissioned by Schering-Plough Corporation and executed by Battelle Medical Technology and Policy Research Center in 1990 analyzed the societal and economic benefits of pharmaceuticals; the first traced the history of the past fifty years; the second projected twenty-five years into the future. The conclusions of the studies are truly stupendous. In the case of polio, the Salk vaccine introduced in 1955 avoided 970,000 cases of which 630,700 would have resulted in paralysis to some degree. The direct costs of treatment saved by the vaccine was $1.3 billion, and the indirect costs, measured in terms of human capital, saved society $11.1 billion. The economic benefits derived from pharmaceuticals over the past fifty years with regard to just four diseases—polio, tuberculosis, coronary heart disease, and cerebrovascular disease— amount to $141 billion. Of course, nobody can put a price on the human suffering from these four diseases—the 1.6 million people who avoided prolonged sickness or death, and the emotional grief of family and friends.

Projecting pharmaceutical benefits for the next twenty-five years, the Battelle Research study concludes that 395,000 serious cases of Alzheimer's disease will be controlled, reducing the direct costs of treatment by $68 billion. Nine million cases of coronary heart and cerebrovascular disease (stroke) will be avoided at a savings of $211 billion. Lung cancer, leukemia, and colon-rectal cancer cases will be reduced by 662,000 at a savings of $15.7 billion. Osteoarthritis and rheumatoid: 1.5 million disabilities avoided at a savings of $181 billion.

Just as the pharmaceutical revolution that emerged at midcentury catapulted us into the modern age of medicine, so too, at this very moment, we are in the midst of yet another scientific revolution in pharmaceuticals, and progress is advancing faster than anyone could have anticipated. From the new frontier of biotechnology and genetic engineering it appears the world will realize the long sought-after but elusive goal of definitive and painless therapies for cancer as well as the control of viral infections, Alzheimer's disease, and other complicated ailments of our day.

And just as it was with the first pharmacological revolution that I watched during my early years of practice, so with this one, American private enterprise has again taken the role as world leader. Biotechnology has discovered how to mass produce pharmaceutical ingredients that previously could only be made in minute quantities. Not only will this technology reduce the cost of production, it will greatly enhance the quality of products. When the aim is to destroy unwanted cells with toxins, the enhanced specificity of generically engineered drugs will see malignant cells attacked while leaving healthy tissue unmolested.

The evidence is overwhelming. Here is an industry that does exactly what American free enterprise is supposed to do. It manufactures a better mouse trap. Spurred by eager competition and the profit motive, it delivers a superior product from which society benefits. It continually seeks to improve its product and it proves its superiority through worldwide acclaim, creating vast export sales that give more Americans good jobs. And it delivers its product efficiently. As a percentage of total health care costs in the United States, prescription drugs account for less than 5 percent, and that represents a *reduction* from almost 9 percent in 1965, according to the Health Care Financing Administration. Prescription drugs, moreover, account for less than 1 percent of our gross national product, with no increase since 1965.[4]

The men and women who make the American pharmaceutical

industry successful do so through diligence and hard work. Beginning with their schooling, they must excel in difficult courses of science and mathematics; and in their daily work, human life itself depends upon their careful adherence to scientific principles. They are modern day pioneers, taking risks, venturing where no one has ventured before, leading society into the future.

One would think that with their record of accomplishment, the media would hold pharmaceutical producers up as role models for young people, as they do basketball players and actors. One would think that Congress would honor them with an award for creating jobs while preventing death and alleviating suffering. But those who view facts from the socialist perspective see things topsy-turvy. From television we get special "documentaries" indicting the industry for greed; from Congress we find proposals to impose tax penalties on the industry and bureaucratic price controls on the products. According to the new religion of liberalism, pharmaceutical producers commit a mortal sin: they earn a *profit!*

Headed by Senator David Pryor of Arkansas, the Senate Special Committee on Aging issued a staff report of sophistic observations upon which legislation is being proposed. One notable example is the charge that the industry spends more on marketing than on research. Karl Marx made the same observation about all capitalist industries when he designed a system that would eliminate what he perceived to be wasted marketing effort. The result was a system that failed to bring needed products to the consumer.

The research-based drug industry depends on its ability to bring a steady stream of improved, patentable products to market. The introduction of new drugs requires extensive and detailed explanations before physicians can begin prescribing them to their patients. To guard against any abuse in the marketing system, the American Medical Association established guidelines that forbid undue inducements to doctors, and the Pharmaceutical Manufacturers Association adheres to those guidelines.

Profits are a major concern in Senator Pryor's committee staff report which charges that the pharmaceutical industry profit margins are three times greater than the average *"Fortune* 500." What is so interesting about this is that the pharmaceutical industry invests four times the all-industry average in research and development. Most American industries attempt to sidetrack the risks of building a better mouse trap by seeking easier short-term profits, which is one reason Japanese industries have gained the upper hand, driving profit margins down further.

The high risk of venturing into a costly research project with an uncertain outcome is evidenced by the 1991 *"Business Week 1000"* survey in which twelve of the thirty largest pharmaceutical firms either lost money or returned less than a bank savings account would have earned shareholders. Most of us look at a tiny pill and assume the ingredients could not cost more than a few pennies; we are unaware that it costs an estimated $231 million to bring a single new drug from concept to the marketplace; and after numerous attempts to produce a new drug in the laboratory, only one in four thousand proves to be nontoxic, effective, and marketable.

It takes an average of twelve years to bring a new drug to market, but just getting it there is not the end of the risk: Duke University economist Henry Grabowski reports that of every ten drugs that eventually make it to market, only three sell enough to recover the developer's research cost. Yes, when a pharmaceutical company finally scores with a winning product, it must produce a very big profit or it could never take the risk of developing new drugs. It is a good thing the American pharmaceutical industry is profitable. We all benefit from those profits.

It is also apparent that minorities benefit from the industry as much as anyone. Allow me to explain: Among the most unhealthy proposals to come from Senator Pryor and his liberal colleagues is their attack on what they call "me-too" drugs. What they view as a me-too drug is any new product that treats a malady that can be treated by an existing product.

Pryor attempted to enact "formularies" for substitution of prescriptions so that me-too drugs could be bypassed for cheaper alternatives. This would have involved the creation of a federal commission to devise tables of drugs that could be substituted for the specific drug prescribed by a physician. In that way, a bargain drug would be swapped for the prescribed drug for Medicaid patients—without the consent of the doctor or patient.

As Senator Pryor should have known, the human body is complex, no two are exactly alike, and each of us reacts a little differently to different medications. Usually those reactions are subtle, sometimes they are violent. Also, different ethnic groups, races, and ages respond differently to medications for genetic and other reasons. For instance, Dyazide, one of many hypertension medications, is considered a me-too drug. Yet, in practice, we find that Dyazide is especially effective for African Americans and senior citizens. These groups have higher incidences of hypertension than the population in general, and the availability of an effective medication is crucial to prevent heart attacks and strokes. Given the current political climate, it is ironic that policies of liberal politicians conspire to discriminate against minorities while industry is eager to serve them.

Another benefit of multiple entries into the market is the unexpected. All drugs have some surprising side effects, and that is not necessarily bad. Often we find that drugs possess properties that are effective against maladies never contemplated by the researchers. While it is true that some new drugs have presented unpleasant surprises that did not surface during the trial tests, we have also had some pleasant surprises: lidocaine, for example, a local anesthetic, was found to be effective in treating cardiac arrhythmia. At present, the Food and Drug Administration (FDA) has almost nine thousand new drug application amendments requesting tests for additional uses, and most of these are for me-too drugs. The more me-too drugs that come to market, the better our chances of saving lives and relieving suffering in unexpected ways.

It would be nice if every new drug that came to market brought a major therapeutic breakthrough. Without question, that is what every manufacturer hopes for; otherwise, nobody would commit hundreds of millions of dollars and a decade or so of effort to a single drug project. But securing a major therapeutic breakthrough is far more difficult than, say, producing a box office blockbuster, and everyone knows how perilous show business is.

Still, Senator Pryor insists that any pharmaceutical firm that produces a me-too drug should lose its research tax credit, if it qualifies; he wants, moreover, to impose price controls to ensure that pharmaceuticals not rise faster than the consumer price index. In short, what Pryor favors is a government-regulated drug market modeled after Canada.

But Canada's controlled drug market has some obvious drawbacks. First, the United States is the world leader in pharmaceutical innovation, and we have already demonstrated the economic benefits derived therein—drug therapies, export sales, and employment. How has Canada fared in comparison? Where the U.S. is number one, Canada is dead last: in recent years, Canada has introduced fewer medicines than any country in the industrialized world. If Canadians did not have the U.S. pharmaceutical industry to rely on, health care would be much more expensive and of much less benefit. And if the Canadian government had not robbed its citizens of the incentive to be more innovative and productive, Canada might have captured a greater share of American pharmaceutical jobs—just as Japan and Europe will capture our jobs if Senator Pryor has his way. In that case, of course, the United States, like Canada, will become a net importer of pharmaceuticals.

Congress should know that first place is a precarious position. Politicians should have learned this not only from our auto industry, which was once the indisputable world leader, but more recently from our electronics industry, which has eliminated a quarter of a million jobs during the past four years, according to the American Electronics Association.

Last year the Council on Competitiveness reported that mistakes in public policy harmed our competitiveness in electronics, and that similar mistakes are now being made with respect to the pharmaceutical industry. The report noted a "disturbing trend" in American industry—the loss of technological leads. And this because of three government-created causes: first, a lack of government support for private sector research efforts; second, inadequate incentives and confusing, often contradictory, economic policies; and third, product liability laws that discourage innovation while providing inadequate protection for consumers.

The U.S. pharmaceutical industry may hold an enviable world market share at the moment, but foreign competition is anxious to topple its preeminence. A 1990 report by Booz-Allen and Hamilton, entitled "The Global Pharmaceutical Industry: Competitive Re-structuring for the 1990s," demonstrates that European and Japa-nese firms are starting to match U.S. investments in drug research and development. And while America's future in the industry rests on its lead in the new frontier of genetic engineering (biotechnol-ogy), the U.S. Commerce Department reports: "Biotechnology has been targeted by the Japanese government for specific attention and support."[5]

It should be apparent to Senator Pryor and his liberal colleagues that we need more incentives to attract investment in drug research, not fewer. With greater research investment not only would the industry's technological lead be held, but consumers would benefit from the advanced therapeutic remedies and the lower prices that greater competition brings. Anytime a new drug enters the market—even if it is not a therapeutic breakthrough—prices are held down by the force of added competition.

Logically, congressional efforts should be focused on removing government-created costs and impediments to the research indus-try. Clinical trials for new medications have already shifted from the United States to Europe and Japan because it is becoming too costly to perform studies here. What that means to the American con-sumer is that new therapeutic advances will not be available until much later, and that the domestic drug market will become less competitive and more dependent on imports. In the end this means we will spend more, and wait longer, for medical treatments.

While Congress has long sought to placate special interests with promises of expanded entitlements or controlled prices—i.e., some-thing for free at someone else's expense—it has neglected its duty to oversee those agencies that are meant to protect the public from harm. A case in point is the Food and Drug Administration which is faced with a bureaucratic logjam of new products waiting to be brought to market. As a result, a growing number of new drugs obtain approval overseas first, thus depriving Americans of the therapeutic advancements and placing American producers at a competitive disadvantage.

Although the approval requirements of most foreign drug review agencies are as stringent as those imposed by the FDA, the average processing time for new drugs is three and-a-half years less than at the FDA. And even though the FDA is mandated by law to conclude the paperwork in the final review process within six months of submission (after completion of all clinical trials), the actual time taken is two and-a-half years.

When, moreover, hundreds of millions of dollars are already invested in research and extensive clinical trials, the time value of that money becomes staggering during the protracted bureaucratic delays. If the American FDA were to operate with the same efficiency as its foreign counterparts, the average cost of bringing a new product to market would be reduced by more than 25 percent.[6]

Nowhere is the FDA backlog more egregious than in the division responsible for approving biotechnology and genetically engineered products, where many momentous breakthroughs are being delayed for years. For instance, despite a mounting backlog, not a single medication in the monoclonal antibody category has been acted upon in the past five years, even though the pending products include life-saving advancements in overcoming organ transplant rejection, septic shock, and cancer.

To grasp fully the gravity of the problem, remember that the knowledge that enables scientists to splice genes has been gained at American universities and research institutes over the past forty years. Those institutions are taxpayer-supported or the recipients of government grants and public donations. We, the American people, paid for the foundations of that knowledge in the hope and anticipation that our nation would prosper from it. It was paid for with the expectation that America would continue as the world's technological leader and that our sons and daughters would avail themselves of that knowledge, secure good employment, and then invest in the knowledge of future generations.

We must also be mindful that knowledge without the ability to apply it is useless. Only the pharmaceutical industry has the ability and incentive to transform raw scientific knowledge into useful products at an affordable price. This fact is exemplified by the history of penicillin, knowledge of which lay dormant for over fifteen years in England before it was brought to American pharmaceutical manufacturers who developed methods to mass produce it.

Filled with sophistic delusions that industries will continue to lead once stripped of all incentive to invest and earn a profit, our liberal congressmen are on the verge of denying Americans the last technological frontier in which we hold a substantial lead. If Senator Pryor is sincere in his expressed desire to secure affordable medicines for the public, he should focus his attention on the inefficiencies of government, not private industry. The American people would then benefit from less costly but more effective health care and better job opportunities.

CHAPTER 7

Drugs, Sex, and Violence

Picture a pot boiling over on the stove. Would it be more prudent to clamp a lid on in hopes it will not explode, or to turn down the fire? The boiling pot is analogous to the eruption of medical costs. Liberal politicians are frantically trying to clamp a lid on with proposed price controls and global budgets, what President Bill Clinton calls a "national ceiling on health care costs," while ignoring the causes of overheated demand—the fire under the pot.

If such controls are implemented, unchecked demand will drive costs to the legal limit, and the health care system will not be able to take care of everybody who needs help—price controls during periods of high demand always lead to shortages. History, moreover, tells us that shortages induced by price controls lead to arbitrary rationing, which denies care to some at the whim of faceless bureaucrats. Then, when controls are finally lifted, prices explode.

What is so ironic about the current health care debate is that not only are liberals failing to address the unwarranted demand, their own social policies are what fired that demand to such appalling levels to begin with. They say our health care system is responsible for higher infant mortality and lower longevity than some other countries. In truth, these problems are not medical ills, but social ills brought about by liberal social policies. Social ills are not the result of poor health care; they fuel the fire under the pot.

Americans, for instance, have always had an affinity for guns—the Second Amendment to the Constitution even assures the right to own a gun. But, as in the case of every right, there is a concomitant responsibility. At one time Americans used guns to civilize a hostile land; today we create hostility in a civilized land.

We used to say that people were murdered by murderers. In those days we had few murders, even though there were plenty of guns. Nowadays we hear that people are murdered by guns, and that we have too many murders because there are too many guns. Just look at this headline from the Washington Post Service: "Guns kill more teens than diseases."

Aren't we missing something here? Unlike a disease, someone must pull the trigger of a gun; that person is the killer, and he should be held responsible. The medical system can control the spread of disease, but gunshot wounds are the result of social ills that must be controlled by clamping a lid on crime, not health care.

Our failure to hold individuals responsible for their actions has led to the highest violent crime rate in the industrialized world. Liberals will retort that we still have stringent penalties for crime, and that, besides, locking up criminals doesn't work. But the penal system worked in the past. Our crime epidemic only dates back to the 1960s, when the rights of criminals were strengthened and the rights of their victims weakened.

Under liberal social policies, crime pays. The National Center for Policy Analysis released a report calculating "expected punishment"—the cost of committing a crime as opposed to statutory penalties. The expected punishment, or perceived cost of committing a crime, was derived by multiplying the probabilities of (1) being arrested, (2) being prosecuted if arrested, (3) being convicted if prosecuted, (4) going to jail if convicted; then multiplying this by the median time actually served for the specific crime. Based on these calculations, a murderer could expect 2.3 years of imprisonment for his crime; a rapist less than three months; the perpetrator of aggravated assault less than two weeks.[1]

The expected punishment for serious crimes has been reduced by two-thirds since the early 1950s, and today seven times as many serious crimes are committed. By reducing the cost of committing crimes, we have increased the demand, and thus the cost, of medical treatment.

Gunshot wounds pose some of the most challenging of all demands for health care services, especially at inner-city trauma units which are inundated with such patients. Bullets, when they don't kill the victim outright, often cut through vital organs, severing arteries and shattering intricate joints. One bullet can create the need for three, four or more surgeries, often requiring the services of neurosurgeons and cardiopulmonary specialists simultaneously. Within milliseconds a single bullet can cause more internal destruction than years of cancer and heart disease, and it can leave the survivor permanently paralyzed and with other chronic disorders—disorders that require medical attention for the rest of the patient's life.

Herculean efforts to repair multiple wounds in a single gunshot patient have been known to cost hundreds of thousands of dollars. In my discussions with hospital administrators across America, I hear the same story over and over: "The vast majority of gunshot victims are uninsured and do not pay their medical bills." For many hospitals the emergency room represents an open door through which money flows out twenty-four hours a day.

Because we have the highest crime rate, we spend more than any other industrialized country treating the victims of crime—a sum that increases dramatically with each passing year. The problem is compounded for American cities with disproportionately high crime rates. To illustrate the inner-city situation, a tally was made of the medical bills of all crime victims admitted to the eleven emergency rooms of Washington, D.C., during a period of two months. The total exceeded $40 million, and the bills of individual patients—two-thirds of whom were uninsured—ranged up to a quarter of a million dollars.[2]

What happens to all those unpaid bills? How can any hospital accommodate the next gunshot or stabbing victim? It's not easy. Those deficits must be paid by someone, so they are added to the bills of all paying patients—one reason we get charged several dollars for a single aspirin.

Hospitals are targets of much misguided rage for such overcharges; and politicians exploit that rage to justify a lid on health costs. But what would happen if the lid were clamped on while crime continued unchecked? Can we really allow politicians to force hospitals to turn away the victims of crime—crime these same politicians failed to control?

It should be apparent that every time a life is taken by crime, the average life expectancy of our population is lowered. After all, life expectancy is the average lifespan of all people in a given society—the younger the crime victim, the lower the average. If youths are dying on the streets as a result of drugs and violence, then life expectancy for the entire nation drops.

Many other factors can affect average life expectancy, but news reports comparing America's longevity statistics with those of other countries usually imply that Americans lag behind due to poor health care or its inadequate delivery. But on closer look, statistical comparisons prove precisely the opposite. American life expectancy at birth is 75.4 years, placing it eleventh among the top fifteen countries worldwide. Even at that, America's massive heterogeneous population impressively leads the smaller, homogeneous populations of Finland, Denmark, the United Kingdom, and New Zealand, each of which has a universal, socialized medical system. Japan is in first place at 78.9 years. But when comparisons are made of life expectancy from postadolescence on, America narrows the gap to fourth place by age sixty-five. America's international ranking improves with age because our longevity statistics are skewed by the high rates of adolescent homicide, suicide, drug addiction, trauma, and by our high infant mortality. For instance, our homicide rate for males fifteen through twenty-four years of age is forty-four times that of Japan.

Similar comparisons are made of infant mortality rates which show that the United States ranks about twenty-second among industrialized nations. Again, Japan enjoys the lowest rate. What the news reports don't tell is that the mortality rate for infants born of unwed mothers of all ages is about 60 percent higher than legitimate births, and that the rate of illegitimate births is twenty-six times greater in the United States than in Japan (26 percent vs. 1 percent of all births).

We know that the teenager's body can procreate long before mental and emotional development allow for responsible parentage. Even on the physical level, the U.S. Public Health Service has listed pregnancy by girls under age eighteen as a risk factor for premature delivery and low birth-weight babies, the major causes of infant mortality. Nationally, the average age of a teenager who becomes pregnant is sixteen, and in large cities that average is significantly lower—as in my hometown of Miami where the average age is fourteen.

You can add to that the problem of common adolescent behavioral patterns of expectant mothers—smoking in an attempt to appear mature, taking drugs and alcohol under pressure of peers, and consuming junk food for pleasure followed by crash dieting to satisfy vanity. Each of these behaviors multiplies the risk of an unhealthy delivery.

Fewer than 1 percent of Japanese mothers are teenagers compared to 13 percent of American mothers. Setting aside the incidence of drug abuse and deleterious maternal behavior among adults—behavior unique to the American scene—this comparison alone indicates medical intervention in the United States is significantly more effective in saving newborns when social factors place them at much greater risk. A comparison of maternal mortality rates also confirms the effectiveness of American medical care: a mother is four times more likely to die during delivery in Japan than in the United States.

If Japan seems too remote or alien to provide a fair social comparison with the United States, similar comparisons between Canada and the U.S. demonstrate the same moral decline and excessive medical demands of our society. The rate of teenage pregnancy is greater in the United States than Canada by a factor of over 240 percent. And in the U.S. almost half of all illegitimate births are to teenage mothers.

It is remarkable that we are able to save as many infants as we do, for while it may be said that we lag in twenty-second place in infant mortality, our incidence of low birth-weight deliveries is higher than thirty-one other countries—providing further evidence of superior medical intervention in a nation marred by parental neglect.

Low birth-weight—the incidence of neonates weighing less than 5.5 pounds—accounts for 75 percent of infant deaths within a month of birth and 60 percent of all deaths before the first birthday. Think of it: low birth-weight increases the likelihood of infant death within the first year by a factor of twenty. The condition is usually preventable, as it is most often caused by the very behaviors just mentioned: drug use, smoking, drinking, and inadequate weight gain during the first and second trimesters of pregnancy. These behaviors frequently coincide with the unwed mother syndrome, and not only among teens.

Historically, infant mortality in the United States has undergone continual improvement, and more neonates survive today than ever before. But improvement came solely from advances in medical treatment, despite the dereliction of parental responsibility. Countries unhampered by this social anomaly have lessened infant mortality rates more rapidly, and with much less medical intervention.

Initial declines in infant mortality over the past half-century came from the control of tuberculosis, cholera, typhoid fever, and other infectious diseases. Later, a technological revolution brought about the neonatal intensive care unit, and, most recently, dramatic progress has come from pharmaceutical breakthroughs, especially the development of surfactant, a drug which stimulates respiration in the tiniest of neonates.

Well over 90 percent of low birth-weight infants are saved in America, more than in any other country. Most are restored to normal health and returned to the care of their mothers, however deficient that care may be. Even those weighing just 1.2 to 2.2 pounds experience an 80 percent survival rate compared to 30 percent just fifteen years ago. Still, each year about forty thousand babies cannot be saved; they die within a year of birth. It is estimated that many times as many are saved but live with severe abnormalities requiring continual medical attention or custodial care. Very low birth-weight infants (weighing less than 2.2 pounds) are twice as likely as those of normal weight to develop congenital anomalies and are at great risk of cerebral palsy, autism, mental retardation, blindness, and deafness. Only a quarter of congenital anomalies are caused by genetic factors, whereas three-quarters are the result of maternal behavioral and environmental factors—e.g., fetal alcohol syndrome (FAS) from drinking during pregnancy and drug abuse.

The financial demands that low birth-weight deliveries have placed on the medical system are staggering: the treatment of severe cases can range up to a million dollars and more. We spend about half a billion dollars a year on hospital bills for the delivery of cocaine babies alone. Add to that the cost of perinatal care and foster care, developmental and special education, and other health services through age five and the annual price tag estimated by the inspector general of Health and Human Services is $20 billion, of which the parents rarely pay a penny.

American public policy has proceeded for decades on the assumption that our high incidence of low birth-weight is caused by poverty, scarce medical resources for low income mothers, or by insufficient nutrition. As a physician, I support measures that extend medical care to those unable to provide for themselves, but gainsaying behavioral causes of low birth-weight deliveries in America has only aggravated the problem.

Poverty is not the cause. Poverty is contributed to by paternal abandonment of family responsibilities. This is easily proved by comparing whites to Asian-Americans, who have a higher poverty rate than whites, but who also have substantially lower incidences of infant mortality. The same is true of Pacific Islanders under American domain. Or one can compare African-Americans to the residents of Puerto Rico, an American commonwealth: Puerto Ricans have much higher poverty rates, but they also have much lower rates of infant mortality.

The problem is attributable to neither race nor racial discrimination. This is evident by comparing the incidence of low birth-weight among immigrant black mothers to American-born black mothers: the rate for American-born black mothers is over 50 percent higher.

Malnutrition is not the problem. The American taxpayer spends over $2.5 billion a year to give mothers eggs, milk, cereal, fruit juice, cheese, and legumes under the Special Supplemental Food Program for Women, Infants and Children (WIC). In over twenty years the program has had almost no effect in combating the incidence of low birth-weight babies in America.

Lack of available prenatal care is not the problem. At an estimated cost of $17.4 billion Congress expanded Medicaid in 1984 to include more low-income women and children, plus free prenatal care for teenagers. At the request of Senator Lloyd Bentsen (D., Texas), a study was conducted by the General Accounting Office to determine the effectiveness of the enhanced program. The study found "little evidence" that free coverage resulted in better use of prenatal care.

Long prior to his conviction on drug charges, former Washington, D.C., Mayor Marion Barry boasted that his city had the most comprehensive prenatal care network in the country—and it was no idle bluster. At a cost of well over a hundred million dollars a year, the district's public health department operates sixteen clinics conveniently located throughout the inner-city, eleven of which offer prenatal care absolutely free to anyone with a household income of less than $20,000. The clinics are open evenings to accommodate working women and are fully staffed: doctors, nurses, dentists, social workers, WIC counselors. They even provide drug treatment referrals. Then there is the Maternity Outreach Mobile program— the MOM Vans, which ply inner-city neighborhoods giving free rides to the clinics, leaving reminders with patients about pending appointments, and going door to door to scout out pregnant women who may be eligible for care at the clinics. And you can add to that the Better Babies campaign, a radio, television, and billboard advertising campaign to promote prenatal care and publicize the availability of free care. The district also has more private obstetricians who welcome Medicaid patients than any other city— again, providing free prenatal care to anyone in need. Problem solved? Low birth-weight under control? Quite the contrary: infant mortality in the District of Columbia is the highest in the nation— treble the national average!

The District of Columbia is not alone in this costly, utopian experiment. Detroit features an equally elaborate prenatal network, and the city also deputized a permanent posse of social workers to ferret out pregnant women of inner-city neighborhoods and drive them to the free clinics. Does it work there? No. Infant mortality in Detroit is second only to the District of Columbia.

Of course, the absence of prenatal care and proper nutrition are causes of high infant mortality in many less developed countries. But in American inner-cities, even where these aids are aggressively promoted and offered free of charge, behavioral patterns preclude their use. In a free society we cannot force-feed prenatal care, much less force a mother to act morally or responsibly. No amount of free food, no amount of free medical care, no amount of income redistribution will induce people to act responsibly. To heap new social welfare programs upon old, failed programs is tantamount to adding stories to a building with a faulty foundation.

In practicing family medicine, one aspect of humanity becomes apparent: people dedicated to family life are healthier than those who are not. That is a gross generalization, of course; the world abounds with tragic exceptions and delightful remissions. But a stream of research reports confirms that general observation of so many doctors.

The reports are too numerous to list, but here are some examples from one article: a study by the Health Care Financing Administration indicates that Medicaid patients who are "high users" of hospitals are three times more likely to be divorced or separated; a University of Michigan study of patients fifty-five and older who had been hospitalized for chronic illness demonstrates that those who were single spent more than twice as much time in the hospital as married ones; the National Center for Health Services Research reports that divorced women suffer more health problems than married women despite the advanced average age of the latter group; and Princeton University demographers note that married men and women of all industrialized countries enjoy distinctly lower mortality rates than singles.[3]

The reasons for these phenomena are numerous and complex, but, clearly, bonding in matrimony is "natural" and healthy for our

species. Tragically, Americans have been abandoning the responsibilities of family life. From the time I entered medical practice in
1938, the divorce rate in America has increased nearly two-
and-a-half times, giving us one of the highest rates in the world.
Simultaneously, many Americans have been forgoing marriage
altogether. Since 1970 the rate of marriage among those under
forty-five has decreased by more than a third.

But the decision to forgo marriage has not deterred many from
bearing children. America has among the highest illegitimate birth
rates in the world—more than a quarter of our neonates are born of
unwed mothers, an 85 percent increase since 1960. But it is no
longer fashionable to ostracize those born out of wedlock, and I am
the first to concede that these children do not deserve to be stig-
matized. After all, it's the unwed mothers and fathers who are
illegitimate!

Since holy matrimony in American culture stems from Judeo-
Christian morality, the fact that single parent households are intrin-
sically less healthy is difficult for many liberals to accept. According
to the liberals' new religion, to choose to bear children out of
wedlock is no more important than to choose Coke over Pepsi; and
should any deficiencies eventuate, they are, in any case, the responsibility of government because child-bearing is a right.

Parenthood is, of course, a right, but like all rights, it is also a
responsibility—for both parents. A father is needed to contribute
financially as well as emotionally to the family he helped create.
Scholarly literature is filled with studies demonstrating that children raised in fatherless homes are more likely than those with
fathers to engage in behavior that leads to the emergency room
door—i.e., drug abuse, alcoholism, prostitution, recklessness, de-
linquency, violent criminality. And those who commit the most hei-
nous crimes are commonly raised by single mothers whose own
behavior is marked by sexual promiscuity. Data from the U.S. Department of Health and Human Services has shown that children of
single parent households are up to 40 percent more likely than
those with two parents to encounter substantive health problems.[4]

Disintegration of the family has taken its greatest toll among
minorities, especially African-Americans and Hispanics, the very

minorities Great Society legislation promised to benefit. Not surprisingly, these populations issue the most overheated demands for medical care. Inauspiciously, over 60 percent of black children in America are born of single mothers.

Critics will charge that I am privileged, and since not all can be so fortunate, the Great Society programs were devised for the less privileged. The critics are correct. I am privileged, privileged to have been raised in a loving family. I owe all of my successes to the emotional and moral support provided by my family (for my failings I have only myself to blame). And I want the underprivileged to enjoy the same advantages.

The advantages my parents provided during my formative years were worth much more than mere wealth or status: when I was lazy they instilled duty; when I was disheartened they instilled fortitude; when I was wicked they instilled morality; and when I was hateful they instilled love. I ask: Can government do that for a child?

When undereducated, unwed teenage girls of any race or ethnic origin give birth, there is little chance they will ever become self-sufficient, and in all likelihood their children and their children's children will lead lives marked by poverty, dependency, and extraordinary medical needs. The simple truth is that people are motivated by incentives, and our current welfare programs create perverse incentives: our government pays unwed teenagers to drop out of school and bear children.

Cash paid under Aid to Families with Dependent Children (AFDC) is not enough to justify illegitimate child-rearing as a career, but to an undereducated juvenile, it adds up: AFDC provides an income where there is none; the recipient need not work to be paid; the recipient need not continue in school; the recipient is absolved from other parental responsibilities because she is also eligible for the Special Supplemental Food Program (WIC) in addition to food stamps, subsidized housing, Medicaid, and free access to public health clinics and hospitals. Moreover, the recipient will be paid additional money for every illegitimate child she bears.

In all there are over ninety welfare programs for which she may be eligible. But it is not so much the free bounty that proves enticing, it is the early invitation to adulthood with absolution of adult responsibilities. In the delirium of adolescence, freedom from re-sponsibility is a powerful incentive.

To qualify for full benefits under AFDC the recipient is prohib-ited from marrying the father of her child(ren) or anyone else. She is also prohibited from prudently saving her income or improving her condition with anything but the most menial employment.

Can we honestly expect that children who bear children under these perverse incentives will provide proper moral guidance for their offspring? Can we expect that they will dutifully maintain a safe, hygienic environment for their children? These are the same mothers who fail to immunize their children for whooping cough, diphtheria, tetanus, measles, rubella (German measles), polio, and hepatitis B, even when the service is offered free at public health clinics. Surveys of various inner-city populations show that, depend-ing on the locale, 40 to 90 percent of two year-olds have not com-pleted immunizations, and, as a result, we are experiencing a resurgence of communicable diseases.

Over the past quarter century America has spent a trillion dol-lars on the War on Poverty, more than on any military war in history, and yet we accumulate casualties more rapidly than ever while liberating very few. It's time to face reality. The welfare recipient ultimately gets only thirty cents of the taxpayer's dollar; the other seventy cents is a powerful incentive for politicians to keep the money flowing.

Some of the most powerful special interest groups, moreover, such as the National Education Association (NEA), lobby inces-santly for socialized medicine to cure high infant mortality and low longevity, especially among inner-city populations. But readers who believe government can deliver health care more efficiently than private medicine would be wise to examine government's record on education. The poor performance of public schools is not for lack of taxpayer commitment.

A Fordham University study of New York high schools during the 1988–89 academic year showed that of the $6,000 spent per stu-dent, less than a third actually reached the classroom. In fact, almost half the money was absorbed at 110 Livingston Street, Brooklyn, where not a single studen was taught, but where over four thousand bureaucrats massaged every penny allotted by taxpayers to "education."5 As John Chubb of the Brookings Institution pointed out, big city public school systems have one administrator for every 150 students; parochial schools have one for every four thousand.6

The problem is not lack of funding, but a morally bankrupt public school monopoly controlled by professional poverty panderers. To understand why Johnny can't read, and why he turns to drugs, sex, and violence, we must focus on the philosophical underpinnings of public education.

As we saw in Chapter Four, the reflection of reality found in the press is distorted by the abiding legacy of Horace Greeley—i.e., the socialist mindset interpolated into the methods of modern journalism. What Horace Greeley did for journalism, John Dewey (1859–1952) did for education.

Dewey's thoughts transformed American public education from being the envy of the world to a national disgrace. He threw the system in reverse. And Dewey's power was enhanced by his leadership roles in the Intercollegiate Socialist Society (now the League for Industrial Democracy) and the American Civil Liberties Union, by founding the nation's first teachers union in New York, and, most significantly, by being honorary president of the National Education Association, the largest and most politically powerful union in America.

John Dewey, in the tradition of Saint-Simon, Fourier, Marx, and Greeley, touted his socialistic agenda as "scientifically" determined. Among Dewey's "scientific" assertion was that self-sufficiency was some sort of mental illness. In a college textbook of his authorship, which was standard issue for teachers-to-be for over half a century, he expressed this absurdity as follows:

From a social standpoint, dependence denotes a power rather than a weakness; it involves interdependence. There is always a danger that increased personal independence will decrease the social capacity of an individual. In making him more self-reliant, it may lead to aloofness and indifference. It often makes an individual so insensitive in his relations to others as to develop an illusion of being really able to stand and act alone—an unnamed form of insanity which is responsible for a large part of the remediable suffering of the world.7

Is it any wonder that adults educated under Dewey's theories seek economic support through race, ethnic, and group identity rather than individual achievement? Is it any wonder that youths so trained seek interdependent social power through street gangs?

Dewey also taught that moral training had no place in education. His humanistic-naturalism held that since moral authority was not found in nature, it carried no weight; therefore, natural impulses were to be encouraged and value judgments established according to the satisfaction derived.

Dewey's humanistic-naturalism meant that man was simply another animal in nature, no more in need of moral guidance than a goat or a rabbit. But no goat or rabbit has been known to abuse drugs and alcohol—immoral behaviors that lead to excessive medical demands. While the rest of the animal kingdom is guided by its instinct for survival, mankind is drawn to self-destructive behavior from which only moral guidance and discipline can protect it.

On this point Dewey attempted to distance himself from fellow naturalists by asserting that when a natural impulse could be shown "scientifically" to be self-destructive, then a value judgment could rule against it. But as every good teacher knows, adolescents believe they are indomitable; while each has been told smoking causes cancer, he also thinks it cannot happen to him. More than a thousand Americans die each day from the effects of tobacco use, and each day four thousand become new smokers, 87 percent of them minors. It is a long stretch for a teenager to connect scientific data concerning future consequences with current behavior. Moreover, even where scientific inquiry does demonstrate self-destructiveness, it may take years of rampant license before sufficient evidence emerges, as exemplified by the AIDS epidemic, which is a consequence of sodomy and sexual promiscuity.

Look at how Dewey's theory is applied in teaching high school sex education. In the popular textbook *Changing Bodies, Changing Lives* by Ruth Bell (New York: Random House, 1980), teenagers give testimonials about how good they feel about having sex, and others tell of their preference for abstention—it's up to the student to choose which is right for him or herself. Syndicated columnist Don Feder points out similar advise for teens in a Planned Parenthood publication which scorns the "myth" that "young women who have more than one partner are easy. Some people, both men and women, prefer to relate sexually to more than one person at a time." And from another Planned Parenthood instructional for teens in Syracuse, New York: "Many people believe that sex relations are only right when they are married. Others decide to have sex outside marriage. This is a personal choice."[8]

The point made is that whether or not the student engages in sex is irrelevant, whom the student has sex with is irrelevant, what kind of sex the student engages in is irrelevant; but how the student "feels" about it is all important. From that feeling one establishes a "personal value judgment" for guidance in sexual practices. Taken to its logical conclusion, pedophilia, bestiality, incest, even rape can be justified. If the behavior in question cannot be scientifically proven destructive to the one who feels the impulse, what are the limits to amoral, stimuli-driven value judgments?

Simply put, Dewey's amoral revolution combined with the perverse incentives of the welfare state have resulted in naked savagery in the most scientifically advanced civilization in history. Our teenage drug addiction, criminality, pregnancy rate, and incidence of sexually transmitted diseases, including AIDS, are higher than those of any other industrialized nation. In consequence, our demand for health care is greater than any other industrialized nation's.

To diehards of the socialist mindset, the solution is not to reintroduce school children to morality and personal responsibility, but to hand out condoms in school. Adams City High School, near Denver, Colorado, was the first to give kids condoms a few years ago, since which time the student birth rate has soared to 31 percent above the national average. In response, school administrators installed a nursery on campus for the students' offspring, thus further absolving kids of parental responsibility.

Adult encouragement of adolescent promiscuity far outweighs the effectiveness of condoms. It is a matter of simple arithmetic: if condoms are 80 percent effective, two of ten sexual encounters pack the potential of pregnancy, infection, or both. Increase the number of encounters and you increase the incidence of pregnancy and venereal disease. Common sense notwithstanding, the practice of distributing condoms in schools has spread from New York to Los Angeles. (Reflect on the current absurdities: children of our inner cities are prohibited from learning the Ten Commandments— "Thou shall not steal, thou shall not kill, etc.; instead, they are taught to use condoms.)

Since Congress enacted Title X of the Public Health Services Act in 1970, the American taxpayer has spent $2 billion to provide free contraceptive services to teenage girls and low income women. During this time several surveys have shown that sexual activity among teens has increased dramatically. It is dismaying for a physician to reflect on the consequences, but during a period of just two years, between 1986 and 1988, the incidence of syphilis among teenagers has risen 62 percent. Is it any wonder, despite all the marvelous medical advancements, that adolescents constitute the only age group of America whose health status has not improved over the past three decades?

During the 1960s President Lyndon Johnson declared his War on Poverty, and Congress passed volumes of social legislation with the promise of creating a Great Society. Great Society legislation changed one thing for certain: the way we view responsibility. We were led to believe that government could supersede family responsibility in assuring acceptable social behavior, that poverty and crime could be controlled by changing the socio-economic conditions rather than by individuals exercising responsibility. We were promised an end to ignorance by instilling a "feeling" of self-assurance in young people rather than by requiring them to learn rudimentary academics, morality, and personal responsibility.

But as the ensuing years have proven, there can be no freedom without responsibility because there is no such thing as freedom from responsibility. Freedom from responsibility has only made people dependent on government, and dependency is no freedom at all.

Health care is not the only thread in the social fabric strained by the weight of the teetering welfare structure; the justice system, the job market, public education, race relations—all are threads of the same fabric, frayed by the same fundamental flaws. Correct the flaws of omnipotent bureaucracies and we will begin to restore the self-sufficient family unit as the catalyst of responsible behavior, and, in so doing, turn down the fire under the pot.

One thing for sure: we will not control unwarranted demand for medical care by creating a government monopoly of medicine. Instead, we must liberate the welfare state with inner-city student vouchers, enterprise zones, lower taxes, and incentives to work and save.

Modern health care is said to be a right, but again, there are no rights without responsibilities: we cannot afford twenty-first century medicine and behave like barbarians. Yes, we can have a great society with health care available to all, but as Winston Churchill said: "The price of greatness is responsibility."

CHAPTER 8

AIDS: The First Politically Protected Disease

I am not a homophobe. As a physician I subscribe to the philosophy that all people must be treated as individuals, with empathy, and with a willingness to assist without regard to the source of the problem: Physicians are homophiles.

Medical practitioners have a threefold purpose: First and foremost, to prevent disease and injury through public health measures and education; second, when confronted with illness or accident, to cure the patient and hasten recovery; third, to relieve the pain and stress of those who cannot be helped by curative therapies. Anyone who pursues a career in medicine assumes an obligation to strive for these objectives.

The first objective, prevention, is the most desirable, of course. Prevention is inexpensive and it helps protect against suffering and death. For many years doctors have spoken out against the use of tobacco in hopes of preventing cancer, emphysema, heart disease, and strokes. Smoking leads all other behavioral factors in causing disease. But it is the use of tobacco that deserves condemnation, not its victims. Should we be branded as homophobes for that effort?

Our compassion and treatment are not diminished for patients who ignored our warnings. Just so with AIDS.

AIDS is in most cases a preventable disease. It was not preventable for some hemophiliacs and transfusion recipients who found that the blood supply upon which their lives depended had been contaminated (before effective screening became available), but it was preventable for those who contaminated the blood supply. It was not preventable for a number of babies afflicted within their mothers' wombs, but it was preventable for many of the mothers who bore them. In short, more than 95 percent of all AIDS victims contracted the disease through their lifestyle behavior; only the remaining 5 percent contracted it from the former under circumstances over which they had no control—and with effective blood-screening methods, these occurrences are diminishing.

How is it that this preventable disease has already killed, and in less time, more people than the Vietnam and Korean wars combined? The answer: AIDS is the first preventable disease in American history to be politically protected. In the press and in our schools—both vital to our mission to educate for prevention— AIDS has enjoyed protection under the new ethos of "political correctness." In government and its bureaucracies, the HIV virus has acquired a sort of civil rights of its own—although there is nothing civil about AIDS, the final manifestation of HIV. Ironically, laws and regulations have been designed to restrict the actions of the vast majority of citizens who are not infected, but nothing has been done to admonish those whose behavior puts them at risk or to inhibit the actions of those able to spread the disease.

On the contrary, medical and public health exhortations to label AIDS as a *sexually transmitted infectious disease* have been rebuffed. Such a designation would do nothing more than subject the AIDS episode to the same proven public health measures applied to syphilis and gonorrhea. Instead, a campaign has been launched to absolve those whose behavior spreads the disease while blaming those whose message, if heeded, could have saved the lives of more than 130,000 victims, as well as the hundreds of thousands, perhaps millions, now destined to die.

A good example of this distorted message is the film *Stop the*

Church, aired by some public television stations, in which the Roman Catholic Church and New York's Cardinal John O'Connor are blamed for the spread of AIDS. In one scene a man invades the sanctity of Saint Patrick's Cathedral in New York City screaming, "You're killing us!" In another example, gay activists calling themselves "Dignity" staged "stand-ins" at the cathedral: during Mass, with their backs to the altar, they shouted obscenities to disrupt the service. Cardinal John O'Connor, who encourages monogamy in matrimony and abstinence rather than condoms out of wedlock, was condemned as "the city's sickest mass murderer."

By what twist of logic can the church be accused of spreading AIDS? The church does not condemn homosexual individuals, the church simply teaches that sodomy—committed by many homosexuals—is immoral and should be avoided. But gay activists, rather than accept responsibility for their promiscuous and lethal behavior, demand that the church abandon its biblical teachings and condone behavior it considers immoral.

What the church terms immoral or sinful can accurately be translated in secular terms as unnatural and foolish. What the church calls sodomy is also called anal intercourse. Whatever you call it, it is the root cause of the spread of AIDS. Not only is AIDS preventable, it is *easily* preventable. By traditional standards of behavior, AIDS is difficult to contract.

The HIV virus requires an unobstructed portal of entry to the bloodstream in order to infect its victim; it cannot survive in the open air very long. Anal intercourse provides the ideal conduit for transmission because the tender tissue of the rectum was never intended to be repeatedly violated by the intrusion of a penis. These violent intrusions result in torn tissue and bleeding lesions that create portals for transmission of semen to the bloodstream. The anus and rectum are not sexual organs; they are the drainpipe of the body's sewer. Anyone foolish enough to play in a sewer can expect unhealthy consequences.

While sodomy explains the most common route by which the HIV virus moves from host to yet another victim, its spread in epidemic proportions is explained by the abandoned promiscuity of the victims among multiple partners, often numbering ten and more during a single interlude. This is not to suggest that all homosexuals engage in this activity, but it is to insist that an aggressive subculture exists that, by promoting this lifestyle, is responsible for the AIDS epidemic.

This frank discussion is intended neither to offend nor to condemn homosexuals, but to jolt people—both homosexuals and heterosexuals—into realizing the importance of being responsible for one's behavior; it is the obligation of a physician so to educate. People who control their hedonistic urges for immediate gratification and instead invest emotionally in sincere, monogamous relationships, enjoy the greater long-term rewards of life; those who succumb to beastly urges and subject their bodies to unnatural activities in search of immediate gratification suffer horrifying consequences.

Unfortunately, since the 1960s our society has increasingly accepted the new religion of liberalism, whose basic tenant teaches that society, not people, are responsible for whatever the action. This doctrine has resulted in depravity and death.

We read the headlines: "AIDS Spreading Fastest Among Heterosexuals." And we hear the axiom: "It can happen to anybody." But in truth AIDS does not threaten those who live according to traditional family values, except in freak instances. AIDS can be spread through heterosexual activity, but again, transmission is through the portal to the bloodstream provided by an open lesion, and ulcerated genital lesions are usually the result of venereal diseases: syphilis, chancroid and genital herpes. We find cases of transmission to and from prostitutes and other promiscuous women with ulcerated venereal lesions; these women have had sexual contacts with bisexual men who, in turn, had previously contracted the HIV virus through anal intercourse. In like fashion, we find women who contract HIV through anal intercourse with bisexual men—again those who had themselves previously contracted it through homosexual anal intercourse. Also, we find that HIV can be spread heterosexually through intravenous drug use—sharing needles with those who, either directly or indirectly, have been contaminated through anal intercourse.

Transmissions between homosexual men outnumber heterosexual transmissions ten to one—even though homosexual men comprise less than 10 percent of the general population—because AIDS is primarily spread through anal intercourse. Notwithstanding the anatomical impediments against transmission from women to men (a woman is seventeen times more likely to contract AIDS from a man than a man from a woman), no overly promiscuous sexual activity is risk free, with or without a condom. It is not sexual preference that deserves condemnation, but rather the promiscuous and unnatural practices of some people, both homosexual and heterosexual.

Certainly the most unaccountable of the uncommon AIDS cases were those of Kimberly Bergalis and Barbara Webb. Kimberly, an intelligent, vivacious twenty-three year old, and Barbara, a stalwart grandmother of sixty-six, contracted the disease in the office of their dentist, Dr. David Acer, through nonsexual means that remain shrouded in forensic mystery. Because of the potential ramifications of this type transmission, the case of Dr. Acer has been investigated by health authorities more thoroughly than any other single-source transmission.

But after all the delving, all we still know is that Dr. Acer was a promiscuous sodomite who contracted AIDS through anal intercourse and then transmitted it to Kimberly, Barbara, and three other patients during the course of dental treatment; and we know also that Dr. Acer failed to abide by standard sterilization practices: he reportedly treated himself with instruments and later used these unsterilized instruments on his patients.

But scientific probes could not even confirm that this wanton neglect was a probable cause of the transmission because the HIV virus does not survive outside of body fluids for very long. Interestingly, a friend of the dentist later told the *Palm Beach Post* that before his death, Dr. Acer spoke of his belief that a cure for AIDS would not be found until it struck mainstream Americans—young people and grandmothers.[1] And indeed, it did strike, right in Dr. Acer's office—the only case in history in which a health care worker transmitted the virus to patients. (More than twenty health care workers have contracted AIDS from patients, usually while handling blood.)

Shortly before AIDS terminated her young life, the virtuous Kimberly Bergalis testified before Congress and the world that she "didn't do anything wrong." Those innocent words of an innocent victim succeeded in enraging gay activists and liberal columnists: "Inciting homophobia!" they cried. "David Acer didn't do anything *wrong* either," they wailed. "This is code" to denigrate homosexuals, they insisted. After all, "anybody can get this disease." They demanded absolution for a lifestyle of sodomy and promiscuity, and never mind the nonparticipant who got in the way.

A vicious campaign has been waged against anyone who dares tell the truth about the spread of AIDS. The AIDS Coalition to Unleash Power (ACT-UP), a national organization, uses disruptive and distasteful tactics against those engaged in public health efforts to explain lifestyle dangers and stop the spread of AIDS through prevention. When Dr. Louis Sullivan, our dedicated, straight-talking secretary of Health and Human Services during the Bush administration, attempted to relay the shocking truth—nearly two-thirds of AIDS transmissions are through anal intercourse between homosexual men and nearly a quarter are through sharing contaminated needles by intravenous drug users—he was shouted down.

During the 1991 annual meeting of the American Medical Association at the Chicago Hilton Hotel, I observed a noisy rabble outside the hotel shouting "Cure AIDS now!" while defacing the walls with "American Murder Association" and other offensive graffiti. (Ironically, while police held the disheveled crowd at bay, our foremost clinicians and researchers were deliberating on how to improve treatments and relieve the suffering of AIDS patients.) ACT-UP members also invaded our nation's Capitol, blocking doorways and shouting from the galleries that Congress must "Cure AIDS now!"

What, then, of the charge that not enough effort is being put forth to find a cure for AIDS? Groundless. *More money is being put into AIDS research than into any other disease.* Federal research funds for AIDS exceed those allotted to heart disease or cancer, even though

AIDS patients are small in number compared to the massive numbers stricken with either of the others. In 1990 heart disease took nineteen lives for every one life lost to AIDS, yet heart research received less than $1 billion that year compared to $1.6 billion for AIDS. Similarly, cancer struck twelve times as many victims as AIDS, yet only $1.5 billion in federal funds went into cancer research.[2]

Much of the research funding earmarked for cancer, heart, and lung diseases is, moreover, actually devoted to AIDS, especially when manifestations of the other diseases are unique to AIDS patients. For instance, it is estimated that one-quarter of the 1991 cancer budget was actually spent on AIDS research.

To visualize more clearly the disproportionate research spending, consider this: in 1991 there were 1,100,000 cases of cancer reported in the U.S. compared to 179,136 AIDS cases. Without adjusting for AIDS research conducted with cancer money, research was $1.55 per cancer case reported compared to $2,841.42 per AIDS case.[3] And while AIDS funding is still being increased, cancer research has declined below its 1980 level. Not surprisingly, reports speak of imminent breakthroughs in cancer therapy that have been stalled due to lack of funding—and most cancers are not preventable.

In addition to federal (taxpayer) funds for AIDS research, private pharmaceutical companies are currently conducting ninety-six different research projects on AIDS, and eighty-eight medicines and vaccines are under development. Since the introduction of AZT and ten other drugs for the treatment of AIDS, life expectancy from the time of diagnosis has been extended from under ten months to over three years, with some patients living up to five years. Mathilde Krim of the American Foundation for AIDS Research anticipates that life expectancy for patients will soon be extended to ten years, and that within the decade a normal life span could be restored, but only with constant medication and treatment.

The cost of treating AIDS patients, however, is astronomical and rising rapidly as new technologies extend the lives of those infected. Fred J. Hellinger, PhD, an economist with the Agency for Health Care Policy and Research, estimates that, currently, it costs over $100,000 to treat an HIV-infected patient until his death. From that, imagine the multiple increases as life is extended by new treatments. In the aggregate, the cost of treating Americans with HIV infections is estimated in excess of $7 billion a year and will probably exceed $10 billion by 1994.[4]

These rising costs, when covered by insurance, are reflected in the rising premiums we all must pay. In hospitals, the costs of treating uninsured patients are shifted to the bills of insured patients; and public hospitals are, of course, supported by taxpayers. At the 1991 International Conference on AIDS, Dr. Dennis Andrulis of the National Public Health and Hospital Institute reported that surveys of public hospitals nationwide showed AIDS treatment facilities were filled to capacity and beyond, while the treatment of AIDS patients accounted for 28 to 36 percent of the responding hospitals' financial losses.

Added to this burden is the legal designation of AIDS as a "disability" under the Supplemental Security Income program. This qualifies many afflicted with AIDS to receive taxpayer monies from the Social Security system, a luxury not granted to those who suffer from cancer, heart disease, or other debilitating maladies. Recently, the qualifying rules were relaxed to include many who are infected with the HIV virus but have not yet shown signs of full-blown AIDS; i.e., those who can still work collect government disability benefits.

The vast majority of Americans—those who live by traditional family value—are paying the price of treating AIDS and of searching for its cure. And they are more than willing to offer further public support for the sake of humanity, because the public by and large is not homophobic. Homosexuals have, after all, made innumerable contributions to science, the arts, entertainment, fashion, music, and business. Many homosexuals are committed to monogamous relationships and many do not violate bodily functions nor pose unusual or excessive problems for themselves and society— HIV does not infect people because they are homosexual, it infects people because they engage in high-risk behavior. Most Americans, myself included, feel strongly that homosexual citizens deserve their privacy and should be left alone to pursue happiness as they see fit.

We must remain mindful, too, that many people who do engage in high-risk behavior are also valuable contributors to society. I, like many Americans, have mourned the loss of friends to AIDS. My heartfelt compassion went out to them during their suffering no less than to those friends who died of cancer or any other debilitating malady. Organizations such as ACT-UP, on the other hand, make little or no positive contributions. Their hostilities may well provoke an unwarranted animosity against homosexuals in general. I fear the belligerent antics of ACT-UP, Queer Nation, and other militant homosexual organizations will suffocate society's compassion; I fear they will eventually strain our nation's tolerance for individual differences, the cornerstone of a heterogeneous democracy.

Moved by the loss of many colleagues, Hollywood personalities, in the name of the fight against AIDS, raise vast sums of money for organizations that attempt to dignify what cannot be dignified rather than curb the behavior that spreads the disease. Unburdened by the responsibilities of family life, homosexual activists have devoted their time and energy to wielding political power, and done it so effectively as to belie their small numbers. In the main, these activists work through three groups: the Human Rights Campaign Fund, a homosexual political action committee (PAC) to finance political candidates; the National Gay and Lesbian Task Force, a parallel group to the Americans for Democratic Action to lobby law makers; and the Lambda Defense League, a homosexual legal advocacy group that parallels and often works closely with the American Civil Liberties Union. These groups push furiously for an agenda that would fundamentally alter the mores of American society—an agenda that, in many ways, is counter to what is necessary in order to stem the spread of AIDS.

Our decade has been designated the "Gay Nineties," the decade in which homosexual activists are determined to culminate thirty years of struggle for their social agenda. Their victory envisions:

- national health insurance to ensure that society at large pays for the AIDS scourge

- laws to give homosexuals the right to adopt children (already won in many jurisdictions through the courts in lieu of legislation)
- laws setting hiring quotas for avowed homosexual schoolteachers
- inclusion of lessons in sex education classes at public schools of sodomy and other homosexual acts (already implemented in many states)
- laws compelling the Boy Scouts and 4-H Clubs to accept avowed homosexual scoutmasters and group leaders to serve as role models
- rules compelling health departments to dispense free syringes to inject cocaine or heroine (already implemented in several cities)
- rules compelling public schools to dispense condoms to students (already implemented in several cities)

As matters now stand, the continual treatment of AIDS patients will cost vast sums of money, but should the homosexual activists' demands for socialized health care succeed, the necessary global budgets will result in less care for the patients on the one hand, and less money for research on the other. This, of course, would only serve to weaken our ability to bring the epidemic under control. But then almost all of the social demands of the activists hamper real efforts to control the disease, especially where teenagers are concerned.

Given that homosexual "couples" are precluded by anatomy from procreating, parents would do well to query the homosexual activists' keen interest in their children. There have always been homosexual schoolteachers, everybody knows that. What is different today is that the activists insist on making the teacher's sexuality an issue so as to promote the homosexual lifestyle—the very same behavioral patterns that caused the AIDS epidemic in the first place.

Most states today mandate sex education in our schools, but very few insist—or even suggest—that family values should be emphasized or that behavior conducive to the spread of AIDS should be avoided. And because so many children come from single-parent households or households where both parents work, few parents find the time to search out what is being taught, much less to influence school curricula. This lack of parental vigilance is exploited by homosexual activists with disastrous consequences.

In most high school classrooms, textbooks and training materials assert that homophobia—likened to race discrimination—is incited by biblical teachings (bad) about sodomy (not bad). As an antidote, the student is taught not only to avoid "value judgments" concerning sexual behavior, but to experiment until he or she discovers which sexual activity—homosexual, bisexual, or heterosexual—is most pleasing to him or her. In the absence of moral guidance, teens are urged to acquire sexual habits according to what "feels good."

A case in point is the popular textbook by Ruth Bell, *Our Bodies, Ourselves.* In it, sexual orientation is depicted in a diagram much like a political spectrum. At one extreme are heterosexuals, at the opposite, homosexuals. The student is given the impression that *most* people fall somewhere in between. Boys and girls can happily explore the many pleasurable possibilities to discover where each belongs on the spectrum. Should the student "find" himself or herself anywhere but at one of the extremes, a lifelong monogamous relationship—the most fulfilling human existence—would be closed off and locked tight.

Another example is a multimedia learning program designed for seventh and eighth graders (twelve and thirteen year olds) entitled *About Your Sexuality* by Deryck Calderwood, PhD. In it, students are cautioned *not* to share the contents of the course with their parents because it may cause a "misunderstanding." The admonishment is made with good reason. Not only are the children given a "Homosexual Bill of Rights" and encouraged to become active in the gay rights movement, they are treated to a color video featuring explicit, frozen-frame demonstrations by two homosexual men, two lesbians, and a heterosexual couple engaged in anal intercourse, oral-anal stimulation, and other acts. The kids are reminded over and over that all of these acts, perversely described as "lovemaking," are "normal" and "natural." One need not be a medical doctor to know that this is anatomically and hygienically incorrect.

Morals aside, serious health risks other than AIDS are also associated with anal sex. The deadly hepatitis viruses, both infectious and serum, are known to be transmitted by some of the very acts depicted in this video instruction. Other diseases include amebiasis, a form of dysentery which can also infect the liver, pleura, and pericardium; giardiasis, which causes chronic intestinal inflammation; and shigellosis, another form of dysentery. These diseases often spread in concert with one another; together they occur so frequently that homosexual men refer to them as the "gay bowel syndrome" (GBS). Early symptoms of GBS can include fever, cramps, and diarrhea with blood and mucus in the stools.

But perhaps the most cruel hoax being played on school kids today, in the absence of any inducement for moral self-control, is the dispensing of condoms as a panacea for immoral behavior. Researchers find that in real-life situations, condoms, when used for birth control, result in a 14 percent pregnancy rate. When used in anal intercourse, which subjects the condom to far greater stresses, studies show condom failures to be 20 to 50 percent.

The actual use of condoms, moreover, falls by the wayside when kids practice what they are being taught—to do what feels good, explore pleasurable possibilities, find yourself on the sexual spectrum. For an adolescent it is a very long step from instantaneous gratification to the discipline of: wearing a condom (AIDS transmission is usually from the party who must wear it to the partner); planning ahead to the occasion of the act; using the condom properly in the heat of passion (most condom failures are due to mishandling).

Not surprisingly, condom usage is least frequent among the most promiscuous teenagers. One federal survey indicates that sexually active teens with a single partner over the course of a year use a condom in 60 percent of sexual encounters, while the usage rate drops to 37 percent for those reporting four or more sexual partners a year.

There has, in fact, been no evidence to indicate that schools have succeeded in preventing pregnancy or sexually transmitted diseases by distributing condoms. On the contrary, some school districts report that, following the practice, a marked increase has occurred in both problems. By making condoms available, sexual promiscuity is encouraged. In anecdotal reports, high school boys admit that because adults provide condoms, the reluctance of girls to engage in sex is easily overcome: "If it wasn't OK, they wouldn't have given us the condoms."

In addition to our schools, homosexual activists have targeted the work place as the new frontier for their political agenda. Bolstered by success in designating AIDS as a disability under the Social Security Act, they have now expanded political protection of the disease under the Americans with Disabilities Act. This raises the prospect of considerable risks for fellow employees and liability for the employer. Should an employer decline to hire an HIV-infected job applicant, he can be accused of discrimination. If, on the other hand, the applicant is hired, the employer is burdened with additional explosive costs if health care is an employee benefit, and the employer assumes liability for any health risk to co-workers.

AIDS itself cannot be contracted through casual contact, but some opportunistic infections associated with AIDS are highly contagious. The potentially fatal tuberculosis (TB) is often found among AIDS patients and it can be transmitted to anyone by coughing and sneezing, as evidenced by the resurgence of TB in certain areas after decades of control and near complete extinction. This resurgence has physicians and public health officials wrestling with multiple, drug resistant strains that will need another national effort to bring TB back under control.

The incidence of cytomegalovirus (CMV) is also very common among AIDS patients, and although it is not dangerous to men carriers, the disease can damage a developing fetus when passed to an expectant mother through casual contact. (This danger was documented early in the epidemic when a pregnant nurse contracted CMV from an AIDS patient and consequently delivered a malformed baby.) Another hazard at the work place arises with the onset of dementia, a common symptom of AIDS. These risks are lessened where workers are not in close proximity to the person infected with AIDS, but they are compounded for obvious reasons when the work place is a hospital or other health care setting; there, transmissions of opportunistic infections have been documented time and again.

Currently, twenty-six states have either officially designated the incidence of AIDS as a handicap or passed some form of legislation requiring employers not to discriminate in hiring employees with AIDS or HIV infections. To resolve the "Catch 22" of liability to co-workers, Ohio and Washington absolve employers of legal responsibility for the transmission of AIDS among employees.

Incredibly, Florida and California have passed legislation to prohibit the use of AIDS tests in determining eligibility for health, life, or disability insurance. Insurers can still decline applicants on the basis of pre-existing heart conditions or cancer, but not AIDS. This is tantamount to forcing an insurer to pay the repair bill for an auto accident that occurred before the application for insurance. The financial burdens of these laws severely lessen the ability of employers to hire more people.

The most shocking—and misguided—homosexual activity, however, has been in the area of public health. When AIDS was first diagnosed over a decade ago, it was found in a few homosexuals in specific locales. With the cooperation of those few homosexual communities, it could have been controlled with relatively few casualties.

As a young physician I devoted a great deal of service to the public health efforts that brought syphilis under control. With almost no public opposition, all patients upon admission to hospitals were tested for syphilis, just as they were tested for a myriad of other conditions. Patients who tested positive were treated by what medications we had. The definitive cure, penicillin, was still years in the future. In any case, the sooner treatment began, the better the chances for the patient.

Each syphilis patient was counseled about the dangers of spreading the disease, and each case was reported to the public health department. A specially trained public health officer interviewed the patient in confidence to determine the probable source of the infection and who else might have been infected. In this fashion we were able to test, treat, and counsel each person exposed, and thus control the spread of syphilis.

Today, in contrast, the efforts of doctors and public health officials to control AIDS have been blocked by political and legal intervention. When it became clear that anal intercourse among multiple partners was the conduit for the rapid spread of AIDS, health officials investigated the many so-called "bathhouses" that operated in cities with large homosexual populations. Typically, such establishments featured a room partitioned by a plywood barrier with a series of openings at groin level through which patrons exchanged sexual favors; no words were spoken and the participants never saw their partners. Similarly, health officials found rows of wide benches upon which patrons would lie face down to await anal intercourse from another person. Again, nothing spoken and no visual contact between the men—the strangers.

Such encounters deride traditional family values: there is no courtship, no affection, no concern, no love, no commitment, no responsibility. And it is from this manifestation of the new liberalism—i.e., individuals are not responsible for their own actions, only society is—that the AIDS scourge took hold. Perhaps the marvelous accomplishments of modern medicine lead people of jaded thinking—and appetite—to believe that nature can be forced to forgive all transgressions, for when health officials sought to close the bathhouses, homosexual activists went to court and secured injunctions against the closures. (The injunctions have since been lifted, but too late to save many thousands of patrons.)

Instead, homosexual activists demanded a cure for AIDS *and* the repeal of state and local laws against sodomy. They met uncanny success in legalizing sodomy in many areas of the country, but an immediate cure for AIDS is not within reach no matter how much funding is devoted or diverted to the cause: AIDS is the result of a virus and we have never found a definitive cure for any virus. With cooperation and proper public health measures, the best we can hope for is to contain its spread and incremental advances and ultimately to commute a death sentence to a life of chronic illness requiring continual medication and treatment.

But, in contrast to the cooperation we received when combating syphilis, doctors in state after state have been confronted with laws prohibiting HIV testing—even when symptoms are present—without prior written consent of the patient. We can routinely test for heart disease, liver disease, cancer, gonorrhea, syphilis, and on and on, but not for AIDS.

Homosexual activists have also cowed legislators into passing strict confidentiality laws that prohibit AIDS cases from being reported to public health officials, thus precluding early treatment and counseling for others exposed or placed at risk. Not even spouses can be forewarned, and since AIDS symptoms do not show up for several years after HIV infection, the opportunities for continued spreading are limitless. Some confidentiality restrictions are so stifling that doctors are unable to relay the diagnosis of AIDS to other physicians to whom the patient has been referred for specialized treatment, or even to notify other health care workers assigned to care for the patient. Currently, eighteen states have passed some form of AIDS confidentiality law.

Other regulations allow only *anonymous* testing of newborns so that health officials can tally the incidences of AIDS at birth. But again, doctors and nurses cannot know the diagnosis, and public health officials have no way of contacting the mother who may be unaware of her infection and her potential to spread it.

The tragic irony of this political intervention is that it has effectively countered protection of homosexuals—as evidenced by the tens of thousands dead—while as effectively protecting the disease. Homosexual activists have established a new civil right: the right of an incurable but preventable disease to spread unabated.

Antisodomy laws have existed in the civilized world throughout history, including ancient Rome and Greece. The time when a rain of brimstone and fire brought ruin to Sodom and Gomorrah was presumably not the only occasion when unnatural customs and rampant promiscuity resulted in social calamity. After all, AIDS did not fall from outer space, nor did it ooze from the depths of the earth. What is new in Western society is not so much AIDS as the pernicious behavior that brought it about.

No civilization has challenged nature with impunity, and no "silver bullet" can render sodomy, promiscuity, and intravenous drug abuse harmless. The problem is not a homophobic system as the activists assert (there is nothing homophobic about urging prevention of disease); the problem is a political movement that refuses to acknowledge the responsibility for personal behavior. Doctors do not condemn homosexuality, they condemn promiscuity, unnatural sex acts, and intravenous drug use, whether by homosexuals, bisexuals, or heterosexuals.

It is time for homosexual activists to stop telling others what to do and start listening to reason. When, during the Bush administration, members of ACT-UP invaded the president's summer retreat in Maine carrying signs that read, "Legalize sodomy—for the fun of it," and chanting, "Cure AIDS now!" President Bush came back with a reasoned retort, a retort the militants would be wise to heed: "Change your behavior."

CHAPTER 9

The High Cost of Living, the Higher Cost of Dying

Medically speaking, the only thing more expensive than living in America is dying in America. Medicare claims data offer a vivid illustration of the degree of the problem. Those sixty-five and older constitute about 12 to 13 percent of the U.S. population, but they consume between 33 and 40 percent of health care delivered. And herein the rub: between 25 and 35 percent of elderly care is delivered near the end of life, the bulk within the last thirty days. When factoring in patients of all ages, it is estimated that half of America's health care bill is attributed to patients in their final year of life.[1]

Granted, people are sickest before they die, and since at times doctors are unable to assess the likelihood of survival, treatment must proceed. But in most cases terminal illness is diagnosable and the imminence of death predictable. All too often advanced technology is applied to prolong death and agony, not life and joy.

With modern technology we can relieve the pain and allay the anxiety of the terminally ill, or we can keep such patients alive for a few more days or weeks of great distress by prodding, probing, testing, and treating.

*   *   *

Take the case of Patient M reported in the *Wall Street Journal*. Patient M was not significant because he was unusual, but because he was so typical. Suffering from bilateral pneumonia, a fractured hip, and gradual respiratory, kidney, and heart failure, his doctors knew he would not recuperate. Still, at the insistence of family, and at the expense mostly of Medicare, he spent his last forty-one days in intensive care at Saint Luke's Roosevelt Hospital in New York City. Treatment included 70 arterial blood gas analyses, 156 blood tests, 38 X-rays, 13 blood transfusions, a cardiac ultrasound, a Swan Ganz catheter, and an arterial line to monitor cardiac output and blood pressure. Total cost: $93,111.00. The late patient's niece was quoted: "I can't see why the doctors shouldn't [have done] as much as possible for him. Cost as a factor should never enter in." Mind you, Patient M was ninety years old.[2]

The same problem arises in caring for the very young. "Baby Doe" decrees mandate that we do everything possible to save all infants, no matter how hopeless. Of the over 100,000 cocaine-affected babies born every year in America, many are deformed, brain-damaged, and withering away in painful seizures. Medical bills can run hundreds of thousands of dollars on a hopeless case, and within a few months, as expected, the infant dies anyway.

In part, the problem arises from our penchant for blaming others for every misfortune that befalls us, even when the occurrence is an act of God. Under the threat of legal action, doctors are no longer free to consider the probabilities of successful treatment; instead they must do everything medically possible.

Perhaps medicine itself has contributed to the problem because, for the first time in history, it is common for children to know their great-grandparents—modern medicine has so extended the lives of loved ones that the inevitable seems unreal to those who have not, as children, seen a relative die.

Whatever the cause, the practice of prolonging imminent death with advanced technology is as unique to the American scene as violent crime, drug abuse, and illegitimacy. While we seek to dignify immorality, we also seek to "undignify" death, and we pay the price with prolonged suffering and higher medical costs.

For those who wish to die with dignity, the momentum of the

system muffles their plea. The current system is so geared to continuing treatment of the terminally ill—even those languishing in a persistent vegetative state—that families of patients sometimes find they are powerless to stop the treatment. I am often asked whether, as a physician, I would actually "pull the plug" on a patient. My answer is yes, I had to several times in the course of my career. In those days the decision was a private one made between doctor, patient, and family. Nowadays—as a result of many court cases, often filed by parties unrelated to those affected—lawyers, judges, and social workers have interceded against the overwhelming will of nature. Families wrenched by the agony of a relative forced to feed and breathe by means of an unnatural technological life-support system are told that they must hire a lawyer and obtain a court order before the inhumane and unnatural treatment can cease.

Let me be quite clear here: withdrawing life support machinery is very different from administering euthanasia. Doctors are not the authors of human destiny; we must not attempt to play God. We intervene against illness and injury when we can, and when we cannot we comfort the patient. Most importantly, a doctor must do no harm. While the debate rages over whether a terminally ill patient has the right to euthanasia, this point is often overlooked: a doctor has no right to terminate the life of a patient.

I said in an earlier chapter that if preventive medicine ever takes hold, we can expect the total cost of health care to rise because the cost of treating an aging population grows disproportionately. As explained above, much of that disproportionate cost can, and should, be eliminated.

But what of the high cost of living with chronic illness during our younger years? Modern medicine has made tremendous strides in extending the lives of patients who would have died just a few years ago. Often, heart and cancer patients can live a normal lifespan with continual medical treatment and repeated surgical interventions, but only by adding hundreds of thousands of dollars to the medical bills of patients who, in the end, will still pay the high cost of dying.

To be sure, there is a certain randomness to the incidence of cancer and heart disease, although genetic factors place some people at greater risk than others. Tragically, though, a great deal of the problem is preventable. A lot of blame is leveled against the medical profession for emphasizing intervention when prevention is so much cheaper. In fact, those touting socialized medicine claim that they will cut the cost of health care by reducing the number of surgeons and specialists while increasing the number of primary care physicians. What we seem to forget, or ignore, is that 95 percent of preventive measures do not stem from doctors and hospitals, but are related to lifestyles, are matters of personal choice.

Almost a decade ago the United States Preventive Services Task Force convened to establish specific guidelines for the use of preventive services in the clinical setting. The objective was to target the sixty most common causes of death and disability in America and to assess the effectiveness of preventive intervention. Before publishing its final report, the twenty-member, multidisciplinary task force reviewed more than 2,400 scientific studies, and the preliminary findings were then critiqued by over three hundred outside experts in the United States, Canada, and the United Kingdom.

After five years of exhaustive study, the task force released its recommendations. In short, "designer" physicals costing hundreds or even thousands of dollars are no more effective in detecting the future occurrence of disease in the average adult than a simple, routine office physical. The medical establishment has been holding nothing back. Children should be vaccinated according to schedule, and their blood pressure and height/weight should be checked periodically. At birth, thyroxine/thyrotropin should be tested; during infancy, hemoglobin/hematocrit should be checked; and at preschool age, eyes should be examined for amblyopia and strabismus. Periodic screening for adults should include height/ weight, blood pressure, cholesterol, Pap-smear, and a clinical breast exam. Mammography, hearing, visual acuity, and thyroid tests are recommended for specific age groups only. All other forms of clinical screening, including electrocardiograms and chest roentgenograms, were found to be of limited value for the asymptomatic patient. That is not to say that other tests are of no value, but in the absence of specific risk factors, other tests are not recommended.[3]

Routine physicals are readily available throughout the United States, and they are relatively inexpensive. Whether or not people notice, every time they visit a primary care physician, they are routinely screened for blood pressure and weight, and they always have been. Not only did the task force not recommend more extensive screening procedures than traditionally administered, physicians were admonished to be more selective in ordering tests and preventive services to minimize the risk of adverse effects and unnecessary costs.

To be sure, doctors must do a better job of counseling patients, but when all is said and done in the clinical setting, preventive health care is up to the patient.

The task force, for example, emphasized the importance of preventive measures such as the use of automobile safety belts. We pass laws to that effect, but only a third of us actually strap ourselves in. Despite recent improvement, the National Safety Council reports we injure and hospitalize seventy thousand people per week on our highways, and nine hundred more die.

In another health area, ponder this. We have come to rely upon government to regulate every facet of our daily lives to protect us from harm, and at great expense, as demonstrated by the vast administrative code and bureaucracy of the Occupational Safety and Health Administration (OSHA). Yet we still have the highest rate of burn accidents in the industrialized world, according to the National Safety Council. Think about it, two-and-a-half million Americans seek medical treatment for burns each year, a hundred thousand of those are hospitalized, twelve thousand die.

The death rate from smoking is twenty-six times greater than the probability of dying from an accident at the workplace, and 462 times greater than the risk of dying from any other form of air pollution. Approximately 80 percent of illness is related to individual vices—poor diet, tobacco use, lack of exercise, alcohol consumption, etc.—and diet alone contributes to six of the ten leading causes of death in America. According to the Center for Disease Control's 1992 "behavioral risk factor surveillance survey," 23 percent of Americans are overweight, up 2 percent since 1987. And surveys show that only 8 percent of the population exercises properly—i.e., at least three twenty-minute sessions a week. Even among younger people age eighteen to twenty-nine, only 5 percent of women and 7 percent of men say they exercise vigorously and regularly.

The public is eminently well informed about the need for regular exercise and weight control, but we seem to lack the will to take responsibility for ourselves. We want to believe that our problems are the fault of someone else, and that, in any case, government can solve them for us. As my good friend Tim Norbech so aptly put it: "We enjoy the most affluent and self-abusive lifestyle in the world, and so we have the medical costs to prove it! There is something to the Japanese proverb that 'good medicine always has a bitter taste.' Maybe that's why the stoic Japanese lead the world in longevity."[4]

CHAPTER 10

———————————ᐯ———————————

Call the Plumber, We're Insured!

An imaginary scenario: It's time to change the oil in your car, so you take it to a mechanic and fill out an insurance claim. Ordinary maintenance and minor repairs are covered under your auto insurance—perhaps subject to a small annual deductible—and the insurance itself is provided as a benefit by your employer. Sounds like a sweet deal. So sweet, in fact, you needn't bother comparing prices for the work to be done. Besides, the garage down the street probably won't do it for less because its customers aren't paying their own bills either.

You can well imagine the increased demand for auto care: nary a scratch nor a squeak would go unattended. Think how the price of tires would inflate. And those rising prices would be compounded by the economics of running small claims through the insurance mechanism because premiums to pay the claims must also pay the agent's commission, state premium taxes, overhead, plus the cost of processing claims.

Suppose this system were applied to homeowners insurance. I can just hear myself the next time my wife asks me to fix a leaky faucet: "Call the plumber, darling, we're insured!" If insurance covered footwear, shoes would become so expensive government would have to ration them.

Yet, we have applied this senseless system to finance health care—and we wonder why prices keep rising. The media, meanwhile, are so busy blaming private medicine for rising prices, they forget that our system of financing health care—and results—stems from government manipulation, not the private sector. While there are many private players in the health-care marketplace, government abolished the free market for medical services decades ago.

Government first attempted to engineer a de facto national health plan by shifting the burden of health care to corporate employers through tax incentives, thus freeing people of responsibility for their own needs. Although the income tax was enacted a quarter-century earlier as a "temporary" measure borne by the "rich," it was expanded during the administration of Franklin D. Roosevelt to become a means of marketplace coercion. Income tax rates were 4 percent in 1939; within five years they had increased sixfold, and the tax was extended to the common worker—taken right from the paycheck. During this period of tax expansion, corporate employers were told to exclude the cost of employee health insurance from the tax, but if the employee purchased coverage on his own, the cost would be subject to the tax. This effectively penalized those who wished to provide for themselves—even the self-employed and low paid workers who were not covered by their employers.

Traditionally, workers saved a portion of their wages to pay for common mishaps, routine care, and incidentals. (In those days a market for health insurance had not developed because there were few cures for catastrophic illnesses.) But under the new system, not only did wages dedicated to savings become subject to the tax, the interest earned on the savings was taxed as well. Moreover, the economic benefit derived from employer-provided health care was excluded from the taxable income of employees.

Concurrently, the Roosevelt administration imposed wage and price controls at a time of great demand for labor due to the war effort, but then ruled that health benefits would not be counted as wages. Companies were free to compete for scarce labor by offering health benefits but not by offering additional money with which to purchase health insurance. Health benefits were also ruled fair game for collective bargaining, and first dollar coverage became the manna of union organizers.

During the ensuing decades the tax burden continued to grow, Social Security taxes and capital gains taxes were hiked, and state and city income taxes were imposed. Employer-provided health care became the primary provider of health coverage for most working Americans by the mid-1960s, and it continued to expand during the decades of high taxes which followed.

In a free market buyers must deal directly with sellers, but that rarely happens in health care. The reason, as explained above, is easy to demonstrate. When you take into account Social Security taxes of, say, 15.3 percent, plus federal, state, and local income taxes of 36 percent, an employee in this tax bracket would have to earn $1,000 to buy $480 worth of health care directly. That is why 90 percent of Americans with private insurance today are covered through their employers or unions, and most of that coverage is subject to a very low deductible or no deductible at all. By the mid-1960s the portion of the total health care bill paid by patients was down to one-half; today that portion is little more than 20 percent.

As a result, what we call health "insurance" is anything but insurance. Insurance is a mechanism by which policyholders share the risk of catastrophic occurrences, which occurrences befall only a few of those sharing the risk. By spreading insurable risks among many policyholders, each policyholder pays a relatively small premium to cover potentially large losses. In order for a risk to be insurable it must be an unpredictable possibility to the individual insured, and because its occurrence is not a certainty, it will only be sustained by a few policyholders at once. In other words, the occurrence of an insured risk may be predictable to a certain percentage of a large group, or risk pool, but who among the risk pool will actually incur the loss and when it will be incurred are unpredictable.

Every homeowner will encounter a leak in the roof occasionally, and every homeowner knows the roof must be replaced every twenty years or so. These expenses are not insurable risks because their occurrence is a certainty, and the homeowner sets money aside in anticipation of them. But there is always a risk that a hurricane or tornado will blow a new roof off, and few can afford to save for such a catastrophe. For this we have insurance.

The same principle should apply to health care. There is no *risk* that a child will sustain cuts and scrapes on the playground—such mishaps occur to all children. There is no *risk* that an adult will occasionally catch a cold or the flu—all do. There is no *risk* that a senior citizen will encounter chronic ailments—such are a consequence of aging. People, however, of all ages face the risk of serious accident, heart disease, and cancer, even though only some will be stricken. Few could afford medical treatment for such uncertain, catastrophic occurrences without sharing the risk through insurance.

Insurance, moreover, should be purchased to suit individual needs. If you drive a Toyota you wouldn't buy insurance for a Rolls Royce. If you live in a bungalow you wouldn't buy insurance for a mansion. Why should a worker with two children equally share the risks of a coworker who has eight children? Why should a bachelor pay for maternity benefits? Why should a nonsmoker share an equal risk with a smoker? That is what happens when employees of a company or union are lumped together in the same, relatively small risk pool of a group policy. (Even large companies have relatively small, heterogeneous risk pools.)

Also, insurance should be portable. When you change jobs you don't change your homeowner's policy, subjecting you to a new deductible and other conditions. If your employer goes out of business you don't lose your life insurance. Why, then, should health insurance be a condition of employment?

Government finagling with the marketplace has only caused higher medical costs, higher insurance costs, smaller paychecks, and a growing number of uninsured workers because fewer employers can afford the rising costs. Consider the inflationary effect of submitting small claims on a typical employer health policy. Suppose a claim is submitted for a $300 bill subject to a $200 deductible and 20 percent coinsurance. Subtract the $200 deductible and multiply by 0.8: the insurer pays $80. Now suppose the same medical procedure is encountered the following year, but inflation has increased the medical bill by 8 percent: the new bill is $324. Subtract $200, multiply by 0.8: the company pays $99.20. Thus, the insurance reimbursement has increased $19.20; that's 24 percent of the previous year's reimbursement—*three times the inflation rate!*

There is more. Suppose the annual deductible and coinsurance limits have been met when a claim is submitted for $25. Insurance administrators say the expense of processing the paper work and issuing the check raises the actual cost of paying the claim to $50— double the net amount of the claim.

Although imprudent utilization of low deductible and nondeductible policies increases costs exponentially, conscientious use of them by any individual beneficiary has no significant effect on a group policy. Clearly, then, there is an incentive to abuse and overuse employer-provided health insurance. This is confirmed by a Rand Corporation study conducted for the Department of Health and Human Services which found that the average beneficiary subject to 50 percent coinsurance spent 25 percent less than the beneficiary of first dollar coverage, even though the coinsurance provision was compensated by wage supplements.[1]

If an individual consumes something, and another produces that which is consumed, and if a third party is called upon to pay the second party for the consumption of the first, then it follows that the third-party payer will want control over consumption or else demand will outstrip its ability to pay, as demonstrated by the Rand study. The first-party consumer will naturally resist any limits on consumption, especially with regard to health care, leaving the third-party payer to attempt controlling the second-party producer. It also follows that if the third-party payer is an employer in the airline business, its ability to oversee the operation of clinics and hospitals used by employees will be no better than a doctor's ability to pilot a Boeing 747. Therefore, corporate employers hire outside contractors, often insurance companies, to negotiate and oversee the delivery of medical care to employees in the financial interest of the employer. But, unfortunately, the contracted middleman is often no more qualified than the employer that hired him, a fact that has spawned yet another frontier for government regulators.

Thus, due to the fundamental flaw of the third-party payer system in health care, a new entrepreneurial industry has emerged which, contrary to popular myth, only drives costs higher than ever. Known as managed care, the industry includes utilization review (UR), preferred provider organizations (PPOs), health maintenance organizations (HMOs), and many variations thereof. Since government, primarily through Medicare and Medicaid, is the largest third-party payer in the country, most of these managed care schemes were hatched by Washington bureaucrats and then copied by the private sector.

In the case of utilization review, a 1992 survey by Faulkner and Gray, Inc. showed that employers and insurance companies paid $7 billion that year to UR firms to question the necessity of care provided to beneficiaries. It stands to reason that if $7 billion was spent to question doctors and hospitals, then another $7 billion must have been spent to hire the staffs necessary to answer those questions. That's $14 billion a year added to the health care bill of employees. And for what in return?

The inspector general of the Department of Health and Human Services reported in 1990 that for 500,000 cataract operations subject to UR, Medicare paid $13.3 million for reviews which denied $1.4 million in medical costs—a net loss to the government of $11.9 million.[2] Another survey in 1990 by Foster Higgins of corporate benefits managers found that half of the respondents confirmed that UR and other managed care strategies had little or no effect on lowering costs. The survey reported that the only measure that did work was increasing the employees share of costs.[3]

If medical benefits are overused, why doesn't managed care solve the problem as does increasing employee coinsurance? Because managed care focuses on catastrophic care, precisely the area that legitimate insurance would cover with few questions and where overuse is least likely to occur. But if UR were to focus on less expensive procedures—the kind of care legitimate insurance has no business paying for in the first place—then the cost/benefit ratio would be even worse and the cost of reviews prohibitive.

If most people are surprised by the ineffectiveness of utilization review, they are even more surprised by the HMO record. HMOs are the most severe form of managed care because most deny patients free choice of physicians, supposedly to cut costs. The liberal media have tried to sell the public on the concept claiming that because HMOs offer first dollar coverage, much like the Canadian and European socialized systems, preventive care would be emphasized and costs reduced. But the truth is that preventive care has more to do with lifestyle habits—diet, exercise, drinking, drug use, sexual behavior—than anything a doctor can do for a patient. Cancer-screening techniques, vaccinations, and other preventive medical measures are only required periodically and are relatively inexpensive.

Still, by law all but the smallest companies are obligated to offer an HMO option when available. Since most people are loath to submit to a plan that dictates which doctor will perform surgery on them, employees drawn to the plans by their first dollar coverage are likely to be younger, healthier, and less likely to need surgery. That leaves higher risk employees in the traditional plans, driving the cost of those plans even higher.

But isn't there a counterbalancing savings to the HMO, especially since younger workers are enrolled? No, managed care is management heavy and therefore more expensive. Besides, the lack of coinsurance is self-defeating, as demonstrated by the Rand study. *Benefits* magazine used the database of its sister company, CobraServe of Clearwater, Florida, to compare the average premiums under employer health plans nationwide. With fifteen thousand different rates in the database, this was the largest survey ever taken to compare rates, and therefore the most statistically accurate. The result: the average monthly rate for HMOs covering single employees was 9 percent *higher* than traditional plans, and for families HMOs were 16 percent *higher*![4] Finagle all they will, bureaucrats and entrepreneurs will never overcome the problem of excessive cost without correcting the basic flaw: the system of third-party payers, whether government or corporate. There is no more efficient or effective method of delivering health care than the private doctor serving the patient who pays a fee directly for the service rendered.

Ultimately, workers bear these excessive costs. When an insurer raises the premium to cover the cost, the employer is left with fewer dollars for wages. From the perspective of the employer, the cost of health benefits is a part of employee compensation. When union negotiators demand first dollar coverage, they are simply taking money off the bargaining table, money that could have been used for salary.

The trade-off of salary for health benefits is not the sweet deal many workers think. According to a study conducted by the National Center for Policy Analysis, health care spending in the United States could be reduced by a fourth if workers and other patients retained responsibility for their own health care spending. To correct perverse tax incentives, the study proposed the use of individual Medical Savings Accounts to cover predictable and routine expenses, coupled with high deductible insurance for catastrophic expenses. Contributions to the accounts would not be taxed, nor would the interest earned. As coauthor John Goodman demonstrated, the resultant economies for patients were impressive in insurance premiums alone: By opting for an insurance deductible of $1,000 rather than $250, a Southern California family would save $1,585 per year in premiums; and a middle-aged man in Miami would save $1,156 per year. As a beneficiary's Medical Savings Account compounded, the insurance deductible would be raised accordingly, thus lowering the premiums.[5]

This logical proposal would solve another problem: the lack of guaranteed renewable health insurance. Nobody would buy a life insurance policy that the underwriter could cancel if the insured suffered a heart attack five years after taking it out. Likewise, there should be little demand for health insurance policies that are not guaranteed renewable.

But under the current system of employer-based health insurance, workers have no choice. Here's why. When life insurance is purchased, the policy is grouped in a very large pool of policyholders of similar risk potential. This is called a risk pool and it is usually much larger than most employee groups, even though each pool is segregated according to the degree of risk. Risk pools enable the underwriter to predict losses better and to set rates that are competitive with other insurers. In this way coverage becomes available to everybody—if not through one carrier, then through another—regardless of age or health status because rates are set to compensate for the degree of risk. (In the case of health insurance, the cost of exceedingly high risks could easily be made affordable through tax credits.)

But with low deductible or no deductible employer-based health insurance, a single policy must cover many varied risks which, being unknown, are not predictable, plus covering a steady stream of small claims which, to a large degree, are incurred at the discretion of covered employees, as demonstrated by the aforementioned Rand study. The insurer has no choice but to apply what is known as "experience rating," which amounts to a tax-induced, prepayment scheme for medical care. Insurers are not offering risk indemnity, they are not charging a certain premium to cover an uncertain loss as they should. They are selling their services to shuffle papers and earn interest on the workers' money. Under this system premiums are set according to the claims experience of each employee group for the previous year, not the potential risk. Should a few workers incur extraordinary claims, premiums are raised the following year, or the policy is canceled. Even if the policy is not canceled, premiums may jump higher than the employer can afford, in which case the policy must be dropped at a time when some workers are seriously ill. Since risks cannot be predicted in a heterogeneous employee group, employer-based policies cannot be guaranteed renewable.

At this point some may ask: Why, then, isn't guaranteed renewable health insurance universally available to individuals not covered at the workplace? Again, the reason lies with government regulation. In order for an underwriter to offer a guaranteed renewable policy, the risk of loss must be predetermined or the insured can be certain that the underwriter, like all gamblers, will go bankrupt eventually. But government insurance regulators in many states make it impossible to determine risk. For instance, in response to the powerful gay lobby, several states prohibit insurers from asking an applicant whether he has been tested for AIDS or whether he has been rejected as a blood donor. Thus, all who previously had chosen to go uninsured and subsequently discovered they were infected could apply for insurance, and the costs of treatment would be borne by policyholders who had been paying premiums all along. The only option left to the insurer, of course, is to apply experience rating, just like group insurance, thus precluding guaranteed renewable policies.

Another example is mandated coverage for adopted children, even children with preexisting conditions. The insurer has no way of knowing how many people will buy a policy with the intention of adopting children afflicted by serious illness. Again, if the insurer cannot predict the risk, it cannot guarantee renewability. Some states try to fix the problem by mandating guaranteed renewability, which only guarantees that premiums will rise unreasonably high.

What is just as galling about government interference in the marketplace for health insurance is the extent to which lawmakers have imposed the wishes of special interests on the insurance-buying public—both individuals and companies—unable to self-insure. I am speaking here of government-mandated benefits for services that would be far cheaper if paid out of pocket, and for other services that people do not need and most do not want—services that are of no help in the treatment of catastrophic injury or illness, and in many cases of no medical benefit whatsoever.

For example, chiropractors are not medical doctors, they are not trained or licensed to treat catastrophic illness. Yet, due to lobbying efforts, all but a few states demand that medical insurance cover the services of chiropractors, and some laws even dictate that reimbursement for office visits be at the same rate charged by medical doctors. In the newspaper this morning I came across a quarter-page chiropractor's ad which read in bold, capital letters: "LICENSED MASSAGE THERAPIST ON STAFF." Directly below it states, "WE ACCEPT INSURANCE ASSIGNMENTS." It would not take many policyholders to run up the premiums for everybody by visiting the chiropractor a few times a week for a massage. And they do!

Another example: almost all states mandate coverage for alcohol and drug abuse. Are these insurable diseases? If they are, they're contagious. The cost of treating substance abuse adds 10 percent to the cost of employer benefits nationwide, a percentage that has doubled over the last decade. And in most cases medical treatments have proven no more effective than self-help groups, such as Alcoholics Anonymous. Forcing people who buy medical insurance to pay for the abuses of others is what I call the "medicalization" of social ills.

Here is a typical example of the analogy we began with about filing claims to change the oil in your car. In the stampede to get on the bandwagon of preventive medicine, many states now mandate coverage for Pap smears, mammograms, immunizations, and more. Florida even prohibits deductibles for routine pediatric check-ups. Think how much more efficiently a free market would accomplish the same objective. When a homeowner installs a fire alarm or burglar alarm, the insurer grants a premium discount. When a teenage driver completes an approved safe-driving course, an insurance discount is available. Likewise, if health underwriters were liable solely for catastrophic occurrences, it would be in their best interests to provide premium incentives for vaccinations and early detection screenings.

The list of state mandates runs the gamut from the routine to the frivolous and even the absurd. Some states mandate benefits for "naturopaths," nonmedical practitioners who prescribe herbs; some mandate the services of acupuncturists, nonmedical practitioners who insert needles to alter the flow of imaginary "chi" energy; some mandate the services of marriage counselors and pastoral counselors; some mandate *in vitro* fertilizations; some mandate coverage for deposits to a sperm bank; and Minnesota even mandates coverage for hairpieces. In 1965 there were only five state-mandated health insurance benefits; today there are about one thousand, and the number is still growing by fifty to a hundred each year.

One would think that in the nation where personal freedom was pioneered, a citizen would be free to choose health insurance according to his or her needs. We would not consider it justifiable to force a homeowner on a mountaintop to buy flood insurance; why then do we force people to buy health insurance with coverages they don't need?

By law, if you cannot afford these unneeded benefits, you may not purchase health insurance at all. In another study by the National Center for Policy Analysis, it is estimated that a quarter of America's uninsured had been priced out of the market by mandated coverages.[6]

Rather than remedy the injustice by restoring the rights of individuals to take home what they earn and buy insurance according to need, President Clinton, Senators Teddy Kennedy and Jay Rockefeller, and other liberal leaders would preempt state regulations with a federal law mandating that all employers purchase health insurance for all employees nationwide. Imagine what the future would hold once Congress took control of health insurance mandates under its "let someone else pay for it" attitude. A classic example of what does happen in countries where governments have grossly overstepped their bounds appeared in the *London Times* (July 25, 1992). The *Times* reported that a Dutch high court upheld a handicapped man's right to be reimbursed by his local council for the services of a female "sexual aid worker." The claimant based his case on a psychologist's opinion that he needed sex at least once a month. Can you imagine what would happen to costs if we mandated coverage for the services of prostitutes? Some people would never get their fill of health care.

CHAPTER 11

———————∿———————

Paper Plague:
The Sickening Saga of
Government Intervention

Nothing raises more anxiety among workers than the future of programs under the Social Security Administration, especially Medicare. They have reason to be concerned.

Politicians call it insurance, but it isn't. For the past three decades beneficiaries have paid into the system only a small fraction of what they have taken out, leaving today's workers to wonder whether anything will be left of their withholding taxes when they retire. For instance, under Medicare Part A hospital benefits, for every dollar contributed by the average beneficiary who retired in 1991, $5.09 was paid out before the first year.[1] And under Medicare Part B, the premiums paid by beneficiaries covered only about a quarter of the plan's expenses; the deficit was made up by general tax revenue. Moreover, at the inception of Medicare, 16 million Americans were enrolled who had never paid a cent into the system, and 7.5 million of them were already paying for private insurance (which has terminated under Medicare).

Medicare, being fundamentally flawed, will continually teeter on bankruptcy, requiring endless taxpayer bailouts. The first Medicare financial crisis was conceded by Congress a mere four years after the system was implemented, and workers were socked with their first quick-fix tax hike in 1970.[2] Upon implementation, Congress told the American people that Medicare Part A would cost $3.1 billion in 1970, but the actual cost was $5.8 billion. That was only the beginning. The public was also told that Medicare would cost less than $9 billion in 1990; the actual cost was $95 billion. Hold your hat, the 1992 bill is expected to top $127 billion!

The Social Security Board of Trustees' 1991 annual report, moreover, admits that the system will go belly-up again as early as 2001 without another taxpayer bailout. The magnitude of the tax hike required is astonishing—about double the current payroll tax—especially given that low income workers, the very workers who cannot afford health insurance for their own families, already pay about 50 percent of their taxes in Social Security withholding. It is mind-boggling to consider that between 1991 and 1995, Medicare and Social Security will have distributed $300 billion of those taxes to retirees whose incomes are over fifty thousand dollars.

Whereas legitimate insurance works on the principle of policyholders prepaying into a "legal reserve" fund to protect them from future catastrophic loss, Medicare collects taxes from today's workers to fund the current spending of retirees. As the birth rate decreases and longevity increases, fewer and fewer workers are left to pay the medical bills of more and more retirees, resulting in higher and higher taxes.

In the year 1900, those sixty-five and over accounted for only 4 percent of the U.S. population. Currently, those sixty-five and over account for 12 to 13 percent of the population, and it is projected that the ratio will double by 2050. We can infer that the portion of total health care consumed by the elderly will also double by 2050, and it will probably more than double because the number of elderly people living into their eighties and nineties will be proportionately greater.

Medicare and Social Security will consume a quarter of the nation's taxable payroll by the year 2000; by 2030 they will consume more than half of the taxable payroll; and by 2060 the burden will exceed 70 percent of the taxable payroll.[3] It is unrealistic to expect that the next generation of workers will be willing or even able to pay the health costs of those who will turn sixty-five by the middle of the next century—and all who will turn sixty-five by then are now living. Unless we devise a plan for current workers to save during their working years in order to pay for their own health needs in retirement, Medicare and other entitlement programs will either cause a serious economic crisis, or they will spur generational warfare resulting in severe limits on care given to the elderly.

The government, moreover, is falsely telling today's workers that the Social Security Administration maintains "trust funds" into which their payroll taxes are placed to take care of the future liabilities of Medicare Hospital Insurance and Social Security. But unlike private insurance reserves and pension funds, the government does not actually maintain investment accounts in trust for beneficiaries; it does not invest the beneficiaries' money in a portfolio of secure, job-creating industries. Instead, government spends the money, writes itself a promissory note, and calls it a trust fund. Even worse, the borrower of those government trust funds, the U.S. Treasury, is already in debt to the tune of $4.2 trillion and is currently running at an annual deficit of $334 billion. This is exactly as if a private employer, insolvent and going ever deeper in debt, were to spend the assets of his company's employee benefit plan and then tell the employees not to worry because the company would give them an IOU. The trust funds may show a positive balance, but the money is gone.

So how is government to repay the notes? The only means government has of raising revenue is raising taxes. And every dollar government borrows, taxes, and spends leaves that much less in the capital markets for industrial expansion and economic growth. In other words, as the Treasury borrows and spends from the government's so-called trust funds it increases the need for taxes, and, as it does so, it reduces the ability of the economy to generate those taxes. Consequently, the American standard of living is doomed to decline.

It may be more appropriate to call Medicare "anti-insurance" than insurance because not only is the system actuarially unsound, the priority of benefits is reversed. Rather than offer absolute protection from catastrophic loss, Medicare encourages nonessential spending with low deductibles while leaving gaps and limits on catastrophic protection.

This happens because politicians appeal to one of our baser desires—the desire to gain something for nothing—thus forcing the system to pay for various and sundries that many beneficiaries can afford out of pocket. To counter this imprudent largess, government tries to control spiraling costs by limiting hospital stays and nursing care, and by placing impediments on the treatment of catastrophic illness.

I once read a letter to the editor of *Private Practice* magazine that illustrated the perverse incentives of the system. A physician from Idaho told of a seventy-five-year-old woman, one of the wealthiest in his town, who asked for a prescription for a new wheelchair—her third in three years. There was nothing wrong with her current wheelchair, she just liked to get a new one each year because she was entitled to it for "free" under Medicare. The doctor declined the request, as I recall, but the persistent patient simply found a doctor who acquiesced.

If an individual is to consume, and another is to produce that which is consumed, and if a third party is called upon to pay the second party for the consumption of the first, then it should be obvious that the third-party payer must have some say over consumption or else demand will outstrip its ability to pay. You simply cannot hand out blank checks drawn on the taxpayers' account and expect that responsible trade will take place. Thus, in every socialist system, government has resorted to price controls and arbitrary rationing, even when the means of production are left in private hands. In the case of Medicare—which was designed on socialistic principles—government has attempted to impose rationing by regulating the providers of health care, largely unbeknownst to the consumers.

As recounted in an earlier chapter, when I argued on behalf of the American Medical Association against the proposed structure of Medicare prior to its enactment, I charged that Medicare would spur uncontrollable demands and drive the cost of health care to undeterminable heights. (The accuracy of that prediction was uncanny, for in 1965, the year Congress enacted Medicare, medical inflation rose just 2.1 percent; but by the end of the first year of implementation the medical inflation rate had zoomed to 6.5 percent.)[4] And I predicted that government would insert itself between doctor and patient and that bureaucrats would soon dictate who would be admitted to the hospital, how they would be treated, and when they would get out.

But the liberal politicians of the mid-1960s assured that none of this would come to pass, and, to abate public apprehension, they even wrote a preamble to the Medicare law prohibiting any governmental control over the practice of medicine. Section 1801 of the law states, "Nothing in this title shall be construed to authorize any federal officer or employee to exercise any supervision or control over the practice of medicine, or the manner in which medical services are provided, or over the selection, tenure or compensation of any . . . person providing health-care services . . ." Although completely ignored in practice, the passage stands unaltered—a monument either to the utopian delusion of its authors, or to the degree of their deceit.

Prior to the enactment of Medicare, medical fees were derived as is any service offered in a free market—they were negotiated. If surgery was deemed necessary, doctor and patient discussed the procedure and agreed to a fee. If the doctor's normal fee was more than the patient could afford, it was lowered, even as low as fifty cents, and installment payments could be arranged. Conversely, wealthy patients were expected to pay more. I will never forget a patient whom I billed the normal surgical fee only to receive a check for double the amount with a note telling me I had charged too little.

When Medicare was enacted it paid doctors the "reasonable and customary fee," in other words, the fair market price for services rendered. And, of course, physicians' incomes rose, because they were paid the full fee for all patients over sixty-five, even those who previously had paid a reduced fee or no fee at all. What none of the Medicare advocates seemed to understand was that when government became the third-party payer for a major segment of the American populace, a segment which consumed over a third of all medical services, the law of supply and demand was jolted and fair market prices were no longer determinable. Wilbur Cohen, the chief designer and champion of Medicare at the Department of Health, Education and Welfare, admitted years later that the political struggle to pass the law had been so consuming that no one thought about such issues as reimbursement alternatives and efficiency.[5]

Some may justly counter that medicine was not a perfect marketplace before government's intrusion, that too many patients were subject to emergencies or too sick to assure fair treatment. But this had not gone unnoticed by the medical profession, and thus a private, social contract was made between doctors, hospitals, the public, and their insurers. Before government intrusion, hospitals upheld the public trust by requiring that doctors with staff privileges maintain membership in their local medical societies, and each society assembled a committee of its most respected physicians to assure that members adhere to the highest ethical standards. These committees would mediate any grievance, including price gouging, brought against a member of the society; and the committees held the power of expulsion, in which event hospital staff privileges would be lost too.

The system was enhanced in many areas by the Foundations for Medical Care under the auspices of local medical societies. Through the foundations, member physicians voluntarily agreed to subject their practices to review by their peers on the bases of the necessity of services rendered, the quality of those services, and the amount charged. The foundations established maximum reasonable charges that members agreed not to exceed. But members were free to charge less than the maximum, and a physician's regular fees were always subject to reduction through negotiation, or waiver due to the patient's inability to pay. Needless to say, Foundations for Medical Care were greeted warmly by the public, and public awareness of them assured that few doctors would prosper without subscribing to the local medical society and peer review.

It stood to reason that if a physician were going to submit voluntarily to peer review, he or she would insist that the reviewers be among the most knowledgeable in the field, and they were. And because the reviewers were volunteers, it was of paramount importance to them that their efforts be received positively and that they enhance the prestige of the medical community. Peer review, therefore, was a continuing educational process for practitioners rather than an adversarial arrangement—like having private tutors throughout your career. In fact, peer review had been used in hospitals as a learning tool for more than half a century before government intervened.

Local medical societies also coordinated charitable care given by member doctors, scheduling rotating shifts at free clinics and augmenting the staffs of public health clinics with volunteers. Each community had its own unique needs, but most doctors spent about 20 percent of their work week tending to the poor. It was a fair trade because to be a doctor in good standing was a great honor in those days, a position of privilege and respect in the community.

When I entered the field under this system there was no federal regulation of medical practice—a federal administrative code had not even been written. A fair marketplace for medical services was maintained entirely through private, voluntary agreements, and care was universally available to any who sought it, regardless of ability to pay.

No system is perfect, although this system worked well, and the public, by and large, was greatly satisfied. But the government challenged the system on the very basis of public satisfaction. Because it was difficult for a physician to prosper without submitting to the scrutiny of fellow physicians, government reasoned that organized medicine held too much power over its members—power government wanted for itself. First, the Foundations for Medical Care were attacked under antitrust legislation, and the court decrees of Pima and Maricopa counties in Arizona, later sustained by higher courts, forced an end to self-regulation. Additionally, hospitals that received federal funds were prohibited from barring doctors on the basis of medical society membership.

Next, the American Medical Association (AMA) was attacked by the Federal Trade Commission (FTC) because its code of ethics restricted the promotional claims of AMA members. The AMA held that a doctor's good reputation should be earned through public satisfaction, board certification, and peer review, not through advertising. Again, the AMA was (and still is) a voluntary association—no law obligates doctors to join. But doctors join because the public demands that doctors subscribe to the highest ethical standards.

The Constitution assures the right of citizens to assemble and agree voluntarily to a code of ethics, but does it also grant government the right to establish "independent" regulatory agencies to interfere in this right? Yet the politically appointed commissioners of the FTC assume the functions of all three branches of government—and without the requisite separation of powers. Thus the AMA was prosecuted by an FTC employee on charges of violating the rules of the FTC, and the case was heard before an FTC-employed administrative law judge—who also acted as jury—who ruled that only the FTC could restrict the promotional activities of AMA members, not the AMA.

When Congress created the FTC it specified that the agency had jurisdiction over entities operating "for profit." Since the AMA was (and is) a nonprofit organization, it would seem that the FTC had no jurisdiction. But the FTC's judge ruled that because the AMA had opposed proposals to socialize medicine during the 1930s and 1940s, and because it had opposed the enactment of Medicare in the 1960s, the AMA was therefore acting for the profit of its members, even if it did not earn a profit itself. This was particularly vexing since when I spoke on behalf of the AMA in opposition to Medicare I made it clear that the pay of physicians would increase under Medicare, and it did. What the ruling really means is that when private citizens speak out against the interests of the federal bureaucracy, then the citizens' rights are diminished. After seven years of litigation the case made its way to the U.S. Supreme Court which deadlocked in a vote (4–4) on the issue of jurisdiction, leaving the FTC in control of AMA promotional affairs.

While the ethics-in-advertising case was still in litigation, the FTC attempted to have the AMA stripped of its authority to accredit medical schools, a public service it had performed for over thirty years in conjunction with the Association of American Medical

Schools. Who, besides the nation's doctors, could possibly determine what needs to be taught in medical schools?

After failing in that attempt the FTC launched a lengthy investigation to show that the AMA restricted applicants to medical schools in order to keep physicians' fees high. The allegation was preposterous. The only applicants the AMA sought to restrict were those not qualified to become first-rate doctors—exactly what the public expected. After several disruptive years the FTC failed to uncover any wrongdoing by the AMA and never even issued a public report on its costly investigation.

Although not entirely successful in all its attacks, the government effectively stripped private medicine of the right to self-regulate. Gone were the antigouging powers of the Foundations for Medical Care; gone were the hospital policies requiring staff physicians to submit to medical society grievance committees when fees were questioned; gone was the AMA's right to restrict promotional activities; gone was the self-regulating, free market for medical services. In their stead, the government took over; it began to regulate every facet of medical practice, usually deriving its power as the third-party payer under Medicare. A healthy, efficient, and affordable system of private medicine was thus drowned in the bureaucratic "paper plague."

In 1972, for services rendered under Medicare and Medicaid, Congress established Professional Standards Review Organizations (PSROs), which were agents of the government assigned to replace peer review by the medical profession. After ten years PSROs proved to be so ineffective and costly that Congress phased them out. But rather than restore the profession's power to self-regulate, Congress in 1982 spawned a new generation of money-eating monsters called Professional Review Organizations (PROs), which are privately contracted agents of government.

America's local medical societies had accumulated vast experience in peer review, but Congress excluded them from participating in the review process. And with good reason; unlike the review process under private medicine, government review organizations were not so much concerned with the quality of care as they were with limiting care to save money—in other words, rationing.

Today, the bureaucracy attempts to establish rigid "norms of treatment" which are reviewed after the treatment is given at central offices with jurisdiction over wide areas. But as every good doctor knows, medicine is as much an art as it is a science—what William Osler described as "an art which consists largely in the balancing of possibilities." Clear-cut answers to medical problems are not so easy to come by; the human body is a complex organism, no two patients respond precisely the same to similar treatments, and there are many alternative approaches to any given illness. Physical ailments are also very often intertwined with anxiety which affects the effectiveness of treatment. Medical decisions involve discretionary judgment, which is difficult to second guess with second-hand information. The closer the reviewer is to the problem, the more effective he or she will be. The review of hospital care, moreover, must be done in the hospital, not from some remote city with medical recipes read from a medical cookbook.

The objective of the government reviewer is to scrutinize the patient's records for medical decisions at variance with the official cookbook, then to deny Medicare reimbursement for the procedure. To the physician the objective is to provide endless paperwork to satisfy the reviewer. The concerns of the patient, which were foremost under private peer review, are now secondary.

Moreover, like any other walk of life, medicine has its share of avaricious scoundrels. Under private peer review, fraud among physicians was almost unheard of, and when it did occur it was easy to isolate because the reviewers were local doctors with immediate access to first-hand information. Under the government's system, all the unscrupulous practitioner needs to escape sanctions is to supply the proper paperwork to the bureaucracy, not proper care to the patient. Just as with all government bureaucracies—from public housing to the Pentagon—crooks, although few in number, subject Medicare to massive fraud costing the taxpayer about $10 billion a year. Every year the Medicare bureaucracy announces with great fanfare a new campaign to catch the crooks, and every year the fraud continues unabated.

Soon after government stepped into the review process the AMA established a policy of working with Washington to ensure the effectiveness of the government's system, especially where it concerned ethical issues and quality care. The AMA arranged with the federal government to supply workable review criteria, only to find that nearly every proposal submitted was summarily ignored. Under Civil Service protection the bureaucrats in charge have no incentive to work effectively or efficiently; on the contrary, they have every incentive to expand their power. Throughout history government has seized power during periods of disarray or crisis. Thus the more the bureaucratic programs malfunction, the more power the bureaucracy stand to gain.

Rather than work with organized medicine to eliminate unethical practitioners, government chooses continually to expand its authority. Instead of focusing on the few bad apples, every doctor in America is subjected to bureaucratic challenge—like indiscriminately blasting away with a shotgun rather than taking aim with a rifle. While honest doctors are burdened and harassed by the bureaucratic morass, crooks find that the paperwork and labyrinthine regulations offer opportunities to manipulate the system with impunity. And promoting oneself to the public, when less than reputable in the eyes of the medical community, is no longer a problem because, with the blessing of the FTC, such practitioners can run alluring ads in the yellow pages and daily newspapers.

What we have today, then, is a review system that has challenged the medical judgment of 73 percent of the nation's physicians in clinical practice, very few of whom have ever actually rendered less than competent, ethical care.[6] How can this be? Instead of attracting the most knowledgeable reviewers, as was done under private peer review, the PROs, which are "for profit" businesses, often hire doctors whose lack of adequate credentials prevent them from practicing at the very hospitals under review. Reviewers also often work under production quotas; in my home state of Florida the PRO was indicted when it was alleged that medical charts were not reviewed by medical people at all. One highly qualified physician who devoted part of his time to reviewing medical charts for the Texas PRO wrote to *Private Practice* magazine to explain his reason for quitting: ". . . I found that my decisions were overruled frequently by the local directors. It turned out that they wanted to match the computer in their

callous and blanket denial of claims."[7] This is why we have horror
stories like the Massachusetts woman who became very anemic after
suffering a severe myocardial infarction. Her doctor wanted to extend her hospitalization until her anemia could be brought safely
under control, but the utilization review committee insisted she be
sent home, and she was. Ten days later, she died there.[8]

Medical judgment is challenged so frequently that doctors find it
necessary to document and record every minute detail of patient
histories and physicals, test results and procedures, dietary instruc-
tions, medications, and therapy plans. Everything that goes into a
patient, and everything that comes out of a patient, is recorded.
Every move the patient makes in the hospital must be registered on
the chart, every nursing shift change requires additional notations.
Nothing is too routine or insignificant to be documented. When I
practiced medicine a patient's history and physical with laboratory
or x-ray findings were recorded on three-by-five cards with only
positive findings put down so that anyone referring to the cards
would know instantly the patients problems. In those days, a surgical chart was one or two pages long and it contained sufficient
information to aid future readers in making appropriate medical
decisions. Today, all findings, positive and negative, must be spelled
out, thus burying the pertinent information in charts often over a
hundred pages long. This is why when you enter a hospital floor it
seems that all the nurses and doctors are behind long desks pecking
at rows of computer terminals rather than at the bedsides of sick
patients.

Once a PRO unjustly challenges a physician's judgment, the physician must appeal or pay a fine of several thousands of dollars, even
over procedures resulting in charges of five dollars or less. A typical
PRO-sanctioned hearing may include the testimony of ten or more
doctors and nurses. In one instance of such a hearing in Illinois,
after two hours of testimony, with stenographer and all, it became
obvious that the reviewers had not read the hospital admission
charts before lodging the denial. Total cost of the proceeding:
about $20,000.[9]

Then there are the legal fees for a protracted defense, which can
be astronomical. Take, for instance, the case of Dr. Melashenko, a

family physician who was charged with performing too many colonoscopies, a procedure usually performed by specialists. It turned out that he had exceeded Medicare's profile for family doctors solely because his clinic was in rural Minnesota where there were no specialists to do the procedure. (Many family practitioners take additional training to learn specialized procedures.) The legal fees for his defense: $113,235—which had to be reimbursed by Medicare.[10] The government's review procedure is analogous to a random police roadblock where traffic citations are issued to every driver coming along; the majority, who are driving within the law, are forced to document their innocence and apply for a hearing, or just pay the penalty to dispense with the matter. Either way, the cost of operating a vehicle goes up—as has the cost of medical care.

That's not the only inflationary impediment government has placed on health care. In 1971 doctors' fees and hospital charges were frozen. Like all government-imposed price controls, the effort failed; when the tourniquet was released in 1975, the medical inflation rate spurted to 12.5 percent.

The bureaucrats then hatched a grandiose scheme to herd all Medicare patients into federally chartered health maintenance organizations (HMOs), corporate ventures initially financed by the taxpayer under the bureaucrats' control—a sort of privatized socialism. In 1972, HEW took money earmarked for "research" and "planning and development" to fund the first one hundred HMOs, and sought another $3.9 billion from Congress to finance over twelve hundred more HMOs by 1980. Teddy Kennedy thought it was such a great idea that he sponsored a bill to pour $8 billion into the untested scheme, more than double what the bureaucrats requested, because he decided that every American should be enrolled (except, apparently, for himself; he never joined one).

When the Health Maintenance Act passed in 1973 it provided provisional funding of $375 million to test the HMO concept. The money was spent to run television commercials and publicity campaigns to lure enrollees with exaggerated promises of preventive health care and with special competitive advantages granted exclusively to HMOs, such as the waiver of deductibles and co-payments, enticements which would trigger criminal prosecution if advanced by private physicians.

But the scheme failed to produce the expected results, and after financing their formation, the taxpayer was again called upon to bail out a number of faltering HMOs. HMO advocates were convinced that they would quickly become the dominate form of health care delivery in America, but after twenty years they have enrolled only 6 percent of the Medicare market and less than 15 percent of the total market.

Experience has demonstrated that about one-third of those who enroll in HMOs drop out within two years. Why? This comment attributed to the director of quality assurance for Humana Health Plans of South Florida, as reported in the Fort Lauderdale *Sun-Sentinel* October 23, 1990, seems to sum up the cause of public discontent: "In any HMO there is financial incentive to hold back on services." Illustrative of the problems is a 1991 General Accounting Office report of Humana's Gold Plus Medical Plan, Florida's largest HMO, which alleged that after being prepaid by Medicare the plan failed to pay for enrollees' emergency care, abused claims payments, improperly denied appeals, and engaged in misleading marketing schemes—all of which Medicare officials failed to do anything about. Moreover, from 1988 to 1991 the Florida Department of Insurance received a record 1,628 consumer complaints filed against Humana's HMOs alone. But it seems the Washington bureaucrats and politicians pushing the HMO scheme had long been aware of the perverse incentives, the pitfalls, for a 1986 McGraw-Hill survey of all proponent members of Congress and the federal bureaucracy showed that not a single one himself enrolled.

Undaunted by the earlier expense to the taxpayer, Congress provided the impetus for a major effort to enroll Medicare beneficiaries in HMOs by passing the Tax Equity and Fiscal Responsibility Act (TEFRA) of 1982. The big push came in 1985 when final regulations pursuant to the act were prepared, at which time Health and Human Services Secretary Margaret Heckler announced it as "another historic step in reforming our Medicare system." The go-ahead was given despite an HCFA-funded study that failed to show Medicare had saved a single nickel under the pilot programs.

While force-feeding HMOs on the public at their own expense, government proceeded to strangle private medicine with onerous new regulations. In 1975, regulations were issued requiring all Medicare hospital admissions to be preapproved by the bureaucracy, a procedure called precertification. In this case the AMA obtained a court injunction to stop non-medically trained bureaucrats from denying hospital admissions, but in 1986 the government authorized the privately contracted PROs to precertify admissions. Typical of the outcome is a 1990 Texas study showing that over a three-year period, 100,000 hospital admissions in the state were reviewed of which fewer than twenty were denied, and most of the denials were for minor, low cost procedures; for every dollar the denials saved Medicare, the Texas program cost more than twenty dollars to administer.[11]

In 1977 the federal government began publishing the names of physicians who received more than $100,000 per year in Medicare claims to shame them into providing less care to the elderly. But of the first 112 names listed, all but thirty-two were published with erroneous data. One doctor said to have received $233,871 in 1975 through his clinic in Illinois had actually retired to Arizona in 1963. He never received a penny from Medicare; it did not exist when he retired. Another doctor who was said to have charged Medicare $258,139 in 1975 had, in fact, died the year before. Moreover, many of the thirty-two listed correctly were actually senior partners receiving payment on behalf of large group practices, most of which were located in Florida where the majority of their patients were retirees on Medicare. A court injunction put an end to this idiocy.

With more experience, government became more inept. In spite of all the historical evidence demonstrating the ineffectiveness and harmful side effects of wage and price controls, in 1984 Medicare froze physicians' fees again, and then in 1987 the maximum allowable actual charge (MAAC) regulations ushered in a new era of complex and unworkable price controls. And while the controls were imposed, government did nothing to stem the tide of unwarranted

costs that it created, such as the malpractice crisis and the expense
of regulatory compliance.

With Medicare costs continuing to soar, 1992 brought implementation of the resource-based relative value scale (RBRVS), the most
sweeping and complicated price-fixing scheme ever. RBRVS neces-
sitated a complete overhaul of the Medicare administrative system,
including new diagnostic and procedure claims codes and another
three hundred pages of bureaucratic regulations. This time the
scheme had been tried before; RBRVS is based on a theory long
since discredited—the "labor value theory" which the central planners of the former Soviet Union tried in vain to make work for fifty
years. Under RBRVS the government sets physicians' fees for specified procedures without regard to medical complications or differences in the quality of care. A practitioner, that is, can no longer
prosper by his or her reputation for providing outstanding care, but
only functions as a mass producer, and therefore frequently as a
dispenser of substandard care. Because government's egalitarian
planners wish to provide equal pay for each medical procedure
performed, there is no incentive for the most capable practitioners
to tackle the most severe cases. All the benefits of a consumer-driven
free market have been ignored.

Under Medicare our system is subjected to the perverse incentives of arbitrary price-fixing, utilization review, concurrent review,
retrospective review, and retroactive denial of payment—making
health care the most heavily regulated industry in the history of our
nation. Government decides whether or not a patient will be admitted to the hospital, whether or not surgery will be performed,
whether or not an assistant will be used in surgery, when a patient
will be discharged, and what and how often procedures and diagnostic studies will be performed—all without ever examining the
patient. Imagine the bureaucratic enormity of annually monitoring
22 million admissions and discharges at 7,000 hospitals with 467
diagnostic-related groups plus 350 million charges from half a
million doctors with 7,000 different encoded procedures.

With so many bureaucrats eating away at the Medicare dollar,
current reimbursements, it is estimated, have been cut to about 50
percent of the actual cost of providing care and complying with

government paperwork. Regulations currently being phased in will phase out the traditional sliding fee scale; they will prohibit physicians from supplementing the cost of care for patients who cannot pay more than Medicare allows by charging more from those who can afford to pay more. Senior citizens will lose the right to pay for medical services on a case-by-case basis without dropping Medicare coverage—and no private insurance is permitted to compete with Medicare.

This violation of the right of contract between private citizens has frightening ramifications. For example, Medicare enrollees are explicitly guaranteed free choice of physicians, but many physicians will simply have to turn away Medicare patients even when the patient is willing to pay the bill out-of-pocket. To avoid denying care to patients who need it most, doctors who can shift the cost of treating Medicare patients to patients covered under private insurance—another reason the cost of private health insurance is unaffordable for increasing numbers of working Americans. And how long will private insurers be willing to underwrite Medicare's shortcomings? That's anybody's guess.

Aside from their unjust ramifications, Medicare regulations are virtually incomprehensible. They are so complicated and change so often that the bureaucracy publishes weekly bulletins filled with explanations, but the explanations themselves are almost impossible to understand. This, of course, is the inherent nature of bureaucracy, for it stands to reason than once regulations are written there is no need for that bureaucrat's job to continue; thus, the rules are rewritten—again and again. Since the rules do nothing to correct the basic flaw of Medicare—the third-party system of payment—they can never accomplish what they were intended to do, and rewriting them always seems necessary.

Before Medicare, the typical physician spent one-fifth of his or her working time caring for the poor; today the typical primary care physician spends one-fifth of his or her time on regulatory paperwork; the average patient visit necessitates the execution of ten document pages.[12] And when time devoted to paperwork by support personnel is added, much more time is spent filling out forms than tending to patients in the typical doctor's office. What has this done to the cost of care? Administrative costs are rising at more than twice the rate of health care in general, making it the fastest growing component of health care costs.[13] For a real eye-opener, consider that between 1980 and 1985, in the midst of the Reagan administration's concerted effort to reduce the regulatory burden on the American public, total health costs rose 85 percent while the cost of administering health care rose 186 percent.[14] This came about because the administration was also determined to cut spending and bring the deficit under control. Since it was not politically feasible to cut Medicare benefits, the bureaucracy promised that with a few more regulations, it would control Medicare costs. The regulations were implemented, and Medicare costs continued to soar due to the added regulatory burden.

Between 24 and 26 percent of medical costs in the United States are attributed to administration, most as a result of regulations intended to limit charges by providers. What is so remarkable about this figure is that all professional fees combined account for less than 20 percent of the nation's health care bill, a ratio that has not risen since 1950. And when I say professional fees, I am including chiropractors and all other nonmedical practitioners who cannot treat catastrophic ailments—ailments which require the most intensive treatments and therefore are the focus of the most burdensome regulations. Medical doctors and doctors of osteopathy, the only practitioners licensed to treat catastrophic illness, account for approximately 13 percent of the total health care bill, and half of that is absorbed by overhead and the expense of regulatory compliance. If government arbitrarily cut the net-before-tax earnings of all medical doctors by 50 percent, it would save the system less than 4 percent. (Actually it would save nothing because most doctors would find more rewarding careers and the resultant shortage would lead to higher costs.) On the other hand, if government rescinded all regulations imposed since the early 1960s, administrative costs would return to their pre-Medicare level of less than 5 percent, giving a net cost reduction of about 20 percent.

Thus far our discussion has focused on regulations affecting medical practitioners, but regulations affecting hospitals have been just as detrimental. Initially, Medicare and Medicaid paid hospitals on the cost-plus system. Under cost-plus, if Medicare patients at a given hospital accounted for 40 percent of occupancy, then 40 percent of the hospital's costs plus a nominal profit margin were prorated to Medicare patients. If a hospital wanted to earn more money, it could not do so by being more frugal in the purchase of new equipment, nor by bargaining with suppliers, nor by reducing energy consumption, nor by devising less costly methods of treatment, nor by rewarding staff for working efficiently; all of these measures would result in less income. The only way a hospital could increase income was to increase costs. And the only thing hospital suppliers needed to do to increase income was to increase prices. They did.

We all know that when a service station opens on a busy corner, top prices can be gotten for gasoline. If a second station opens at the same intersection, the first station will be forced to lower prices to maintain enough sales volume to remain profitable. And if a third and then a fourth open, an all-out gas war will likely erupt. But under the government-imposed third-party payer system in health care, consumers have had no incentive to seek out the best prices, and under Medicare's cost-plus system, health care facilities had no incentive to lower prices in the face of competing facilities. In the free market, when more service stations are built, gas prices go down; under Medicare when more hospitals are built, health costs go up.

Medicare actually encouraged the building of more hospitals. Since Medicare initially covered only in-hospital charges, thousands of patients were hospitalized daily for minor procedures and diagnostic tests. Had these patients been spending their own money in a free market, they would have been treated as out-patients at a fraction of the cost.

With hospital costs skyrocketing the bureaucrats finally recognized the folly of their system. But rather than admit the fundamental flaw of the third-party payer system—an admission that would signal government's failure in the health care marketplace—they exacerbated matters with further oppressive regulations.

To try to limit the expansion of health care facilities, the bureaucrats came up with a certificate of need (CON). Before a new hospital or nursing home could be built, or before an existing facility could buy new equipment or add capacity, a CON had to be applied for. Alarm bells should have rung all around, for as we know the public is better served when more service stations compete at an intersection, just as the public is better served by greater hospital capacity in a given community. Even if CONs should succeed in limiting capacity, the restricted supply would still give no incentive to reduce health costs in the face of unlimited demand.

CONs disrupted the marketplace in other ways too. For instance, the product life cycle phenomenon tells us that when a new technology receives widespread market acceptance the price of the product drops dramatically. This is clearly illustrated in the case of personal computers, which today sell for little more than a thousand dollars and yet have as much computing power as mainframe computers which just two decades ago sold for hundreds of thousands of dollars. Thus, when CONs restrict the market for medical technology, prices are kept artificially high.

I have observed the CON process on a number of occasions, and its only measurable outcome was unnecessary red tape resulting in long delays and excessive legal fees. The outcome was immeasurable in terms of unwarranted suffering and loss of life. In one case with which I was intimately familiar, a private nonprofit hospital had raised sufficient cash donations to purchase a CAT scanner. A CON was denied on the grounds that a CAT scanner was already located at another hospital a few miles away. But the great lifesaving advantage of a CAT scanner is its ability to direct surgeons in emergency head injuries and stroke cases. In many of these cases the patient cannot be stabilized sufficiently to be transported, and if the patient is moved, the time entailed can see brain hemorrhaging that often causes death or permanent paralysis—a terrible price to pay just so bureaucrats can continue their senseless intervention in a field about which they know nothing. In this particular case the decision was appealed and overturned, but the legal fees borne by the hospital came to nearly $50,000—money that should have been used to save lives.

CONs were embodied on a voluntary basis in the Comprehensive Health Planning Act of 1966, but six years later Medicare and

Medicaid began penalizing health care facilities that did not conform. Not satisfied, in 1974 Congress passed the National Planning and Resources Act granting the secretary of HEW awesome new powers to control health care facilities, including the imposition of mandatory CONs nationwide. Immediately upon passage the AMA went to court and succeeded in paring down several blatantly unconstitutional provisions of the law, but the surviving provisions still concentrated more federal power over private citizens and local communities than any previous peacetime act of Congress.

Teddy Kennedy, as chairman of the Senate Subcommittee on Health, created a mechanism in the planning act through which the bureaucracy would eventually reign over his vision of socialized medicine. It embodied a multilayered Soviet-style central planning pyramid with the HEW secretary at the helm of a national advisory council which oversaw the state planning agencies, the state coordinating councils, and finally over two hundred local health systems agencies. The HEW secretary appointed all members of the agencies in consultation with the governors, and in an incredible act of governmental stupidity, two-thirds of the appointees had to be individuals with no education or experience in health care, the very field over which they made life and death decisions. To make matters worse, half of the nonmedical members were politicians and bureaucrats. Under the act all states would be required to have certificate of need laws which were administered by the health systems agencies.

By 1978 the ultimate nightmare came true when the Washington bureaucracy arbitrarily dictated the number of hospital beds per thousand population permissible in any community. The local health systems agencies then ordered some hospitals to close and others to seal off wards, floors, and entire wings. Fortunately, public outcry was shrill enough to embarrass the Carter administration, and the orders were withdrawn.

Before Congress finally ended this idiocy the bureaucracy had spent over $2 billion just administering the planning act. (Despite all this, certificates of need and local planning agencies still survive under the laws of several states.) According to the Center for the Study of American Business, every dollar government regulators spend causes private industry to spend an additional twenty dollars in compliance costs.[15] This means that over the life of the planning act $40 billion was unnecessarily added to the nation's health care bill, not a penny of which went to treat patients.

In 1983, by an amendment to the Social Security act, Congress changed the method of reimbursing hospitals to something called the prospective payment system. Again, the regulations were changed without addressing the fundamental flaw of the third-party payer system. Under the prospective payment system hospitals are paid according to Diagnostic Related Groups (DRGs), similar to the RBRVS price-fixing scheme recently applied to doctors. Medicare unilaterally set prices on 467 DRGs; if a hospital loses money on a complicated case, that money has to be recovered through cost-shifting to privately insured patients or by overpricing sundries not covered by the DRGs, such as aspirins. In the first year after enactment the Health Insurance Association of America reported that the amount of costs shifted from Medicare and Medicaid patients to private patients had increased more than 50 percent. Medicare's price-fixing schemes also give an incentive for health care facilities to shun, in any way they can, the sickest of senior citizens. This is evident from the American Hospital Association's estimate that in 1993 hospitals will lose an average of $900 on each Medicare patient treated, resulting in a total deficit of $9 billion.

In summation, we often hear proponents of national health care cite the excessive cost of administering medicine as reason to do away with the multiplicity of private health insurers and replace them with a single-payer government-run system. But in truth, America's excessive administrative costs are due solely to regulations under Medicare and Medicaid, including the cost of running the bureaucracy itself, a monstrosity that has given us the highest ratio of health care bureaucrats to health care providers in the world.

We need not wonder what a government-run single-payer health care system would be like; we have seen it in action with Medicare for nearly thirty years. In fact, House Ways and Means Committee

Chairman Dan Rostenkowski (Dem. IL) is so proud of Medicare's record in controlling health costs that he used it as a model for his proposed national health care system.[16] Hard to believe given public knowledge that the cost of Medicare has doubled every five years since 1970. By now the truth of this axiom should be obvious: "Government has no solutions; government is the problem."

CHAPTER 12

—————∿—————

Toxic Torts:
When Lawyers Make the Laws

I would not want to live in a society without lawyers any more than I would want to live in a society without doctors or schoolteachers or farmers. The finest man I have ever known, my late stepfather who raised me from infancy, was justifiably proud of his noble profession. Without lawyers like him society would have been at the mercy of quacks, con artists, and thugs.

But profound changes have taken place since my stepfather's day in court, and these changes have affected society in general and health care in particular. Today we find ourselves increasingly at the mercy of those who take advantage of a civil justice system that has run amok. With each passing day our society slips closer to barbarism; no one feels secure that his or her possessions will not be seized pursuant to an unforeseeable injury claim; and no one feels sure that if he or she is wronged compensation will be paid in less than five to ten years, if ever, and then only after being slashed by legal fees, expert witness fees, and litigation expenses. It seems that no matter which side of a dispute you may fall on, the legal process has become a game of chance at which only lawyers cannot lose.

I know of no one, with the exception of trial lawyers, who sincerely believes that the changes in the legal process over the past thirty years are healthy for society. Even among lawyers themselves, discontent has become commonplace. In a recent readership survey taken by *California Lawyer* magazine, most of the respondents indicated they were unhappy with their careers, and 81 percent said "hardball tactics and uncivil behavior" were still on the rise in the legal profession.[1]

So blatant are the legal assaults on common decency, so outrageous are the judicial decrees, so unwieldy the legal process, that the vice president of the United States felt impelled to address the American Bar Association (ABA) in 1991 and say, in effect, enough is enough, we must reform. On that unprecedented occasion former Vice President Quayle pointed out to the swollen bar that there was one lawyer for every 335 people in America compared to one for every nine thousand in Japan, and that our civil justice system placed us at a competitive disadvantage by imposing litigation and liability costs, both directly and indirectly, which might exceed $300 billion each year—$100 billion more per year than the total cost of the savings and loan bail-out. Given that the United States constitutes only 5 percent of the world's population, surely no fair-minded person could fault him for posing these rhetorical questions: "Does America really need 70 percent of the world's lawyers? Is it really healthy for our economy to have 18 million new lawsuits coursing through the system annually? Is it right that people with disputes come up against staggering expense and delay?"

Surely the vice president was right to question the imposition of "arbitrary" and "freakish" punitive damages when he suggested that they should not exceed the total compensatory damages to which they are related. Surely he was justified in suggesting that in place of the contingency fee we should adopt the English rule of having the opponent in a lawsuit pay the legal fees of the prevailing party. Surely he used sound reasoning when he proposed that testimony by so-called expert witnesses be limited to sound scientific theories, and that "junk science" be barred from the courtroom.

The response was unnerving. Rather than offer constructive co-operation, the presiding ABA president, John J. Curtin, embarked on this irrational tirade: "Anyone who believes a better day dawns when lawyers are eliminated bears the burden of explaining who will take their place—who will protect the poor, the injured, the victims of negligence, the victims of racial discrimination, and the victims of racial violence."

Setting aside the fact that the vice president did not suggest we eliminate all lawyers, just how do lawyers protect the poor when for every dollar won by plaintiffs in tort claims up to two-thirds is taken by lawyers in fees and other litigation expenses?[2] How are the poor served by lawyers when in many regions the single greatest overhead expense inflating the bill for a physician's office visit is malpractice insurance? How are lawyers protecting the poor when up to 95 percent of the cost of a child's vaccine—the most effective means we have of preventing deadly and crippling diseases—goes to legal liability expenses?[3]

DEMISE OF THE CONTRACT

Our legal problem is multifaceted, much like the problem of unaffordable health care, of which the legal problem is but one facet. The first facet of the legal problem involves the breakdown of the doctrine of *stare decisis*—"let the decision stand"—a judicial policy lending stability to the rule of common law so that citizens can predict with reasonable certainty the legal effect of their conduct. Our long tradition of common law governing contracts and torts, inherited by the American colonies from the courts of England and sustained by the courts of the United States, gave us a staid civil relationship under which all parties to a transaction understood what was expected of them, and liability under the law of torts was predictable according to a person's actions.

In 1929 the classic but rare case of medical malpractice arose when an eighteen-year old lad, embarrassed by a tiny scar on his hand, called on a physician for help. The physician attempted to graft skin from the boy's chest to his hand, an impossible cosmetic feat given the technology of the day. In the end the boy's hand was permanently marred by a grotesque clump of hairy tissue. The court found in the boy's favor because the doctor had breached his contract. Why breach of contract? Although not in writing, under common law patients contracted with their doctors, not necessarily for a certain outcome, but for a certain standard of care according to contemporary technology and medical methods.

Since then the judicial system has taken a radical turn as evidenced by this example of another physician who lost a malpractice suit, but not for failing to deliver proper care. In 1981 a Chicago pediatrician administered the proper dosage of a whooping cough vaccine to a small girl, a procedure required by law before a child could be enrolled in school because whooping cough is among the deadliest of childhood diseases. The same doctor had administered the same vaccine to hundreds of other children without adverse side effects. The vaccine had been approved by the Food and Drug Administration (FDA) and the doctor had procured it from a reputable manufacturer. The effectiveness of the procedure was scientifically unquestioned; without such immunizations untold numbers of young lives could be lost nationwide. Still, due to the innate constitutional makeup of certain children, there is a remote possibility of adverse side effects from vaccines—an unpredictable and freak mishap. In this case it was alleged that the vaccine subjected the child to multiple convulsions. Her parents sued and a judgment of $5.5 million was won, an amount far exceeding the limits of most malpractice policies.

Unlike the 1929 case, the doctor had performed according to contract. Why, then, was the judgment entered? By the time this case arose the courts had summarily discarded the common law contract in such cases, and in its stead they imposed tort liability. Had the contract survived, a simple, efficient, and inexpensive solution to this type of tragic loss would be possible: medical accident insurance—an arrangement by the patient, the health care provider, and the insurance underwriter whereby for a nominal premium the patient would receive a specified sum and the provider would be absolved from financial responsibility if he or she delivered the prevailing standard of care. Payment would be made immediately and the entire sum would go directly to the patient without any deduction for legal fees or litigation expenses. Doctors could then continue to provide the level of care expected of them without fear of financial ruin, and affected patients could go about the difficult task of putting their lives back in order without enduring years of depositions and pretrial discovery.

The overall societal advantages of such a contractual system would be immeasurable. Verdicts similar to the Chicago incident have been repeated thousands of times, and have had a variety of harmful results. Due to the unpredictable nature of these mishaps and the inflation of awards by emotion-driven jurors, especially when children are injured, many manufacturers of vaccines have been forced to withdraw their products. As a consequence we encounter repeated shortages of life-saving vaccines, and the costs of the available supply are inflated by 2,000 to 5,000 percent. The Center for Disease Control is often forced to ration vaccines to public health clinics and to stockpile supplies to avoid future shortages. Most tragically, the development of new vaccines has been severely hindered. Recent news reports that the introduction of an AIDS vaccine has been inhibited by liability concerns illustrate the problem.

But even should the suggested contractual system be adopted, in the current legal climate, no such common sense approach to compensation for unavoidable mishaps would stand because the courts have eroded the integrity of the contract and replaced it with a distended tort liability. That is, even if such a contract were agreed to in writing prior to treatment, the courts could disregard its terms and permit the patient to sue, and, pursuant to the collateral source rule, money already paid under the accident policy would not mitigate a liability award.

In his book, *Liability: The Legal Revolution and its Consequences*, Peter Huber illustrated the demise of the contract with the 1958 California case of *Vandermark vs. Maywood Bell Ford*. Six weeks after Chester Vandermark purchased a new car the brakes allegedly failed, resulting in an accident and bodily injuries. Unlike the Chicago vaccine, the vehicle was apparently defective. A party had been wronged, but was the dealer to blame as well as the manufacturer?

In this case a written contract limited the dealer's responsibility to replacing defective parts, but claims beyond the scope of mechanical repairs could have been made against accident insurance which was readily available. To be liable under the common law of torts the defendant would have to have committed a wrongful act or omission independent of the contract and thereby have breached a legal duty owed the plaintiff, which breach would have to have caused the injury. Although our compassionate sentiments may tell us that the dealer profited from the sale of a defective product and therefore should be responsible for the injuries, the fact was the dealer had no way of knowing the brakes would fail in six weeks and could not have prevented the accident—i.e., no breach of duty by the dealer caused the injury; thus the expressed warranty limits in the contract and the need for accident insurance.

But in 1964 the California Supreme Court held that the contractual limits to liability were immaterial, that the dealer was an integral part of the overall car-making industry and therefore subject to strict liability (liability without fault). Previously, strict liability was only applied in rare circumstances against tort defendants who engaged in extra-hazardous undertakings—e.g., the keeping of lions and tigers over which safe control could not be assured. But in the Vandermark case, strict liability was applied against people engaged in ordinary commerce. In other words, the commission of a wrongful act or neglect of duty was no longer the central issue in applying tort liability; instead, an economic interest had become not only a new, but a more important criterion.

With common law thus corrupted, Americans soon found that they could not protect themselves from legal liability through prudent actions and contractual consent, but could be held liable simply for being in the wrong place at the wrong time.

Even in cases that were clearly matters of tort law, blame was often levied solely on ability to pay. For instance, in the infamous case of *Bigbee vs. Pacific Telephone* (1983), a drunken driver careened off the road, jumped the curb, crossed the sidewalk and rammed into an occupied telephone booth. Clearly a tort had been committed against the hapless occupant of the phone booth and the drunken driver was at fault. But because the driver had little money, the occupant of the phone booth sued the phone company. But could the phone company have prevented the injury? Not unless it had

encased the booth in steel armor. Then the phone company could
have been held liable for injuries to the drunken driver, like the
Florida developer who was sued by a driver who fell asleep and
struck a boulder in the decorative landscape. Nevertheless, the
California Supreme Court ruled that the phone company could be
held liable and even added in a footnote to the opinion: "Imposition
of liability would not be unduly burdensome to defendants given
the probable availability of insurance for these types of accidents."

The court attempted to right the wrong done to one victim by
creating another victim. Courts in the new era are no longer concerned with finding fault of the blameworthy or protecting the
property rights of the blameless, but instead seem to be running a
lottery to redistribute wealth.

Since doctors, hospitals, and the manufacturers of pharmaceuticals and medical devices deal with people who are already sick and
injured, they are, willy-nilly, held responsible for the greatest share
of life's tragedies. According to a 1987 study by the American
College of Obstetricians and Gynecologists, 70 percent of the nation's obstetricians have been sued for malpractice at least once, and
many have been sued by mothers who used cocaine, alcohol, or
tobacco during pregnancy. In my hometown of Miami, neurosurgeons pay an average of $185,000 a year in malpractice pre-
miums. That means that every work week the doctor must recover
$3,700 from patients just to cover the cost of insurance. It has not
taken long for the new tort edicts to price millions of working
Americans out of the medical marketplace.

CONTINGENT JUSTICE: ONLY IN AMERICA

By 1965 all of the states had embraced another facet of the legal
problem, the contingent fee, which has fueled a frenzy of frivolous
lawsuits under the new edicts. The contingent mechanism provides
financial incentives for a host of unsavory attorney practices—
including barratry (incitement of litigation) and champerty
(whereby a person not a party to a suit supports the prosecution in
return for a share of the judgment)—the commission of which
would draw stiff criminal penalties in all other developed nations.

Under the English rule, which is applied in some form almost everywhere but the United States, the loser of a civil lawsuit must pay the attorney's fee of the prevailing side. The poor are thereby assured of representation in court no matter how minor the dispute, and successful plaintiffs are assured they will receive just recompense without deductions for attorneys' fees.

By contrast, the American contingent fee encourages lawyers to file flighty claims in hopes of striking a big verdict, and, at the same time, it discourages lawyers from accepting cases wherein the damage awards will be modest, regardless of the merits of the case. For instance, one Florida patient had no problem finding a lawyer to sue for the loss of clairvoyance after undergoing a CAT-scan. Since the plaintiff was a professional psychic, the claim for lifetime loss of income was sizable.

Without the English rule, moreover, defense lawyers representing wealthy clients with weak cases can prolong litigation in hopes of wearing down the plaintiff to the point that an unjustly low settlement offer will be accepted—a tactic most effective on those badly injured and in dire need—and at the same time keep the fee-clock ticking several years longer than necessary. By contrast, the English rule encourages defendants with weak defenses to settle quickly and avoid unnecessary legal fees from their opponents.

Still, some will query why the contingent fee is not appropriate to lawyers when so many nonlawyers are only rewarded when successful—e.g., insurance agents earn commissions when they sell policies; they earn nothing when they don't. But keep in mind that lawyers are officers of the court and are empowered to file claims of wrongdoing against members of the public. They can compel the accused to spend years defending a claim, sometimes bankrupting the defendant even when the claimant is not successful. Lawyers with doubtful claims often extract settlements from those not equipped to fight, or who simply calculate that it is cheaper to settle—and liability insurers recoup the loss by raising premiums.

The contingent fee provides an overwhelming temptation for lawyers to abuse their coercive power. If policemen, who are also officers of the court, were paid a contingent fee of 40 or 50 percent for every traffic fine collected they would flood the courts with citations for imaginary infractions, just as lawyers do with malpractice and product liability suits.

Contingent fees are demanded, too, in cases where there is no contingency, where the facts speak for themselves and success is certain. Here again, the poor—the very people lawyers profess to help—are most vulnerable because they cannot afford to pay an hourly fee.

Perhaps the most damning indictment of the contingent fee is the exorbitant amount of the fees. Typical of court-approved settlements in my area of South Florida—and this example is only noteworthy because it is so ordinary—is one in which a baby suffered cerebral palsy, allegedly the fault of a physician. Without considering the merits of the claim, and I have no knowledge of the particulars, the case was settled without a trial, a fact which should have drastically reduced the lawyer's fee. But Circuit Court Judge Ignatius Lester of Monroe County approved the $1 million settlement then reduced the plaintiff's take by $550,000. Pursuant to a 45 percent contingent fee, $450,000 of the reduction went to the plaintiff's attorney plus an additional $100,000 in legal expenses. Not bad for a case settled without a court fight. By comparison, only $300,000 of what was left went to the care of the child and $75,000 went to each of the parents.

Fees like this are commonplace in the contingency business, but peanuts compared to the fees earned in multi-million dollar cases. New York trial lawyer Max Toberoff, whose estimated income in 1988 was $12 million, according to *Forbes*, boasted to the magazine that he settled five cases over the phone for $15 million while trying a malpractice case in which he won another $11.5 million. Other examples of estimated contingency earnings that year: $450 million for Joseph Dahr Jamail of Houston; $40 million for Herbert Hafif of Claremont, California; $14.5 million for Walter Umphrey of Beaumont, Texas. In all, *Forbes* provided over fifty examples of multi-million contingency fee incomes. Mind you, these were the personal incomes of individual lawyers, not their law firms.[4]

I do not begrudge hard-working lawyers a fair wage, nor do I plead pity for the poor doctors, but it is important to put the lawyer's compensation into perspective. Deirdre Fanning of *Forbes* observed: "It appears that the only people consistently making as much money as trial lawyers in America are Wall Street money men and entertainers. Doctors? Relatively small stuff. Only a handful of doctors make over $1 million from their craft. Even nontrial lawyers—those involved in securities, divorce and lobbying—regularly earn million-dollar plus salaries."[5]

While it may be true that a handful of doctors with exotic specialties make a million dollars—although I don't know any who do—the average physician ends up with about $150,000 after paying the malpractice premium and other pretax expenses. Gerald Michaud of Wichita, Kansas, a lawyer noted for filing polio vaccine suits, was estimated by *Forbes* to have earned $18 million in 1988. By contrast, the average family physician who administers the vaccine earned $96,000 that year.

To most working Americans $96,000 represents a very comfortable living, although it is not excessive considering the average doctor's sixty-hour work week, the odd hours spent on call, the eleven to sixteen years of required study, the $150,000 invested in that education, plus the cost of expensive medical equipment needed to open a practice. And that is not all. Today, the first hurdle a doctor must jump upon entering practice is the malpractice premium, most of which ends up in lawyers' pockets. It's obvious that lawyers' fees are driving up the cost of medical care, not doctors' fees.

ASK AN EXPERT

Plaintiffs who win big jury awards are often dismayed to find that after their lawyers take the lion's share, another 20 to 30 percent of it winds up in the pockets of so-called expert witnesses. And in some states these witnesses may command contingent fees just like the lawyers, which means that the expert can make a million dollars for a few hours of testimony. Even where that is not allowed, many experts find that by testifying in just a few big cases they command more money than they earn in a year working full time at their craft. As Walter Olson points out in his book, *The Litigation Explosion*, medical experts charge $15,000 to $20,000 per case for malpractice testimony.

This gives rise to two critical questions: how much influence do the experts have on the jury's decision, and how reliable is their testimony? To answer the first question we must consider the makeup of the jury—who sits in judgment?

Historically, juries were made up of peers of the defendant, commonly neighbors and colleagues of the accused. Eventually, it was decided that for jurors to be impartial they should not know the defendant. Fair enough, but unfortunately, like so many other movements in jurisprudence, the courts lost balance and completely abandoned the principle of a jury of peers. Today, prospective jurors are carefully screened to make certain not only that they do not know the defendant personally, but that they know nothing about his or her field of endeavor. But when the accusation involves malpractice or liability for the manufacture of pharmaceuticals or high-tech medical equipment, a juror must have special knowledge, even in-depth knowledge, of the technology or professional methods to arrive at a just finding. Thus another facet of the legal problem arises: jurors are 100 percent reliant upon the testimony of expert witnesses.

Why are such huge sums paid to expert witnesses for opinions rendered in court when the same experts would render such opinions in a professional context for a fraction of the cost? Could it be that expert testimony is tainted by money? Could it be that the very testimony upon which jurors must rely most is the most unreliable?

When out of earshot of the jury, lawyers cynically refer to their star experts as "saxophones," because they can call on them to play a different tune according to the occasion. Jurors, of course, lacking even rudimentary training in the expert's field, have no means to suspect when the sweet-sounding testimony is off key. Even worse, experts are permitted to draw legal conclusions based on hearsay evidence and scientific fantasy. The expert simply turns to the jury and swears that in his or her professional opinion the defendant caused the injury to the plaintiff by malpractice, or that some medication caused the pregnant mother to deliver a deformed child. The expert need not even have examined the patient to draw such conclusions. The expert can swear to scientific conclusions which are at variance with all the scholarly literature worldwide. And the expert can so testify even when his or her own professional society, which provided the expert's credentials, finds the theories testified to invalid.

Of course, the jury also hears the opposing lawyer's cross examination and his own expert. But the experts need not convince the jury either way to induce an unjust verdict, all they need do is confuse the jury with scientific mumbo-jumbo, in which event jurors are left to rely on the only other resource available to them to reach a decision: their emotional response.

Once again, this radical departure from common sense was instituted over the past thirty years. Dubious scientific theories used to be banned from the courtroom under the Frye rule, but the 1960s saw the courts loosening the restrictions on who was qualified to testify to what theories. In 1975 Congress burst the leaking dam by passing liberalized rules of evidence, which were soon copied by most of the states. By 1984 the federal appeals court in Washington, D.C., even proffered that unless a scientific theory could be palpably disproved, the jury should determine its merit. Today, people may sue for anything the imagination can conjure up, and the onus of proof to the contrary is upon the accused. (How, I wonder, does one disprove that a patient lost her psychic-powers in a CAT-scan?)

This is not to suggest that all expert witnesses are insincere. But even when there is an earnest difference of opinion among experts, lay juries are ill equipped to determine upon which side the preponderance of evidence lies.

A good example of the egregious harm inflicted on society by the current rules of evidence is the case of Bendectin. For the nearly twenty years that the drug was marketed, obstetricians worldwide were virtually unanimous in crediting Bendectin with safely controlling nausea and vomiting during pregnancy, a condition often severe enough to jeopardize both the mother and her developing child. Bendectin was the only truly effective drug to treat morning sickness. At a cost of hundreds of millions of dollars to the maker, the drug underwent many years of review, of testing and retesting, with the result that the Food and Drug Administration not only approved the drug, but it reconfirmed that Bendectin was safe for both mother and child, and the United Nations' World Health Organization concurred with that finding.

Still, a few expert witnesses—one doctor primarily—testified in lawsuits all across the country against the manufacturer, claiming that in their professional opinions Bendectin caused or contributed to birth defects. The manufacturer won almost all of the cases by citing the worldwide scientific community's opinion that the paid experts' conclusions were without foundation. But in some cases jurors were confused by the scientific evidence, and the results were stupefying: in one case $95 million was awarded to compensate for a single birth defect, an amount that even the judge found excessive and reduced to a paltry $20 million. And although defeat in a single case was financially devastating, victory was hardly less so: the cost of defending a single case could mount to more than a million dollars. To add tragedy to travesty, the manufacturer set aside a $120 million fund to settle another seven hundred pending lawsuits against it, and then withdrew Bendectin from the market. No manufacturer will again dare to market a morning sickness drug in the United States.

One need not look far to find a recent example of a malpractice case in which the jury was easily swayed by expert testimony. A sixty-eight-year old retired policeman, William Lenahan, slipped a disc in his back and Dr. Douglas Martin of Palm Beach County, Florida, performed a laminectomy for him on Christmas eve, 1986. Soon thereafter a persistent discharge developed at the incision, so Dr. Martin readmitted his patient to the hospital where he drew cultures of the fluid and confirmed an infection. Since there was no indication that the discharge was spinal fluid and since there was no sign of meningitis, Dr. Martin prudently decided against a spinal tap which would risk contamination of the spinal fluid. The infection was soon treated, the discharge cleared, and Lenahan was sent home. Follow-up examinations showed that Lenahan's recovery from surgery was rapid and he was walking two miles a day at the completion of physical therapy—there was no indication of further infection or of possible meningitis.

In the meantime, Lenahan asserted that his slipped disc was the result of a parking lot fray while working as a security guard a month before the surgery. He filed a claim for workers compensation to cover 100 percent of his medical bills, and he filed suit against his sparring partner from whom he eventually collected $400,000 in an out-of-court settlement. Lenahan and his wife, Phyllis, later claimed before a workers compensation judge that his recovery had gone awry and that Phyllis would have to care for him the rest of his life. In January 1989 the workers compensation judge awarded Phyllis $10.50 per hour, twenty-four hours per day, to care for her husband for as long as he lived, plus granting William Lenahan another $315 per week for a total of more than $100,000 a year.

It was that latter claim of a recovery gone awry that landed Dr. Martin in court in February of 1991, accused by the Lenahans of malpractice. The suit claimed that William Lenahan suffered memory loss, reduced intelligence, paralysis of the left side, a 75 percent loss of vision, impaired hearing, diminished reflexes, and loss of balance—all the result of hydrocephalus caused by undiagnosed meningitis following surgery. Strangely, of the several well-qualified specialists who testified against Dr. Martin, none ran a brain scan on the patient until Dr. Martin's lawyer obtained a court order on the eve of the trial. The scan showed no evidence of hydrocephalus, but even the negative result failed to impress the untrained jury because one hired expert confused the issue by testifying to "unidentified bright objects" on the scan. The patient's alleged condition, moreover, was potentially curable, but nobody involved seemed interested in treating him—their only interest was in suing Dr. Martin.

When Phyllis Lenahan testifyed to her husband's plight, several jurors wept openly. Then the experts came on stage. A neurologist from New Hampshire, who had been hired by the plaintiff's lawyer for a dozen previous cases, had not even examined the patient when he told the jury that it was his opinion Lenahan's dementia was the result of imperfectly treated meningitis, which he blamed squarely on Dr. Martin. But the grand finale came when a neurology professor from Miami, who also testified regularly for Lenahan's lawyer, shuffled the wobbly William Lenahan in front of the jury where he handed Lenahan a jacket so the jurors could see him fumble about, unable to put his arm through the sleeve. He then asked the plaintiff how many nickels were in a dollar, and Lenahan replied, "A whole bunch of them, I guess." And when he asked where they were, Lenahan looked up at the ceiling and cried: "Church!" It didn't take the jury long to come back with a verdict of $2.5 million.

But throughout the courtroom drama Dr. Martin's trained eye caught things that the jury didn't. Before teetering past the jury box Lenahan shifted his cane from his left hand to his right, yet his left side was supposed to have been paralyzed. Later Dr. Martin saw him pull a handkerchief from his pocket—with his left hand. Dr. Martin hired a private detective.

During the ensuing months the private detective followed Lenahan with a video camera. Before the trial even ended, Lenahan allegedly had had no problem counting out enough nickels to buy a $250,000 yacht on which the camera later caught him making repairs. He was also taped trotting up four flights of stairs, chasing his wife's Cadillac down the street, and dancing a jig. One day the detective alleged that Phyllis Lenahan drove her husband to a mall where he ran in to make a few quick purchases, and on another day the detective said he followed William when he drove from his home in Port Saint Lucie, Florida, to his vacation home in the Florida Keys, a distance of 240 miles over which he reached speeds in excess of eighty miles per hour.

Charged with fraud and grand theft, the Lenahans have been convicted. Dr. Martin's insurance company is fighting to get its money back, although the judge ruled that Lenahan's attorney could keep $500,000 of the contingent fee.

But to go back a step: if Lenahan had suffered dementia as he claimed, there was still no sound evidence that Dr. Martin was at fault or that meningitis had even occurred. Given the history of the patient's earlier recovery combined with the negative brain scan, the preponderance of evidence should have led to the conclusion that the dementia, if it existed, arose from another source. All of which demonstrates just how easily a lay jury is confused by expert testimony. As one member of the jury explained to Christine Evans of the *Miami Herald*: "We were impressed by all these forty-five dollar words. I mean, here we are, a bunch of laymen, and here they are, a bunch of experts. What do you do?"[6]

I have no reason to suspect that anybody connected with this case was aware of the Lenahans' alleged shenanigans because no one gave the plaintiff a proper neurological examination—which would have quickly exposed the alleged fraud. On this point Dr. Martin's lawyer, Hayward Gay, raised a good question: "Why didn't really smart, good doctors like these probe in more depth?" The answer is obvious: they weren't hired to probe, they were hired to testify. They were paid more to testify than they could earn by probing and healing sick people. And, according to the rules of evidence, they weren't required to probe any deeper before forming an opinion and attesting to it. The rules are designed to obscure the truth, not expose it. As Mr. Gay also commented: "The truth is we've probably been fooled before, and we'll probably be fooled again."[7]

ASSESSING THE DAMAGE

It is a paradox of our time that public opinion surveys show that most people think jury awards are excessive, yet that same public performs jury duty—and the pattern continues. As witnessed in the Lenahan case above, juries are treated to courtroom theatrics intended to confuse the technical facts and stir the emotions, which partially explains the phenomenon of excessive verdicts.

But there is another facet to the legal problem: the definitions of compensable damages have multiplied in recent decades. Under common law as we knew it, the right to damages for an injury was severely restricted to actual monetary losses by the victim alone. For instance, there was no remedy for wrongful death because there was no living victim—the right to sue passed with the victim. This being far too stringent for our enlightened era, the legislatures enacted remedies to relatives of victims for pecuniary damages, meaning that those who were dependent on the victim—whether the victim was injured or killed—could recover the amount of lost income. Mostly through the courts' interpretations of those laws and the courts' willingness to accept speculative loss claims, the meaning of pecuniary and other losses to both victim and family has been expanded.

Today it is not unusual for plaintiffs—including the injured party and anyone else who can think of a reason why the injury affects him—to claim damages for pain and suffering, loss of support, loss of services, loss of voluntary assistance, loss of prospective inheritance (for grandchildren), loss of parental guidance, loss of enjoyment of life, loss of consortium, hedonic damages (the value of the victim's future pleasures), posthumous pain and suffering (e.g., the New York family of an auto accident victim that was awarded $1.5 million extra for the four seconds of pain suffered by the victim before dying), and, of course, mental anguish. Add a couple of million for this, a couple million for that; pretty soon you have a sizable verdict.

Damage awards are usually payable in a lump-sum only, but most of the losses for which they compensate would only be incurred over time—usually a lifetime. For instance, why should an award for lost income be paid immediately when the wages it replaces would have been paid weekly? The "tort tax," which is reflected in the price we pay for health care, would be greatly reduced if insurers could satisfy damage awards with lifetime annuities, which would also serve to protect the plaintiff's principal balance.

Of course, assigning dollar amounts to noneconomic damages— estimated as being one-half of total malpractice awards—raises another problem for juries. How is a jury expected to award recompense for pain and suffering?

In a classic example of how sympathy can override reason without legislative guidelines, a Florida jury awarded $6.8 million to compensate for all expenses and potential losses for generations to come, then tacked on an additional $3.2 million for the pain and suffering of the paralyzed victim. To be eligible for noneconomic damages in most states the jury must find that the defendants caused the injury through negligence. In this case, as in so many others, the jury seemed blind to the fact that the injury which medical personnel attempted to treat occurred when the victim left a bar one night, dived into a pond, and broke his neck.

I have even more difficulty with this next case. Among the most remarkable medical achievements I have seen is the advent of the artificial heart valve. Unfortunately, not all valves work as expected, and of the 85,000 patients worldwide who received the Bjork-Shiley Convexco heart valve made by Shiley of Irvine, California, 310 of them, less than one-half of 1 percent, did not survive. But 51,000 of those whose lives were saved by the valves, together with their spouses, sued the manufacturer for emotional distress claiming they feared the possibility of future valve failures. The company settled with all but one thousand of the valve recipients and their spouses for a total of $140 million. Shiley ceased production of the valve.

Another source of inflated damages which is in need of reform is the collateral source rule. This rule prohibits the introduction of evidence indicating that a plaintiff has been compensated for his injury from a source other than the defendant. For instance, in cases like *Lenahan vs. Martin*, the fact that all medical bills and convalescent care are paid by workers' compensation insurance cannot be disclosed to the jury when the plaintiff claims for the same damages from the defendant. Thus the plaintiff may collect twice for the same injury. In the Lenahan case the plaintiff would have collected from three sources: workers' compensation, the defendant in the parking lot incident, and Dr. Martin.

The doctrine of joint and several liability also contributes to damage inflation. Under this rule plaintiff lawyers play what they call the 1 percent game. By naming everybody who so much as lays eyes on the patient in a surgical malpractice case, including the anesthesiologist and the family practitioner who recommended the surgeon, the plaintiff's lawyer hopes the jury will find each one at least 1 percent at fault, which, under the law, makes each defendant 100 percent responsible for payment of the award. If the surgeon is held 99 percent at fault and the referring family doctor 1 percent at fault for a $3 million verdict, but the surgeon's insurance and personal assets only amount to $1 million, then the family doctor must cover the other $2 million to the full amount of his or her worth.

Jurors believe that with multiple deep pockets there is no harm in being extra generous to the plaintiffs. Some states have enacted the more equitable solution of several liability under which each defendant pays in proportion to blame, thus lessening the incentive to

name defendants who are not really culpable and forcing juries to
relate damages and blame more realistically.

Punitive damages pose the most difficult problem for juries and
the greatest opportunity for exaggerated awards. Like contingent
fees, they are unique to the American system. In Japan they do not
exist at all, and the few European jurisdictions that recognize the
concept apply them only according to the degree of loss, not the
perceived depth of the defendant's pocket. The reason foreign
judicial systems restrict punitive damages is that they are, in essence, criminal sanctions; civil courts operate under different rules
of evidence and different standards for weighing evidence than
criminal courts. Under the rules of civil procedure juries are often
unable to distinguish malicious wrongdoing from unfortunate out-
comes.

Pharmaceutical manufacturers, for instance, are repeatedly
socked for hundreds of millions of dollars in punitive damages, the
application of which requires that the jury find the manufacturer
acted maliciously in introducing a product. Since all drugs undergo
many years of intensive research and testing to satisfy the stringent
requirements of the Food and Drug Administration, and the FDA
must approve the drug before its introduction, it is virtually impossible for a manufacturer to have acted maliciously unless it also
defrauded the FDA, which, of course, is a criminal offense carrying
serious consequences.

Tort victims, moreover, are fully compensated for every loss imag-
inable, including mental anguish, before punitive damages are applied; punitive damages are just a final kick in the groin to teach the
defendant a lesson. Defendants deserve to be compensated, but the
application of punishment by fines should be the sole province of
government—the proceeds should go to some public good, not into
the pockets of lawyers and litigants.

Our laws don't often limit how much may be claimed in punitive
damages, nor do they offer juries much guidance in applying them.
As a result, punitive awards are arbitrary and capricious. The *ad
damnum* clause of the plaintiff's pleadings states the amount of
monetary damages claimed, which may have no relationship to the
actual damages sustained. For instance, when trial lawyer Stanley

Rosenblatt of Miami recently filed a class action suit against a maker of breast implants, he demanded $100 million in punitive damages. Why? "The number appealed to me," he told a reporter. "What am I to do? Pretend that I picked some scientific, engineer's slide-rule type of calculation? No. One hundred million dollars, it had a nice ring to it."[8] If we don't permit policemen to go to court demanding huge traffic fines just because they have a nice ring to them, why should we permit lawyers to do it?

TORTS ARE TOXIC TO YOUR HEALTH

Torts are toxic to the delivery of affordable health care. Seventy-eight percent of America's physicians and 87 percent of hospital based physicians (surgeons, anesthesiologists, etc.) report that they order tests that are unnecessary except to avoid being wrongly accused of malpractice, as was Dr. Martin in the aforementioned case after he declined to subject his patient to a spinal tap just to prove the absence of meningitis.[9] From 1982 to 1989 the cost of physicians' liability insurance tripled, growing at an average annual rate of over 15 percent, more than four times the general inflation rate.[10]

The costs of pharmaceuticals and medical supplies have been similarly affected, not surprising given that the number of multi-million dollar awards in product liability cases tripled in the past ten years. The number of product liability claims filed in just the federal district courts increased by 983 percent between 1974 and 1988.[11] The litigation explosion has not only driven up prices, it has curtailed both the development of new drugs and vaccines, and the availability of physician services. This curtailment has been felt most by women in their child-bearing years because under the current liability climate, no drug manufacturer dares develop or market drugs intended primarily for expectant mothers. And, according to a 1990 survey by the American College of Obstetricians and Gynecologists, more than 24 percent of doctors qualified in obstetrics decline high-risk cases—the very mothers who need their care the most—and one out of eight refuse to deliver babies at all.

The medical records in 80 percent of malpractice claims against physicians lacked any evidence of negligence, according to a 1990 Harvard University study; and 60 percent of all malpractice claims were resolved in the physician's favor, according to a 1987 study by the General Accounting Office. Clearly, our judicial system has become a lottery in which the claimant stands a good chance of winning even without evidence of negligence. But the flood of frivolous cases has bogged down the system to the point where the truly wronged cannot get their cases heard in a reasonable time. What we have is not a health care crisis, but a judicial crisis.

Obviously, our judicial system has failed because lawyers made the laws, and they made the laws to benefit themselves. Lawyers are the dominant force in Congress and in most state legislatures. At last count, fourteen out of eighteen of the president's cabinet-level posts, and nearly half of the congressional seats, were occupied by lawyers. Moreover, when it comes to special interest funding of political candidates, nobody outspends the multimillionaire membership of the Association of Trial Lawyers of America and its counterparts at the state level. In Louisiana the trial lawyers group boasted in 1991 that thirty of the thirty-nine new members of the state senate were elected with its backing, and in the state house the tally was twenty-two out of twenty-nine.

To become a reality, genuine tort reform will require strong national leadership. That poses a problem. According to a CNN-sponsored study by the National Library on Money and Politics, nearly 40 percent of the 1992 campaign contributions to President Clinton—himself a lawyer—came from lawyers, five times the amount from any other source.

During the 1992 presidential campaign, David H. Williams, president of the Arkansas Trial Lawyers Association, seeking donations for the Clinton campaign from colleagues around the country, told how Governor Clinton had blocked an Arkansas tort reform measure in 1987. As reported by the *Wall Street Journal*, he wrote: ". . . I remember a bill that had whistled through the Arkansas House and Senate that would have given immunity from liability to 'good Samaritan' doctors who provided medical care to indigent patients . . . Once again, we got on the horn. . . ." And once again,

Governor Clinton vetoed the bill. "I can never remember an occasion," Mr. Williams wrote, when Mr. Clinton "failed to do the right thing where we trial lawyers were concerned."[12] Now it is time for President Clinton to do the right thing where the health of the American people is concerned.

CHAPTER 13

——————/\——————

What's the Solution?

Most health care proposals coming out of Washington are Wizard of Oz solutions, an analogy I have borrowed from Roger MacBride's *A New Dawn for America* (1976). Think back to the *Wizard of Oz*, that inspiring Judy Garland classic film, and recall the awesome, imposing wizard with his thundering timpani and billowing smoke. When Dorothy and her troop caught up with the omnipotent wizard at Emerald City, expecting him to fulfill his many promises, Dorothy's dog, Toto, sniffed out the fraud behind the facade. There was no wizard, just an ordinary man manipulating a contraption to make people believe he could solve their problems. When Dorothy rebuked him for being such a bad man, he protested: "I am a very good man. I'm just a very bad wizard." The moral of the story was that the solutions for Dorothy's friends had been within themselves all along—the Tin Woodsman found his heart, the Scarecrow his wisdom, and the Cowardly Lion his courage. There was no such thing as a wizard who possessed the ability, and therefore no wizard could solve their problems for them.

For the past thirty years the wizard in Washington has been promising to solve our health care problems, and every year he blows more smoke as our problems worsen. In truth, the wizard turns out to be just a bunch of politicians—ordinary men and women at best—manipulating a huge, imposing bureaucracy with no heart to care for the needy, no wisdom to manage health care efficiently, and no courage to admit its shortcomings. The wizard in Washington is incapable of delivering on his promise.

To solve a problem one must first identify the cause. Ask people on the street what is wrong with American health care and they will tell you it costs too much. But ask the same people whether they have experienced difficulty paying for medical care and the vast majority will indicate that they are adequately covered. And ask whether they are satisfied with their own private doctors and the overwhelming majority will say yes. Public opinion polls have borne out these responses over many years; and yet the same polls demonstrate increasing dissatisfaction with our system of health care.

Public opinion, however, is not the paradox that it first appears to be. Dissatisfaction with the health care system certainly does not arise from the care given: that is the very strength of our system; as President Clinton says, "America provides the finest care in the world...."[1] If you are not 100 percent satisfied with the care given by one doctor, you choose another just as you would choose another grocer if not fully satisfied with him. Freedom of choice is sacred to Americans, and in medicine it is crucial because healing is as much an art as it is a science—when a patient feels uneasy with a physician, the resultant anxiety can inhibit healing even when the treatment given is technically proper. It is therefore not unusual to find people who are displeased with doctors in general, but are delighted with their own doctors. That is the strength of a system that permits each patient, no matter how idiosyncratic his or her needs may be, to seek out the one physician who delivers care to suit him.

Another reason for the high level of satisfaction with the quality of health care is the promptness of its delivery. This too is sacred to Americans. Just as we demand twenty-four hour a day restaurants with fast service, we expect our ailments and injuries to be tended to immediately—no six- or nine-month waits for a hospital bed, no queues for surgery. And we expect prompt attention to be delivered with state-of-the-art equipment, facilities, and pharmaceuticals.

When it comes to battling cancer, heart disease, or AIDS, Americans say, "Only the best will do."

So why the dissatisfaction with our health care system? Because people are anxious about the prospect of losing their employer-provided insurance and being left unable to afford adequate care on their own. With health care prices so high and the savings rate of Americans so low—one-fourth the savings rate of the Japanese—the fear is not unfounded. Of course, if patients could demand a better deal for their money through free market incentives, and if tax laws permitted workers to buy their own catastrophic insurance and save for predictable expenses, there would be so few uninsured Americans that government could subsidize their coverage without strain.

But government deems otherwise. Of the health care solutions advanced in Washington, most appear to have been drafted with no consideration at all for the causes of the problems, and most seek to change the good about our system while failing to correct the bad. Most proposed solutions do nothing to encourage savings or to restore market prices, but instead would impose expenditure ceilings, price controls, and third-party universal coverage. This, of course, is the type of system used in most other industrialized countries. But those systems lack the most cherished attributes of our health system: freedom of choice, prompt service, and state-of-the-art equipment, facilities, and pharmaceuticals. Most Americans, fortunately or unfortunately, are not aware that our health care system is uniquely able to deliver this type of service.

In order to solve the problem of overpriced health care we must understand what has disrupted the marketplace. It would be well to recount the points detailed in this book:

1. Under the third-party payer systems of Medicare and tax-induced, employer-based health insurance, we no longer have a free market in which people can exercise their innate wisdom as they do when buying a car or shopping for groceries.

2. Due to the imposition of third-party payers, and to the wizard's feeble attempts to blow a smokescreen of bureaucratic regulations over this fundamental flaw of Medicare, the delivery of health care is top-heavy with paperwork and administration.

3. Because tax laws discourage Americans from saving for predictable health care costs, we are dependent on inflated health insurance policies with low deductibles.

4. By subverting the insurance function with employer-based coverage, smaller heterogeneous underwriting groups have replaced large homogeneous risk pools, and experience rating has replaced legal reserve indemnity funding.

5. Special interest lobbyists have induced lawmakers to mandate insurance coverage of frivolous, nonmedical services and products.

6. Excessive health care demands have resulted from violent crime, drug and alcohol abuse, tobacco use, sexual promiscuity, the breakdown of the family, junk food diets, and sedentary lifestyles.

7. An unpredictable tort system, which functions somewhat like a lottery, inflates the cost of liability for the provision of health care and the manufacture of medical equipment, supplies, and medications, and induces doctors to overtreat and overtest.

How did these disruptions come about? First, the wizard in Washington promised that health care would be a right: workers would be cared for by their employers, retirees by government under Medicare—and the third-party payer system was born. Next the wizard promised a Great Society in which people's problems would be solved by government rather than by individual responsibility and self-sufficiency, thus creating a dependent underclass which was propped up by an ineffective and morally bankrupt public education monopoly. And last, the wizard's tribunals allowed people to seek recompense in court, regardless of blame, for all of life's mishaps.

What will the wizard do next? At this time, the so-called Clinton plan is still undergoing change, but President Clinton has promised to make all employers provide health care for their workers; to reduce regulation and paperwork; to preserve quality and choice; to control costs without rationing; to eliminate fraud and abuse; and to improve the economy by limiting what the nation spends on health care.

To accomplish this the president wants to appoint a central planning committee, the National Health Care Board (NHCB). Because health care is consuming too much of the nation's wealth, the NHCB's foremost mission will be to limit what Americans may spend on health care, whether privately or through public or charitable sources. But, as discussed in chapter five, national wealth is created through production, and when one sector of the economy is productive, it not only does not deplete the production of other sectors, it actually helps it. But when government arbitrarily limits a productive sector it reduces the gross national product (GNP), both directly and indirectly, because all sectors lose commerce from the restricted sector. Thus, when government limits one sector, in this case health care, the percentage of the GNP attributed to that sector will not be reduced proportionately because the GNP itself will also be limited by the government's intervention.

This economic reality notwithstanding, the NHCB will seek to establish a national expenditure target and from that it will dictate a comprehensive health care budget for each state. This is known as global budgeting, the common denominator of the health care system of Canada, Britain, and other countries that have ingested socialized nostrums.

The president has pointed out that government's health care spending is a major contributor to the national debt; it is therefore, of course, detrimental to the economy, a problem he hopes to solve by applying the spending cap. But, as we saw in chapter eleven, Medicare is not based on the actuarial principle of beneficiaries contributing to a legal reserve fund to cover future expenses, but is instead based on the socialistic principle of today's workers paying for today's beneficiaries. Unfortunately, due to a decreasing birth rate the ratio of workers to retirees has also been decreasing. Thus, by applying the NHCB's spending cap rather than providing a prefunding vehicle so that workers can pay their own medical bills during retirement, the result will be rationing by fiat—exactly what the president doesn't want.

The Clinton plan would also empower the NHCB to restrict the use of new technologies which it feels would lead to increased spending. But, as shown in chapter six, most new technologies do not produce inflation, but, instead, new and better treatments for ailments which were previously not treatable or were treated less effectively. New technologies do increase total spending on health care, but they also return sick people more quickly to healthy and productive lives.

Nowhere are the advantages of new technologies more pronounced than in pharmaceuticals. On this front President Clinton favors Arkansas Senator David Pryor's plan to strip research tax incentives from any manufacturer that increases prices faster than the consumer price index. This would be counterproductive because, as chapter six explained, when research pushes back the frontiers of science the cost of that research increases much faster than the cost of bread and butter. This is not difficult to understand when one considers that the Wright brothers launched American aerospace research from a garage with ordinary tools and minimal financing, while today we spend hundreds of billions of dollars sending satellites, probes, and shuttles into space. One can only imagine the benefits, including a definitive cure for cancer, that will come from more costly pharmaceutical research. Yes, drug prices do rise faster than the cost of bread and butter, but the cost of an AIDS vaccine will be minuscule compared to the cost of treating AIDS.

Initially, the Clinton plan would allow, at least in theory, for our traditional indemnity coverage, under which patients choose their own doctors and have a say in their own therapy. But financial disincentives would eventually eliminate these options. According to the "managed competition" scheme which the president touted during his election campaign, workers will be taxed, at least to some degree, on the benefits of employer-provided indemnity plans. (This provision may be postponed due to union opposition, but since it is integral to the theory of managed competition, it will have to be phased in over time.)

Additionally, the Clinton plan proposes that the NHCB fix a fee schedule for doctors and hospitals that accept private patients, presumably based on Medicare's cumbersome resource-based relative value scale (RBRVS) and diagnostic related groups (DRGs) discussed in chapter eleven. This, of course, translates into more paperwork and administration, not less. Currently RBRVS and

DRGs reimburse only about 50 percent of the actual cost of services to Medicare patients, forcing health care providers to shift the uncompensated costs to privately insured patients. But once the fee schedule is applied to private patients, health care providers will no longer be able to deliver quality care. It is no coincidence, moreover, that some of the most egregious Medicare and Medicaid scams—surpassed only by incidences involving HMOs—have developed under the government's price-fixing schedules. In one example, a few unscrupulous entrepreneurs set up diagnostic clinics on wheels that swept through neighborhoods offering kickbacks to patients willing to submit to phony medical tests, and the taxpayer got the computer-coded bills for thousands of small charges that could not be effectively monitored.

Price-fixing just leads to increasingly burdensome regulations for honest practitioners, and provides financial incentives to perform too many tests and procedures while paying too little attention to the real needs of individual patients. Quality medical care is cheaper in the end, but it cannot be mass produced.

Ultimately, the president's plan will change the way health care is delivered in America. Within each state health care providers will establish "organized systems of insurers, hospitals, clinics, and doctors" which will negotiate with third-party payers—employers and government—for a "capitation fee" within the NHCB's budget limit. This is managed competition, which the president touted during his campaign debates but which he failed adequately to explain. What does it really mean? In essence, it means that Americans will be coerced out of indemnity plans and herded into health maintenance organizations (HMOs).

But we have already seen that HMOs limit the patient's right to choose a doctor; that they generate the greatest number of consumer complaints; that they are more costly than traditional insurance plans because they impose a layer of nonmedical managers between the doctor and patient; and that the most egregious Medicare frauds—involving hundreds of millions of dollars in a single incident—have been committed by HMO entrepreneurs.

When a patient without a third-party payer sees a private physician, the incentive for the physician is to satisfy the patient at a cost the patient can afford, meaning better care at less cost. When government or an employer prepays a capitation fee on behalf of a patient, the incentive for HMO managers is not to deliver better care for less, but to cut corners. Once again, this perverse incentive incites more intensive government regulation, not less. And more regulation gives rise to more indirect costs, exactly what the president doesn't want.

The only rationale for the HMO formula is that it provides a mechanism for imposing the NHCB's national budget limit, something that cannot be enforced with traditional indemnity plans. As President Clinton puts it, it gives him a "hammer" to enforce budgetary discipline. This is because HMOs are modeled after the British socialist system of using general practitioners as gatekeepers to more costly, specialized care.

In the British National Health Service system, the hospital-based nephrologist, for instance, must work within a government-imposed global budget to secure equipment and personnel to treat patients suffering from chronic renal failure, a disease ending in certain death without treatment. To operate within the budget, Britain's rate of dialysis treatment is held to less than one-third the rate of the United States, even though there is no medical reason for denying care in most cases. For obvious political reasons, Britain has no law specifying who will be turned away in order to keep within the budget; that decision is left to doctors. Aside from the handicapped, who are usually denied treatment, age seems to be the most decisive factor—the rate of dialysis treatment tapers off for patients over forty-five; patients over sixty-five almost never receive treatment in Britain. In the United States, by contrast, virtually all renal patients are treated. Given that there is no legitimate medical reason these patients should not be treated, if patients and their families had free access to specialists the British nephrologist would be placed in the embarrassing position of contradicting the assessment of the referring doctor, or of admitting to the patient that the denial of treatment was for budgetary reasons. All patients must therefore go to their primary care physicians before they can see a specialist no matter how obvious the need for specialized treatment. The primary care physician quickly learns the budgetary limits of specialized care and limits the number of patients referred accordingly.

This has led to haunting decisions. On one occasion, when researchers from the Brookings Institution pressed a British general practitioner to tell what he would say to the family of a sixty-five-year-old woman with kidney failure, he explained: "I would say that mother's or aunt's kidneys have failed or are failing and there is very little that anybody can do about it because of her age and general physical state, and that it would be my suggestion or my advice that we spare her any further investigation, any further painful procedure, and we would just make her as comfortable as we can for what remains of her life." Another British doctor remarked to the researchers that everyone over fifty-five is "a bit crumbly" and therefore not suitable for dialysis therapy.[2] Not surprisingly, politicians, labor bosses, industrialists, and blue bloods have no difficulty bypassing the gatekeeper in Britain, and we can expect that under the Clinton plan the rich and powerful will have no problem applying their influence on HMO managers while the rest of us wait outside the gates to specialized care in blissful ignorance.

Perhaps the most instructive lessons about global budgeting come from Canadian health care administrators. The Canadian situation is less critical than the British because global budgeting did not begin there until 1971, whereas the British have been at it for forty-five years. In Canada, budgets are set for the provinces by a political process while care is provided by private doctors and hospitals, similar in those respects to the Clinton plan. Thus, a Canadian hospital is paid a set sum each quarter according to the size of the population served. Also like the Clinton plan, since patients do not directly control their own health care spending there is no real incentive for health care providers to deliver care more efficiently, and they don't; they simply treat patients as they come and when money runs low patients are put on waiting lists.

With a few notorious exceptions, the Canadian system treats emergencies adequately; to do otherwise would be political suicide. And the system treats less costly ailments without hesitation, a practice that satisfies the great majority of voters who are not seriously ill, providing them with the false sense of security that the system will respond efficiently when they really need it. In other words, those with sniffles and upset stomachs are tended to promptly. But all others join the queue, even though about one-quarter of those waiting for surgery are classified "urgent." In the case of open heart surgery many never make it to the operating table—witness the *Ottawa Citizen* of February 4, 1989, which reported that twenty-four heart patients had died awaiting heart surgery in British Columbia the previous year. But in an odd twist, in order to assure adequate resources to treat emergencies, administrators fill hospital beds with what they call "bed blockers," patients who no longer need hospitalization, only extended nursing care. They achieve two objectives: they avoid having too many beds available for patients awaiting costly surgical procedures; and they can oust a "bed blocker" to make room when a genuine emergency case arrives.

Another result of global budgeting in Canada is a phenomenon called "queue jumpers." Like the Clinton plan, Canadians are not permitted to pay for medical care in excess of what the government budgets. And because hospitals are prepaid to care for a given population, similar to Clinton's capitation fee, Canadian hospital administrators are anxious to make money on the side by accommodating foreign patients who are legally able to pay for the service. While the Canadian citizen waiting in a surgical queue has already paid for the service through taxation, a foreign patient, a queue jumper—usually American—is operated on immediately. Moreover, since Canadian hospitals do not receive any more money from treating Canadian patients, it behooves administrators to attract queue jumpers with bargain rates, which is one reason Canadian rates appear to be so much less than American rates. Since the Canadian taxpayer has prepaid the hospital's overhead, the administrator need only charge a nominal sum over the cost of surgical supplies to justify admitting a queue jumper.

This problem cannot be dealt with under the Clinton plan because to deny foreigners access to American health care facilities would be to deny Americans jobs, and to attempt to regulate the practice would require a massive—and futile— effort, exactly what the president wants to avoid.

Just how unwieldy are these global-budgeting problems for Canada? Think about this: when the premier of Quebec, Robert Bourassa, needed surgery for melanoma (skin cancer) he did what thousands of other Canadians of means have done. He bypassed the queue by flying to Washington, D.C., where he paid for his treatment out of his own pocket.

The following is just a sampling of the waiting periods for Canadians who cannot afford to leave the country: in the province of Newfoundland, the average wait for a coronary bypass is over one year, the wait for a hemorrhoidectomy is over three months; in Manitoba, the average wait for hip surgery is ten-and-a-half months, to remove a herniated spinal disc the wait is three months, and cataract surgery takes an average of five-and-a-half months; in Nova Scotia, patients wait an average of almost eight months just to fix a hammer toe; in British Columbia, the wait to drain fluid from a patient's ear canal is almost three months; and in New Brunswick, the average wait for a vaginal repair or a hysterectomy is almost four months.[3] Long waiting periods for medical treatment are found in all Canadian provinces as well as in all countries that practice global budgeting.

What is just as unsettling from the American perspective is the unwarranted wait for diagnostic procedures under global budgeting, even when the occurrence of cancer is suspected and timely treatment may be crucial. For instance, as I write, it is Christmas eve in Miami; earlier, my office partner, a general surgeon, received a call from another physician concerning the discovery of a suspicious mass in a patient's breast. Arrangements were immediately made with the hospital, and he has gone there to perform a biopsy. In the Canadian province of Manitoba the patient would have had to have waited three weeks for the biopsy, a dangerous delay that causes the patient horrendous anxiety. The same pattern exists all over Canada because the availability of high technology lab equipment is restricted by the government.

This is exactly what the Clinton plan will do for the United States. These restrictions supposedly assure more efficient use of expensive technology by eliminating the duplication of equipment in the same locale. In a free marketplace, however, more capacity means more competition and therefore lower prices and better service; wherever there is unmet demand vendors quickly move in to satisfy it. But when technology is regulated it means unwarranted waits for limited resources. More examples: women in the Canadian province of Prince Edward Island wait from four to eight months for mammograms, and the province has not a single CAT scanner to detect brain tumors and post-trauma hemorrhaging. With a population of more than half a million, Newfoundland has only one CAT scanner, forcing nonemergency patients to wait an average of two months to be diagnosed. By contrast, CAT scanners in the United States are more than three times as plentiful per capita than in Canada and almost six times as plentiful as in Britain.[4]

Obviously, the Clinton plan promises the impossible. Government cannot preserve high quality health care, prompt service, and freedom of choice without allowing patients to pay their own bills and without allowing health care providers the freedom to meet demand; government cannot reduce the regulatory burden or control fraud under a third-party payer system; government cannot apply price controls without creating shortages and rationing care; and government cannot strengthen the economy by limiting total health care spending any more than it can boost the economy by limiting what we spend on shoes. If government could solve problems through central planning and budgeting, the Soviet Union would be the sole surviving superpower and the United States would have collapsed; West Germany would have been taken in by East Germany; and North Korea would be the envy of South Korea. Ironically, while the rest of the world is turning away from central planning and government-controlled markets, the wizard in Washington is proposing these failed concepts to solve our health care problems.

Although the current Clinton plan is naturally taking center stage, we should not discount other movements toward a Canadian-type system. Until two months before his election to the presidency, Bill Clinton endorsed the "pay or play" concept, and he may switch back to it if his current plan runs into trouble. This idea, in its various forms, has also been advanced by Senator Teddy Kennedy, Senate Majority Leader George Mitchell, and the chairman of the

Pepper Commission on Comprehensive Health Care, Senator Jay
Rockefeller. The plan would require all employers either to buy
workers health insurance or pay a tax. The catch is that the tax
would be 6–9 percent of payroll, about half the cost of health
insurance—in other words, a bait and switch ploy. Even employers
currently providing health insurance would be impelled to drop the
coverage and pay the tax.

Thus, we would end up with government as the single (third-
party) payer of health care, a Canadian-style program which would
increase the federal budget by almost one-third and require $339
billion in new taxes, according to the National Center for Policy
Analysis.5 Worse, having destroyed all that is good about our current system, the new system would do nothing to slow skyrocketing
health care costs, as demonstrated by the fact that inflation-adjusted
per capita health spending has been growing faster in Canada than
in the United States in recent years.6

Whether government alone provides health coverage or whether
employers and government share the burden is, in truth, immaterial; the end result is a cumbersome, inefficient, and expensive
system with restrictions dictated by bureaucrats and insurance administrators that are not in the interests of patients, but in their own
interests. Government bureaucracies and corporations are not
health care consumers; only people consume health care, and only
people possess the heart, wisdom, and courage to make hard health
care choices with intelligence and compassion.

Why, with such a wealth of worldwide evidence and such a long
history of failed attempts to fix health care by government fiat, do
politicians continue promising grandiose solutions that cannot possibly work? Perhaps because they labor under utopian delusions.
We saw in chapter four how these delusions made their way from
economically sick England to healthy America. Sidney Webb, the
father of the Fabian Society, wrote the socialist treatise, *Industrial
Democracy*, and devised the plan of permeation whereby socialist
ideas were implemented by mainstream political parties, and he
devised the doctrine of gradualness whereby socialist policies were
implemented in stages. In chapter three we saw how gradualness
was applied in the United States with the passage of Medicare.

Politicians don't use the word socialism to describe their programs, but the current health care proposals in Washington mean that workers will be denied access to money they earn, which money will be spent according to government dictates. Furthermore, government will regulate delivery, set prices, and direct capital in the health care industry. To the informed observer, this system looks and acts like socialism; why it is not called socialism is best explained by Derek Shearer, President Clinton's close confidant in charge of economic affairs at commerce. In explanation of the curious title of his treatise, *Economic Democracy* (1980), he said in the magazine, *In These Times*: "Socialism has a bad name in America, and no amount of wishful thinking on the part of the left is going to change that in our lifetimes. . . . The words Economic Democracy are an adequate and effective replacement."[7]

It really does not matter whether a program is called socialism, industrial democracy, economic democracy, or managed competition. What matters is the knowledge that only a free market system provides consumers freedom of choice, and only a free market gives producers the incentive to provide higher quality service at prices consumers can afford. Perhaps those under the spell of utopian delusions are to be commended for their good intentions. Whatever the case, President Clinton and our congressional leaders may be very good men, but they are very bad wizards.

What the people need to solve problems in the health care market is primarily some basic consumer information, the freedom to choose their own providers, and the ability to use their own earnings to pay for it. That simple formula works just fine for the procurement of food, even though we are not all nutritionists; it works fine for the procurement of automobiles, even though we are not all mechanical engineers; and it works fine for the procurement of houses, even though we are not all architects. That is the essence of a free market, and it will work fine for health care if we withdraw the wedge of third-party payers that separates patients from providers.

Several alternative proposals have been floated that would take health care out of the political arena and restore a common sense marketplace. Two well thought-out plans are:

An Agenda for Solving America's Health Care Crisis
The National Center for Policy Analysis
1265 North Central Expressway, Suite 720
Dallas, Texas 75243
(214) 386–6272

A National Health System for America
The Heritage Foundation
214 Massachusetts Avenue, N.E.
Washington, DC 20002
(202) 546–4400

Both plans put the patient back in the driver's seat—in charge of his or her own money—with an adequate road map to make intelligent consumer decisions; both expose health care providers to the rigors of a consumer-driven marketplace; both provide assurance that every American will receive appropriate health care regardless of income; and both provide a vehicle for consumers to save for incidental and future medical expenses. If I had to make the tough call of which plan to endorse, I would go with the National Center for Policy Analysis (NCPA) for its comprehensive simplicity and logical consistency.

The NCPA plan was drafted by a multidisciplinary task force of researchers from forty think tanks and universities including the Cato Institute, Stanford University's Hoover Institution, the Fraser Institute of Vancouver, British Columbia, the American Enterprise Institute, and the National Federation of Independent Business Foundation. In summary, the plan would restore a worker's right to control his or her own health care dollar by removing the tax penalty on consumer-purchased policies and the tax incentive to replace wages with health benefits. Under the current system the aggregate national deduction for employer-provided health insurance is about $48.5 billion per year ($485 for every family). Yet, the subsidy is not available to most of the 37 million uninsured Americans, a major reason so many are uninsured. To correct this, the

employee, the self-employed, and the unemployed would be afforded a tax credit equivalent to the tax subsidy currently offered
for employer-provided plans. For low income families whose tax
credit exceeds their tax liability, the unused credit would be refund-
able. This would make health insurance affordable to the poor
whether or not coverage is provided by an employer.

To make health insurance personal and portable, each employee
would be free to choose an individual policy which would remain
with the employee in the event of a job change. Each would choose
the most suitable coverage among all policies offered in the marketplace; current law, in contrast, mandates that all employees be
offered the same coverage on the same terms. With insurance benefits included in gross wages and with premium tax credits available
on the employee's individual tax return, each employee would
pocket the savings for prudent choices and bear the cost of wasteful
ones.

To encourage Americans to save for incidental medical expenses
while insuring for catastrophic expenses, the NCPA plan calls for
individual "Medisave" accounts with deposits receiving the same tax
incentives given the purchase of health insurance. This would give
individuals direct control over their health care spending, thus
eliminating costly insurance and administrative costs, freeing responsible consumers from the penalties of fellow workers who abuse
low deductible group policies, and eliminating the dictates of third-
party payers. As deposits accumulate, the insurance deductible
would be raised, thus compounding the savings.

The NCPA plan also calls for federal law to permit the sale of
insurance free of state-mandated benefits. This would greatly reduce the cost of insurance, especially for younger workers who
comprise a disproportionate number of today's uninsured population. This plan would also foster greater freedom of choice because
insurance would be purchased according to need, and patients
desiring such services as chiropractic or acupuncture would be free
to pay an additional premium or pay directly from their Medisave
accounts.

Workers would also make tax deductible deposits to Medical IRA
(MIRA) accounts which would supplement and eventually replace

Medicare coverage in retirement. In this fashion we would eventually relieve the taxpayer of the Medicare burden as each generation would pay its own way in retirement. The MIRA savings would be the private property of each retiree—out of reach of the politicians who have raided the Medicare trust fund. (President Clinton's bonus for the economy lies here, not in global budgeting, for invested capital from savings is the lifeblood of a capitalist economy, and this plan would relieve the health care portion of the government's deficit.)

Medicare and Medicaid have become price-fixing schemes which limit access to medical care by regulating the terms and conditions under which services can be delivered. Therefore, the NCPA plan recommends that Medicaid patients be granted the right to draw on an account, negotiate prices, and add their own money if necessary to purchase medical services. Similarly, Medicare patients during this phase-out period would be given the right to negotiate prices and supplement payments for services where Medicare is paying less than is needed for reasonable care. This would eliminate the danger of service shortages and government rationing.

Hospitals would be required to quote pre-admission prices either on a per diem basis or as a flat rate for each procedure. This would become a universal practice, much as hotels quote prices over the telephone. Thus, patients could compare prices with relative ease, and since the vast majority of hospitalizations are not emergencies, competitive pricing between hospitals would set the pace for all admissions. Consumer groups could also monitor prices and guide patients.

Finally, the plan allows for patients to circumvent the cost of tort liability with federal legislation permitting the use of voluntary agreements. For example, by mutual agreement a hospital could secure a life and injury insurance policy on a patient prior to surgery in exchange for an agreement not to sue. Not only would the hospital's rates be reduced for those who agreed, but if it came to that, litigation costs would be eliminated, payment would be immediate and certain, and patients would have the added assurance that the quality of care was being closely monitored by the underwriter whose money was at risk.

It took three decades for government to create our health care problems, and neither this nor any other plan will relieve the pain overnight. But it turns us in the right direction, and even the immediate savings would be dramatic. For instance, for many of today's uninsured the extension of tax incentives presently enjoyed by the more affluent under employer-provided coverage would have the net effect of reducing the cost of health insurance by 50 percent. And by overriding state insurance mandates for nonmedical, unnecessary services, the savings could be as much as 30 percent. Replacing first dollar and high deductible insurance with Medisave accounts would bring equally dramatic relief, as would tort reform, and the privatization of Medicare would slay the most burdensome and costly regulatory dragon in history. In the aggregate, it is reasonable to estimate that the total bill for health care today could be cut in half. But that does not mean that total health care spending would be equally reduced, for in a free society we are free to demand more and better services, and medical research promises many wonderful advancements for longer, healthier, and more productive living.

This approach to reform moves away from a regimented system in which faceless bureaucrats and impersonal insurance companies make health care decisions for us, dictating how much and for what we may spend our money. But the only way we can take back what is rightfully ours is to let the president and congressmen know that we want it back.

What we are really talking about is freedom of choice. You can demand to be paid your full wage and to spend and invest as you see fit. You can demand the highest quality health care at the best price. You can demand a health care system responsive to your needs, not the needs of bureaucrats, HMO entrepreneurs, third-party administrators, or your employer. You can demand a health care system that is efficient and competitive under the only system that fosters efficiency and competition: the free market system. You can turn back the socializers, you can turn this movement around, you can take control of your own health care destiny.

The choice is yours.

Notes

——————————/\/\——————————

CHAPTER 2: FROM SICK ENGLAND TO HEALTHY AMERICA

1. George Bernard Shaw, *The Intelligent Woman's Guide to Socialism* (New York: Brentano's, 1928), p. 186.
2. Mina Weisenberg, *The L.I.D., Fifty Years of Democratic Education, 1905–1955* (New York, League for Industrial Democracy).
3. Anne Freemantle, *This Little Band of Profits: The British Fabians* (The New American Library, 1960), p. 233.
4. David Shannon, *Socialist Party of America* (New York: Macmillan, 1955), pp. 55–56.
5. Clifton Brock, *Americans for Democratic Action* (Washington: Public Affairs Press, 1962), p. 49.
6. Francis X. Gannon, *Biographical Dictionary of the Left* (Boston: Western Islands Publishers, 1969), Consolidated Volume One, pp. 17–26.
7. Brock, *Americans for Democratic Action*, p. v.
8. *The Young Worker*, June 1923, p. 4.
9. Gannon, *Biographical Dictionary*, Consolidated Vol. One, pp. 419–421.
10. Freemantle, *This Little Band of Profits*, p. 234.
11. Brock, *Americans for Democratic Action*, p. 69.
12. Milton and Rose Friedman, *Free to Choose*, Appendix A. "Socialist Platform of 1928" (New York: Avon Books, 1979), p. 229.
13. Weisenberg, *The L.I.D.*, p. 26.
14. Frank D. Campion, *The AMA and U.S. Health Policy* (Chicago: Chicago Review Press, 1984), p. 156.
15. Ibid., p. 159.
16. Ibid., p. 160.

17. *Encyclopaedia Britannica*, 15th Ed., Vol. 16, p. 968.

18. John Dewey, *Individualism Old and New* (New York: 1930), p. 119.

CHAPTER 3; FIGHTING FOR NOBLE TRADITIONS

1. Henry J. Aaron and William B. Schwartz, *The Painful Prescription: Rationing Hospital Care* (Washington: The Brookings Institution, 1984).

2. Clifton Brock, *Americans for Democratic Action* (Washington, Public Affairs Press, 1962), p. 181.

3. Francis Gannon, *Biographical Dictionary of the Left* (Boston: Western Islands Publishers, 1969), Consolidated Volume One, p. 25.

4. Frank D. Campion, *The AMA and U.S. Health Policy* (Chicago: Chicago Review Press, 1984), p. 255.

5. Ibid., p. 256.

6. Ibid., p. 521.

7. Gannon, *Biographical Dictionary*, Vol. 2, p. 495.

8. Richard Harris, "Annals of Legislation: Medicare, We Do Not Compromise," *New Yorker*, July 16, 1966.

CHAPTER 4: HIDING THE TRUTH : HOW THE PRESS DOES IT

1. *Miami Herald*, January 23, 1992, p. 3C.

2. Herbert L. Matthews, *New York Times*, July 16, 1969, p. 1-A; editorial, July 28, 1959, p. 26.

3. "Uncle Scrooge's Babies: U.S. Scimps on its Future," editorial, *Miami Herald*, December 26, 1991, p. 22A.

4. Lauren Chambliss and Sharon Reier, "How Doctors Have Ruined Health Care," *Financial World*, January 9, 1990, p. 47.

5. Wall Street Journal/NBC Poll, "Voters, Sick of Current Health Care System, Want Federal Government to Prescribe Remedy," *Wall Street Journal*, June 28, 1991.

6. *Miami Herald*, March 8, 1992.

7. Peggy Rogers, "System Failing 4-Year-Old Girl," *Miami Herald*, February 2, 1992, p. 20A.

8. Based on the combined estimates derived from current membership surveys taken by the American Medical Association (Chicago) and the American Hospital Association (Chicago).

9. Jacquee Petchell, "Impoverished Cancer Patients Fight Illness, System," *Miami Herald*, February 3, 1992, pp. 1A, 8A.
10. Jon Gabel, Howard Cohen, Steven Fink, "Americans' Views on Health Care: Foolish Inconsistencies?" *Health Affairs*, Spring 1989, p. 111.
11. Robert Knight, "Snuffing Out the Lights: The Labor Department Goes After the Salvation Army," Heritage Foundation Executive Memorandum, October 3, 1990.
12. Ibid.
13. Philip Freidin, "Proposed Law is Doctors' Ploy," *Miami Review*, January 24, 1992, pp. A32–3.
14. American Medical Association Special Task Force on Professional Liability and Insurance, "Professional Liability in the 1980s, Report I," October 1984; and "Professional Liability Update," November/December 1990.
15. Michael Levay, M.D., "Observations from a Young Swedish Doctor on Holiday in America," Los Angeles County Medical Association *Physician*, September 23, 1991, p. 23.
16. Lauren Chambliss and Sharon Reier, "How Doctors Have Ruined Health Care," *Financial World*, January 9, 1990, pp. 46–51.
17. *Miami Herald* editorial, October 2, 1991.
18. Martha Musgrove, "A Second Opinion on Doctor-Dictated Health-Care Costs," October 9, 1991.
19. "Physicians give free service," *This Week: Priority Briefing for Medicine's Leaders* (Chicago: American Medical Association), Vol. 2, No. 10, March 23, 1992, p. 3.
20. Jacquee Petchel, "AMA agrees health care needs changes," *Miami Herald*, May 19, 1991, pp. 1B-2B.
21. *Journal of the American Medical Association*, Vol. 265, No. 19, May 15, 1991.
22. "AMA Refines Health Access America," *This Week* (Chicago: American Medical Association), Vol. 2, No. 10, March 23, 1992, p. 1.
23. *New York Times*, editorial, November 8, 1991.
24. John D. Harbron, "Why are U.S. critics attacking Canada's lifesaving Medicare?" *Miami Herald*, February 14, 1992, 17A.
25. Ed Lopez, "Ontario's gain is Florida's loss: Effort to cut health costs will hurt state," *Miami Herald*, September 12, 1991, p. 1C.
26. *Health Management Quarterly*, Vol. XI, No. 1, 1989, p. 12.
27. *Maclean's*, February 13, 1989, pp. 32–3.

28. *Winnipeg Free Press*, February 15, 1988, p. 12.

29. *Toronto Globe and Mail*, October 12, 1989, p. 1A.

30. Ibid., July 28, 1988, pp. 7A, 15A.

31. Clyde H. Farnsworth, "Recession hits Canada's health system," *Austin-American Statesman*, New York Times Service, November 29, 1991, p. A28.

32. Charles Fourier, *The Social Destiny of Man: Or, Theory of the Four Movements*, 1808, Engish Translation 1857; also see *Treatise on Domestic Agricultural Association*, 1822; and *The New Industrial World*, 1830.

33. Horace Greeley, "Social Science" column, *New York Daily Tribune*, February 7, 1843, p. 1.

CHAPTER 5: A SLIT OF THE WRIST OR A SHOT IN THE ARM: DOES MEDICINE REALLY BLEED THE ECONOMY?

1. Paul Harvey, "Let someone else pay for it," Los Angeles Times Syndicate, 1992.

2. Hilary Stout, "Job Hunters See Remedy in Health Care," *Wall Street Journal*, Workplace, February 12, 1991.

3. "Delta People Urged to Meet the Challenge," Delta Air Lines *Dispatch*, May 14, 1992, p. 1.

4. "AMA Backs New Category of Hospital Worker," *Private Practice*, October 1988; survey, *Nursingwood Journal*, January 1992.

5. Milton Friedman, as a guest on Louis Rukeyser "Wall Street Week," February 21, 1992, pegged total taxation at 40 percent of national income.

6. Oskar Morgenstern, *On the Accuracy of Economic Observations*, 2nd ed. (Princeton, NJ: Princeton University Press, 1963); an excerpt can be found in *National Income Statistics: A Critique of Macroeconomic Aggregation* (Washington, D.C.: Cato Institute, 1979).

7. "The percentage of GNP devoted to health is a handy way to compare us to other countries—but not a great way," *Benefits*, May 1991, p. 13.

8. George F. Will, "Peace Might Reveal More Than American Left Wants to See," Washington Post Group, 1990.

9. Jacques Krasny, "Searching for Solutions to the Health Care Crisis," *Backgrounder*, No. 4 (Tallahassee, FL: James Madison Institute).

10. When hospitals under socialist systems with government-imposed budgets cannot afford to turn over limited beds to more patients in

need of high cost procedures, administrators engage in the practice of "bed blocking": keeping patients longer than necessary to avoid making beds available to the next in line for surgery.

11. Steven Globerman, *Waiting Your Turn: Hospital Waiting Lists in Canada* (Vancouver: Fraser Institute, May 1990).

CHAPTER 6: APPLES TO ORANGES: COMPARING OLD AND NEW TECHNOLOGIES

1. Joseph L. Bast, Richard C. Rue and Stuart A. Wesbury, Jr., *Why We Spend Too Much on Health Care* (Chicago: Heartland Institute, 1992), p. 45.
2. "The Development of Biotechnology and Its Challenges," *Industrial Perspective*, Pharmaceutical Manufacturers Association, July 1991; "Facts at a Glance," 1991 edition, Pharmaceutical Manufacturers Association, p. 10.
3. "1989 Annual Summary," *Morbidity and Mortality Weekly Report*, U.S. Department of Health and Human Services.
4. "Facts at a Glance," pp. 28, 29.
5. "America's Pharmaceutical Industry: A Key Competitive Force," *Industry Perspective*, July 1991.
6. Pharmaceutical Manufacturers Association calculation; data source: J.A. DiMasi, Ph.D, Tufts University.

CHAPTER 7: DRUGS, SEX, AND VIOLENCE

1. "Why Does Crime Pay?" *Policy Backgrounder* No. 110 (Dallas: National Center for Policy Analysis, June 3, 1991).
2. American Hospital Association *News*, February 24, 1992, p. 7.
3. Bryce J. Christensen, "In Sickness and Health," *Policy Review*, Spring 1992, pp. 70–2.
4. Secretary Louis Sullivan, "America's Ailing Families: Diagnosing the Problem, Finding a Cure" (Washington, DC: Heritage Foundation, 1992).
5. Dana Wechsler, "Parkinson's Law 101," *Forbes*, June 25, 1990, p. 52.
6. Dennis Kelly, "Poll on schools: More books, less bureaucracy," *USA Today*, October 17, 1991, p. 1-D; see also John Chubb and Terry Moe, *Politics, Markets, and America's Schools* (Washington, DC: Brookings Institution, 1990).

7. John Dewey, *Democracy and Education* (New York: Macmillan, 1916), p. 44.
8. Don Feder, "Family planners celebrate teen sexuality," Creators Syndicate, Inc., March 6, 1991.

CHAPTER 8: AIDS: THE FIRST POLITICALLY PROTECTED DISEASE

1. *U.S.A. Today*, June 11, 1992, p. 3-A.
2. "Sounding Board," *New England Journal of Medicine*, January 9, 1992, pp. 128–32.
3. Rebecca Crandall, "Research Funding and the Media," *Jama*, September 4, 1991, p. 1279.
4. *Hospitals*, January 20, 1992, p. 18.

CHAPTER 9: THE HIGH COST OF LIVING, THE HIGHER COST OF DYING

1. Ronni Scheier, "Who Lives? Who Dies? Who Decides?" *American Medical News*, January 7, 1991, p. 4.
2. Nicola Clark, "The High Cost of Dying," *Wall Street Journal*, February 26, 1992.
3. The U.S. Preventive Services Task Force, *Guide to Clinical Preventive Services* (Baltimore, MD: Williams and Wilkins, 1989).
4. Timothy Norbeck, *Connecticut Medicine*, March 1990.

CHAPTER 10: CALL THE PLUMBER, WE'RE INSURED!

1. Willard G. Manning, "Health Insurance and the Demand for Medical Care: Evidence from a Randomized Experiment," *American Economic Review*, June 1987, pp. 251–277.
2. Thomas M. Burton, "Firms that Promise Lower Medical Bills May Increase Them," *Wall Street Journal*, July 28, 1992, p. 1-A.
3. Howard Larkins, "Despite Results, Firms Purchasing Managed Care Strategies," *American Medical News*, February 25, 1991, p. 9.
4. "When You Survey a Large Enough Group to be Statistically Accurate, HMO Premiums are More than Most People Think," *Benefits*, May 1, 1991, pp. 5, 34.
5. John Goodman and Gerald Musgrave, "Controlling Health Care Costs with Medical Savings Accounts," National Center for Policy Analysis, Dallas, Texas, Report No. 168, January 1992.

6. John Goodman and Gerald Musgrave, "Freedom of Choice in Health Insurance," National Center for Policy Analysis, Dallas, Texas, Report No. 134, November 1988.

CHAPTER 11: PAPER PLAGUE: THE SICKENING SAGA OF GOVERNMENT INTERVENTION

1. John K. Iglehart, "Health Policy Report: The American Health Care System," *New England Journal of Medicine*, April 2, 1992, pp. 962–7.
2. Committee on Finance, U.S. Senate, *Medicare and Medicaid* (Washington: U.S. Government Printing Office, 1970).
3. John C. Goodman and Gerald Musgrave, "Health Care After Retirement: Who Will Pay the Cost?" National Center for Policy Analysis, Dallas, Texas, Report No. 139, June 1989.
4. Marjorie Smith Mueller and Robert M. Gibson, "National Health Expenditures, Fiscal Year 1975," *Social Security Bulletin*, February 1976.
5. *Texas Medicine*, August 1990, p. 47.
6. "Internists Blast Medicare Carriers," *Medical World News*, April 11, 1988.
7. *Private Practice*, January 1989, p. 23.
8. Ibid., p. 18.
9. Ibid., p. 22.
10. Ibid., January 1992.
11. Louis Goodman, Ph.D., Texas Medical Association, Austin, Texas.
12. "Medicare's hassle factor," *American Medical News*, October 19, 1990, pp. 3, 34.
13. Reinhardt, "The Medical B-Factor: Bureaucracy in Action," *Washington Post*, August 9, 1988.
14. Daniel Callahan, Ph.D., "Old Age and New Policy," *Journal of the American Medical Association*, February 10, 1989, p. 905.
15. *National Review*, March 18, 1988, p. 22.
16. S. Rich, "Medicare Cost Curbs: Fit for Universal Duty?" *Washington Post*, August 20, 1991, p. A-13.

CHAPTER 12: TOXIC TORTS: WHEN LAWYERS MAKE THE LAWS

1. "Attorney Angst," *USA Today*, March 5, 1992, p. 1-D.
2. "Torts Control," *Wall Street Journal*, February 4, 1986, p. 30; "The Lawsuit Crisis," Insurance Information Institute, New York, April

1986, p. 3; D. R. Hensler, et al., "Trends in Tort Litigation: The Story Behind the Statistics," Rand Corporation, No. R-3583-ICJ, 1987.

3. Peter Huber, "Consent and Coercion in the Law of Accidents," *The World and I*, February 1989, p. 471.

4. *Forbes*, October 16, 1989, p. 204.

5. Ibid., p. 213.

6. Christine Evans, "A Case of Impairment," *Miami Herald*, June 23, 1991, p. 1-J. 4-J.

7. Ibid.

8. John Donnelly, "In this case, the number is $100 million," *Miami Herald*, January 29, 1992.

9. L. Harvey, et al., "Physician and Public Attitudes on Health Care Issues," American Medical Association, 1989.

10. "The Costs of Professional Liability in the 1980s," Center for Health Policy Research, American Medical Association, 1990; E. Slora, et al., "Medical Professional Liability Claims and Premiums, 1985–1989," and "Socioeconomic Characteristics of Medical Practice 1990/1991," American Medical Association.

11. "Industry Perspective: Product Liability Reform," Pharmaceutical Manufacturers Association, July 1991.

12. "The Clintons and the Lawyers," *Wall Street Journal*, August 27, 1992, p. A-10.

CHAPTER 13: WHAT'S THE SOLUTION?

1. Letter to the American Medical Association, September 8, 1992.

2. Henry J. Aaron and William B. Schwartz, *The Painful Prescription: Rationing Hospital Care* (Washington, DC: Brookings Institution, 1984), pp. 35–6.

3. Michael A. Walker, et al., "Waiting Your Turn: Hospital Waiting Lists in Canada," Fraser Forum, February 1992.

4. "The Truth About Socialized Medicine," *Private Practice*, March 1992, p. 19–25.

5. Aldona Robbins and Gary Robbins, "What a Canadian-Style Health Care System Would Cost U.S. Employers and Employees," National Center for Policy Analysis, Dallas, Texas.

6. Edmund F. Haislmaier, "Problems in Paradise: Canadians Complain About Their Health Care System," *Policy Backgrounder* No. 883, Heritage Foundation, Washington, D.C., February 19, 1992.

7. *Wall Street Journal*, September 10, 1992, p. A-14.

Index

_____/_____

A

Acer, David, 166
Adolescence
  health status in, 160
  sexual promiscuity in, 158–160
Adopted children, mandated insurance
  coverage for, 194
Advocacy journalism, 76, 82, 83
Agency for Health Care Policy and
  Research, 168
Aging
  Congressional committees on, 42, 138
  and health care costs, 124
AIDS (acquired immune deficiency
  syndrome)
  confidentiality law for, 177
  contagious diseases associated with, 174–
    175
  cost of treating, 125, 168–169
  disability designation for, 169, 174
  and drug use, 165, 167
  HIV testing, 177
  incidence among Haitian refugees, 123
  life expectancy for, 168
  medicines and vaccines for, 168
  non-sexual transmission of, 166–167
  policies concerning, 17
  political protection of, 163–178
  preventability of, 163
  research money spent for, 167–168
  sexual transmission of, 158, 164–166
AIDS Coalition to Unleash Power (ACT-
  UP), 167, 170, 178
Aid to Families with Dependent Children
  (AFDC), 155–156
Alcoholics Anonymous, 195

Alzheimer's disease, 137
Amebiasis, 173
American Artists Congress, 25
American Bar Association (ABA), Quayle's
  address to, 221–222
American Civil Liberties Union, 25, 157, 170
American College of Obstetricians and
  Gynecologists, 226, 239
American Committee for Protection of
  Foreign Born, 27
American Council on Soviet Relations, 27
American Dental Association, 72
American Enterprise Institute, 256
American Federation of Labor (AFL), 32
American Federation of Labor-Congress of
  Industrial Organizations (AFL-CIO),
  49, 60, 67
  coalition with ADA, 74
  in Congressional lobbying, 41, 58, 70
  health committee of, 86
American Federation of State, County and
  Municipal Employees, 86
American Foundation for AIDS Research,
  168
American Hospital Association, 72, 86,
  100, 218
American Medical Association (AMA), 34,
  48–49
  attack on, by FTC, 203–205
  decision to lobby in Congress, 39–40
  media misinformation about, 102–103
  on Medicaid, 50, 72–73, 102–103
  on Medicare, 64–66, 68–69
  1991 annual meeting of, 167
  pharmaceutical guidelines of, 138
  presidency of, 11, 39, 52, 62, 71

American Medical Association (*continued*)
  speakers' bureau of, 11, 46, 55
  union's smear campaign against, 52–55, 57
American Public Health Association, 76
American Railway Union, 24
Americans for Democratic Action (ADA), 59, 60, 67, 73
  break with communists, 30–31
  in coalition with AFL-CIO, 74
  in Congressional lobbying, 43, 73
  description of, 27
  formation of, 26–27
  leadership of, 48, 49
  in 1948 elections, 30–33
  permeation tactics of, 28
  supporters of, 46, 47, 50
American Writers Congress, 25
American Youth Congress, 25
Anal intercourse
  church's stand on, 164
  health risks associated with, 164–166, 173
  legalization of, 176, 177–178
Anderson, Clinton, 52, 71
Anderson, M. D., Cancer Center, 118
Andrews, Edson, 18
Anesthetics
  administration of, 14
  technological advancement in, 130–131
Aneurysms, treatment of, 129–130
Angioplasty, 132
Antibiotics, 4, 19, 128
Arnall, Ellis, 17
Arthroscopic techniques, 132
Artificial heart valve, damage awards against, 237
Association of American Medical Schools, 204–205
Association of Trial Lawyers of America, 240
Automobile safety belts, 183
Azine, Harold, 65, 70
AZT, 168

B

Ball, Robert, 51
Barry, Marion, 152
Bascom Palmer Eye Institute, 118
Battelle Medical Technology and Policy Research Center, 136
Bell, Ruth, 158, 172
Bendectin, lawsuits against, 231–232
Bentsen, Lloyd, 152
Bergalis, Kimberly, 166, 167
Beta blockers, 136
Biemiller, Andrew, 41, 52, 74
Bingham, Barry, 27

Bingham, Jonathan, 50
Biotechnology, 137, 142, 143
Bjork-Shiley Convexco heart valve, damage awards against, 237
Blasingcame, Dr., 62
Block, Al, 15–16
Block, Evelyn, 15–16
Blood test requirement for marriage license, 17
Blue Cross/Blue Shield, 19, 38, 72
Booz-Allen and Hamilton, on pharmaceutical industry, 142
Bourassa, Robert, 252
Bowles, Chester, 48, 50
Breast implants, damage awards against, 239
Brisbane, Albert, 109
British Broadcasting Corporation (BBC), 23
British Bureau of Socialist International, 23
British health care system. *See also* Great Britain
  delivery of health care under, 249–250
  employment opportunities in, 116
  global budgeting in, 246
  socialization of, 24
British Labour party, 22–24
British trade union movement, 22
Brook Farm (Massachusetts), 109, 110
Brookings Institution, 44, 51, 157, 250
Brotherhood of Sleeping Car Porters, 30
Brown, Jerry, 87
Bureau of Labor Statistics, 116, 118
Burn accidents, 183
Bush, George, 87–88, 104, 167
Butler, Paul, 47
Bypass surgery, 136

C

Calderwood, Deryck, 172
Camillus House, 90
Canada, teenage pregnancy rate in, 125
Canadian health care system
  average length of hospitalization in, 126
  controlled drug market in, 141
  cost comparison with U.S. health care, 120–127
  delivery of services in, 104–106, 126, 250–253
  employment opportunities in, 116
  global budgeting in, 246, 250–253
  per capita health spending in, 254
  queue jumpers in, 251
Cancer research, 137, 168
Cardiac arrhythmia, 140
Carey, James, 49, 58
Carstenson, Blue, 52
Carter, Jimmy, 114–115, 217

Castro, Fidel, 80
Cataract treatment, 132
Catfish Club, 15
Cato Institute, 256
Center for Disease Control, 124, 133, 183, 224
Center for Study of American Business, 217
Cerebrovascular disease, 136
Certificate of need (CON), 215–217
Cesarean sections, media misinformation on, 97–98
Chiles, Lawton, 86
Cholera, 150
Chubb, John, 157
Churchill, Winston, 24
Citizens Medical Committee on Health (Florida), 19
Civil justice system, 220–222
    contingency fees in, 226–229
    damage awards in, 235–239
    expert testimony in, 229–235
    rules of evidence in, 231
    tort liability in, 222–226
Clark, Ira, 107
Cleveland Clinic, 118
Clinton, Bill
    campaign contributions to, 240
    central planning committee, 245–246
    delivery of health care services, 248–250
    fee schedules, 247–248
    forced spending for, 196
    and freedom of choice, 243
    global budgeting and health care delivery, 250–253
    health care plan of, 253
    managed competition under, 247, 248
    "pay or play concept," 253–254
    restrictions on new technologies, 246–247
    spending caps in, 145, 246
    stand on tort reform, 240–241
CobraServe, 191
Cohen, Wilbur, 50, 51, 54, 74, 202
Collateral source rule, 237
Collins, LeRoy, 16, 19, 43, 46, 48
Committee of One Hundred for National Health Insurance, 76
Committee on Political Education (COPE), 53, 60
Communist-front organizations, 25, 27
Communist International, 26, 38, 44
Communist party, 26, 30, 59
Comprehensive Health Planning Act (1966), 216

Condoms, dispensing of
    and adolescent promiscuity, 159–160
    and rise in pregnancies, 173–174
    and rise in sexually-transmitted diseases, 173–174
Conference of Progressives (1946), 30
Congenital anomalies, 151
Congress of Industrial Organizations (CIO), 30, 32
Consolidated Omnibus Budget Reconciliation Act (COBRA), 101
Consumer price index (CPI), 130
Contingency fees, 221, 226–229
Cooper, Maurice, 19
Coronary heart disease, 136
Cost-plus system of payment, 214–225
Council on Competitiveness, 134, 141
Crime, expected punishment for committing, 146–147
Cruikshank, Nelson, 51–52, 58
Cuban American National Foundation, 79
Cuban Americans, 80, 82
Curtin, John J., 221–222
Curtis, Representative, 74
Cytomegalorvirus (CMV), 174

D

Dade County Medical Association, 40, 44
Damage awards
    and collateral source rule, 237
    compensable, 235–238
    and doctrine of joint and several liability, 237–238
    payment of, 236
    punitive, 238–239
Dana, Charles, 109, 111
Darrow, Clarence, 24
Davis, Arthur Vining, 63
Death, prolonging imminent, with advanced technology, 179–181
Debs, Eugene, 24–25
Dementia, 174
Democratic party, 30, 31, 110
Detroit, Michigan, infant mortality rate in, 153
Dewey, John, 36, 157–159
Diagnostic Related Groups (DRGs), 218, 247–248
Dickinson, Frank, 34
Diphtheria, 135
Dirksen, Everett, 61
District of Columbia, infant mortality in, 152
Dixiecrat, 31
Docking, George, 50
Domagk, Gerhard, 13
Douglas, William, 28

Drug use
  and health care costs, 125, 151
  and spread of AIDS, 165, 167
Duodenal ulcer, treatment of, 136
Dyazide, 140
Dysentery, 173

E

Eisenhower, Dwight, 43, 50, 52
Elderly, medical neglect of, 44–45
Elections
  of 1948, 29–33
  of 1964, 73–74
Electrical Workers union, 49
Emergency medical treatment, uninsured's
  right to, 99–100
Emerson, Ralph Waldo, 109
Employer-provided health insurance
  experience rating in, 193–194
  forced, 196
  incentive to abuse and over use, 189
  risk pools in, 192–193
  tax incentives for, 186–187
Employment opportunities, in health care
  industry, 112–120
Engels, Friedrich, 24–25, 109
England. See Great Britain
English rule, versus contingency fee, 227
Entitlement, 88
  socialist notion of, 115
Erysipelas, 135
Espionage Act, 25
Euthanasia, 181
Ewing, Oscar, 34–35
Experience rating, 193–194
Expert testimony, in tort liability cases,
  229–235
Exploratory surgery, 128

F

Fabian Society, 22–23, 254
  on gradualism, 35, 43, 49, 50, 51, 75,
    254
  on permeation, 23–26, 28, 35, 76, 254
Falk, Isadore, 51
Family life, 12
  influence of, on health, 153–155
Fanning, Deirdre, 229
Faulkner and Gray, Inc., survey on
  utilization review, 190
Feder, Don, 159
Federal Security Agency, 34
Federal Trade Commission (FTC), attack
  on AMA by, 203–205
Fetal alcohol syndrome (FAS), 151
Finletter, Thomas, 50
Fleming, Alexander, 18

Florida Academy of Trial Lawyers, 93
Florida Medical Association, 40, 44
Florida Medical Committee for Better
  Government, 40
Florida Public Health Committee, 17
Fojo, Robert, 107
Food and Drug Administration (FDA), 140,
  223
  processing of new drugs by, 142–143
Forand, Aime, 52
Forand bill, 51–52
Forced income distribution, 84
Fordham University, study of New York
  high schools by, 156
Foundations for Medical Care, 202, 203, 205
Fourier, François-Marie-Charles, 108–109,
  110
Fraina, Louis, 26
Franklin, Benjamin, 115
Fraser Institute (Vancouver, B.C.), 256
Freeman, Orville, 50
Friendly, Fred, 60
Frye rule, 231

G

Galbraith, John Kenneth, 50, 121
Gay bowel syndrome, 173
Genetic engineering, 4, 137, 142, 143
Germany, life expectancy in, 38
Giffin, Walter, 13
Gilbert, E. A., 16
Gingrich, Newt, 104, 105
Global budgeting, 246, 250–253
Goldberg, Arthur, 50
Goldwater, Barry, 73
Goodman, John, 192
Gordon, Jack, 98
Government
  differing views of, 83–85
  intervention of, in health care industry,
    5–7, 242–259
  and mandated insurance coverage, 194–
    195
Grabowski, Henry, 139
Gradualism, Fabian doctrine of, 35, 43,
  49–50, 51, 75, 254
Graham, Bob, 86
Gram negative bacteria, treatment of
  infection from, 19
Gram positive bacteria, treatment of
  infection from, 14, 19
Granick, Ted, 61
Grant, Ulysses, 110
Great Britain. See also British health care
  system
  life expectancy in, 38
  socialism in, 22–24

Great Society (Johnson), 5, 6, 42
Greeley, Colorado, 111
Greeley, Horace, 108–111, 157
Green, William, 32
Greer, Pedro, 90
Gross national product (GNP), percentage of, attributed to health care, 114, 119–120, 123, 137
Gunshot wounds, health care services for, 147

H

Haitian refugees, AIDS in, 123
Hallstrand, Harold, 18
Harkin, Tom, 112
Harriman, Averell, 47, 50
Harvard University studies
    on malpractice claims, 240
    on U.S. industry, 134
Harvey, Paul, 112
Hawthorne, Nathaniel, 109, 110–111
Health, Education and Welfare, U.S. Department of (HEW), 34, 49, 67, 74
Health Access Florida, 93
Health and Human Services, U.S. Department of, 34, 167, 189, 190
Health and Rehabilitative Services, Florida Department of, 93
Health benefits
    tax breaks for, 186–187
    trade-off of salary for, 192
Health care
    administrative, 213–214
    and AIDS, 168–169
    alternative plans for, 255
    average length of hospitalization, 126
    cost of, 15–16, 21, 76
    delivery of, 243–244, 248–250
    effect of civil justice system on, 124, 223–226, 239–241
    effect of Medicare on, 197–219
    effect of social ills on, 145–153
    government-imposed price controls on, 209, 211–212
    government intervention in, 5–7, 242–259
    for homeless, 91–92
    increased demand for, 130–131
    in job creation, 112–120
    limitations on facility expansion, 215–216
    in postwar United States, 20
    quality of American, 243–244
    waste in, 119
Health Care Financing Administration, 137, 153

Health insurance, 187–188
    employer-provided, 186–187, 189, 192–194, 196
    government interference in marketplace for, 186–187, 194–195
    increased cost of, 57
    risk pools in, 192–193
    third-party payer system in, 190–191
Health Insurance Association of America, 218
Health Maintenance Act (1973), 209
Health maintenance organizations (HMOs), 190, 248
    effort to enroll Medicare beneficiaries in, 210–211
    financial incentives to hold back services by, 210
    funding of, 209–210
    ineffectiveness in, 191
Heart attack, 133
Heart disease, 168
Heckler, Margaret, 210
Hellinger, Fred, 168
Hepatitis viruses, 173
Heritage Foundation, 103, 256
Higgins, Foster, 190
Hillquit, Morris, 24
Hispanic Americans, 80
Hitler, Adolf, 28, 39
HIV virus. *See* AIDS
Holland, Spessard, 17
Homeless, medical care for, 91–92
Homosexuals/homosexuality
    activists' agendas, 170–171, 174
    and AIDS, 162–166
    in school sex education, 171–172
Hoover, Lou Henry, 37
Huber, Peter, 5, 224
Humana Health Plans of South Florida, 210
Humana's Gold Plus Medical Plan, 210
Human Rights Campaign Fund, 170
Humphrey, Hubert, 59
    support for ADA, 33, 43
    in television debate on King-Anderson bill, 36, 55–58
Hurlong, Representative, 74
Hussey, Dr., 62
Hysterectomies, media misinformation on, 97, 98–99

I

Iacocca, Lee, 95
Illegitimate births
    and infant mortality rate, 148–149
    rates of, 154
    welfare incentives for, 155–156

Immigration, and health care costs, 123
Immunizations, 4, 19, 156
Independent Citizens Committee of Arts, Sciences, and Professions (ICCASP), 30
Infant mortality rate, 81, 150
  causes of, 148–153
  in Japan, 148–149
  in United States, 148–149, 152, 153
Infectious diseases, 4, 135, 150
Intercollegiate Socialist Society (ISS). *See* League for Industrial Democracy (LID)

J

Jackson Memorial Hospital (Miami), 106–107
Japan
  average length of hospitalization in, 126
  health care cost measures in, 88
  infant mortality rate in, 148–149
  life expectancy in, 148
  maternal mortality rates in, 149
Javits, Jacob, 46
Johnson, Lyndon, 72, 73, 74, 160
  programs of, 5, 42
  support of, for King-Anderson bill, 75
Joint and several liability, doctrine of, 237–238

K

Kemp, Jack, 80
Kennedy, Edward, 76, 86, 196, 209, 217, 253
Kennedy, John, 23, 46–47, 49, 62
  assassination of, 73
  support for ADA, 47, 48, 72
  in television address on King-Anderson bill, 64–68
Kerr, Senator, 71
Kerrey, Bob, 107
Kerr-Mills legislation, 50–51, 54, 72–73, 102. *See also* Medicaid
King, Cecil, 52
King-Anderson bill, 52–53, 54. *See also* Medicare
  decline in public support for, 70, 74
  defeat of, 71–72
  presidential address on, 64–68
  supporters of, 60
  television debates on, 55–58, 60
  union support for, 58, 64, 66, 74
Kleinman, Carol, 117
Koop, C. Everett, 57
Krasny, Jacques, 122
Kravitz, Rabbi, 15
Krim, Mathilde, 168

L

Labor-value theory, 212
Lahey Clinic, 119
Lambda Defense League, 170
Lane, Anne Marie, 106–107
Laproscopic techniques, 132
Larson, Leonard, 52, 62
Lawrence, David, Jr., 79, 86
League for Industrial Democracy (LID), 26, 27, 33, 35, 157
  leadership of, 25, 36, 157
  original name of, 24
Lenahan, William, 232–235
Lend-Lease, war debts under, 24
Lerner, Max, 27–28
Lester, Ignatius, 228
Lewis, Alfred, 26
Liberal Republican party, 110
Liberalism, 33–36, 42, 43, 165
Lidocaine, 140
Life expectancy
  for AIDS patient, 168
  effect of crime on, 148
  effect of pharmaceuticals on, 135
  in United States versus England and Germany, 38
Loeb, James, 26, 50
London, Jack, 25
London School of Economics, 23
Los Angeles Times, 82
Low birth weight, and infant mortality rate, 150

M

MacBride, Roger, 242
MacDonald, Ramsey, 23
MacDonald, Torbert, 68
Madison, James, 86, 111
Madison, James, Institute, 122
Magnetic resonance imaging (MRI) scan, 128–129, 133
Malnutrition, and infant mortality rates, 151–152
Malpractice claims, 20, 240
Harvard University studies
  on malpractice, 240
  on medical care for poor, 92–93
  on tort liability, 222–224, 226
Malpractice insurance, cost of, 93–95, 124
Managed care, 189, 190, 247, 248
Manhattan Institute for Policy Research, 5
Manitoba Medical Association, 106
Marshall Plan, 33
Martin, Douglas, 232–235
Martin, Dr., 45
Martin, Wayne, 19
Marx, Karl, 24–25, 109–110, 138

Mas, Jorge, 79
Massachusetts Medical Society, 64
Maternal mortality rates, 149
Maternity Outreach Mobile Program
    (MOM Vans), 152
Maximum allowable actual charge (MAAC)
    regulations, 211
Mayo Clinic, 118
McCarthy era, blacklisting during, 25
McCulloch, Frank, 50
McEntee, Gerald, 86
McGraw-Hill, survey on HMOs by, 210
McLaughlin, Loretta, 6
McNamara, Patrick, 44, 45, 46, 67
Measles, 135–136
Medicaid, 101, 102, 190, 258. *See also* Kerr-
    Mills legislation
    bureaucratic problems in, 91
    expansion of, 152
    payments to hospitals, 214–215
    review of services under, 205–209
Medical IRA (MIRA), tax deductible
    deposits to, 257–258
Medical profession
    government intervention in, 203–219
    monetarization of, 57–58, 90
    practitioners' threefold purpose, 162
    shortage of physicians in, 34
Medical Savings Accounts, 192, 257, 259
Medicare. *See also* King-Anderson bill
    cost of, 57, 76
    coverage of, 52
    diagnostic related groups, 247–248
    effect of, on health care costs, 197–219
    effort to enroll beneficiaries of, in HMOs,
        210–211
    expansion of, 42
    federal spending on, 88
    financial crisis in, 5–6, 198–200
    government controls under, 36, 258
    and gradualness, 254
    Part A/B, 197
    payments to hospitals, 214–215
    precertification for hospital admissions,
        211
    regulations of, 213
    reimbursements in, 5, 131
    resource-based relative value scale, 212,
        247–248
    review of services under, 205–209
    third-party payer systems of, 190, 244–
        245
Melashenko, Dr., 208–209
Me-too drugs, 139, 140
Miami, University of, School of Medicine/
    Jackson Memorial Hospital complex,
    118

Miami Herald
    campaign against Cuban Americans, 79,
        82
    coverage of health care issues, 86–87, 99,
        100, 102, 104, 106
Michaud, Gerald, 229
Michigan, University of, 153
Military action, and health care costs,
    123–124
Milk dairies, inspection of, 16
Mills, Wilbur, 72, 74
Mitchell, George, 253
MOM Vans (Maternity Outreach Mobile
    Program), 152
Moncton Hospital of New Brunswick, 106
Morgan, Howard, 50
Morgenstern, Oskar, 120–121
Moynihan, Daniel, 56
Murphy, Charles, 50
Murphy, Francis, 14
Murray, Philip, 30
Musgrove, Martha, 100

N
National Center for Health Services
    Research, 153
National Center for Health Statistics, 82
National Center for Policy Analysis (NCPA),
    192, 254
    health care plan of, 256–258
    report on cost of committing crime, 146–
        147
National Citizens Political Action
    Committee (NCPAC), 30
National Conference of Christians and Jews
    Brotherhood Award, 43
National Council of Senior Citizens, 52–53,
    64, 67
National Education Association (NEA),
    156, 157
National Federation of Independent
    Business Foundation, 256
National Gay and Lesbian Task Force, 170
National Health Care Board (NHCB), 245–
    249
National income statistics, bureaucratic
    manipulation of, 120–123
National Institutes of Health, 134
National Library on Money and Politics,
    study on campaign contributions, 240
National Negro Congress, 25
National Planning and Resources Act
    (1974), 217–218
National Safety Council, 183
National Student League, 25
Nestingen, Ivan, 50, 54
New Deal (Roosevelt), 33

News media, misinformation in, 79–111, 114, 115, 128, 132–133
New York City, homeless shelters in, 91
New York Times, 107
New York Tribune, 108
Niebuhr, Reinhold, 27
Nitroglycerin, 136
Nixon, Richard, 46, 83
Norbech, Tim, 184
North American Phalanx (New Jersey), 109
North Atlantic Treaty Organization (NATO), 33

O

Occupational Safety and Health Administration (OSHA), 183
O'Connor, John, 164
Ohio Medical Association, 76
Olson, Walter, 229
Organization for Economic Cooperation and Development, Health Data File of, 126
Oschner Clinic, 119
Osler, William, 206
Oswald, Lee Harvey, 73

P

"Pay or play" concept, 253–254
Peer review, 202–203
versus PROs, 205–208
Penicillin, 4, 18–19, 143
Pepper, Claude, 37–42, 44, 45, 47
Pepper Commission, 42, 86, 254
Perkins, Mr., 16
Perlman, Philip, 48
Permeation
Fabian doctrine of, 23–26, 28, 35, 76, 254
fission of old united socialist front and new order of, 29–36
Pharmaceutical industry, 19, 133–134
argument against government control of, 140–144
in Canada versus United States, 141
economic and social benefits of pharamaceuticals, 135–138
FDA processing of new products, 142–143
investment in research and development, 134–135
profits versus development expenses, 138–139
proposed restrictions on, 247
Pharmaceutical Manufacturers Association, 135, 138
Planned Parenthood, 159
Plastic surgery, 7, 126–127
Pneumonia, mortality rate for, 13

Polio, 135, 136
Pollack, Rick, 86
Population adjusted basis, 101
Poverty, and infant mortality rates, 151
Precertification procedure, 211
Preferred provider organizations (PPOs), 190
Prenatal care, and infant mortality rate, 81, 152–153
Presidential campaigns
Goldwater versus Johnson, 73
press coverage of, 86–88
Wallace versus Truman, 29–32, 39
Pressman, Lee, 30
Preventive care, patient's responsibilities in, 181–184, 191
Preventive Services Task Force, U.S., guidelines for preventive services in clinical setting, 182
Price controls, 38, 83, 209
Price fixing, 20
Princeton University, 153
Product liability claims, 239
Professional Review Organizations (PROs)
costs incurred by, 208–209
versus peer review, 205–208
Professional Standards Review Organizations (PSROs), 205
Progressive Citizens of America, 30
Prontosil, 4, 13
Proxmire, William, 46
Pryor, David, 138, 139, 140, 142, 247
Public education
Dewey's influence on, 157–159
federal government's involvement in, 42
Public Health Service, U.S., 34, 149
Public Health Services Act, Title X of, 160
Public health standards, need for, 17–18
Pulitzer, Joseph, 110

Q

Quayle, Dan, address to American Bar Association, 221
Queer Nation, 170

R

Race, and infant mortality rates, 151
Railway Brotherhood, 32
Rand Corporation study on employer-provided health insurance, 189, 191, 193
Rauh, Joseph, 48
Reagan, Ronald, 65
Reinauer, Richard, 65
Republican party, 29, 110
Resource-based relative value scale (RBRVS), 212, 247–248

Reuther, Walter, 26, 32, 36, 41, 48
  death of, 76
  power of, 53, 61, 76
  support for King-Anderson bill, 58, 60,
    75
Ribicoff, Abraham, 49, 62, 71
Risk pools, 192–193
Robins, R. B., 48
Rockefeller, Jay, 42, 86, 196, 254
Roman Catholic Church, 164
Roosevelt, Eleanor, 50
Roosevelt, Franklin, 15, 29, 32, 33, 186
Rosenblatt, Stanley, 238–239
Rostenkowski, Dan, 219
Rymer, Ernest N., 38

S

St. Mary, Dr., 45
Saint-Simon, comte de, 109
Salk vaccine, 136
Salvation Army, 92
Sankey Commission, Miners' Federation on,
    23
Schering-Plough Corporation, 136
Schlesinger, Arthur, Jr., 49, 59
Scripps Clinic and Research Foundation,
    119
Second International, socialist alliance of,
    28
Sex education in schools
  application of Dewey's theory in, 158–
    159
  treatment of homosexuality in, 171–172
Sexually-transmitted diseases. *See also*
    AIDS
  and condom dispensing, 173–174
Shaw, George Bernard, 22, 23, 35
Shearer, Derek, 255
Shearon, Marjorie, 51
Shigellosis, 173
Smathers, George, 58, 63, 71
  ▸ bid for Senate, 39, 40, 41
  political connections of, 61, 62, 64
Smith, "Boney," 14
Smith, Howard K., 60
Smoking, 158, 183
Social ills, medicalization of, 145–153, 195
Socialism, 80, 255
  in Great Britain, 22–24
  in United States, 24–36
Socialist party of America, 24, 25–26
Socialized medicine
  advocates of, 98
  attempts at, in United States, 32, 34–36,
    38, 42
  in Great Britain, 44
  taxes to support, 87–88

Social Security, 35, 43, 47
  administrative costs under, 56
  federal spending on, 88
Social Security Act, 47
  disability designation under, 174
Sodomy. *See* Anal intercourse
Soviet Union
  British support for, 23
  march of, into Eastern Europe, 29, 31
  support for U.S. aid to, 39
  view of, as utopian society, 25
Special Supplemental Food Program for
    Women, Infants, and Children (WIC),
    152, 155
Spector, Sidney, 44
Spivack, Lawrence, 61
Stalin, Joseph, 39
Stanford University's Hoover Institution,
    256
States' Rights party, 31
Streptococcal infections, 4, 13, 135
Streptomycin, discovery of, 19
Stroke, death rate from, 133
Students for Democratic Action, 32
Sulfa drugs, 4, 13–14, 128
Sullivan, Louis, 167
Supplemental Security Income program,
    169
Sweeney, John, 86
Syphilis, 17, 135, 160, 175–176

T

Taft-Hartley Act, 31
Tagamet, 136
Tax Equity and Fiscal Responsibility Act
    (TEFRA), 210
Taxes
  for marketplace coercion, 186
  to support socialized medicine, 87–88
Tax Foundation, 76
Teachers union, 157
Technology, 4
  advances in, and health care costs, 128–
    144
  loss of American lead in industry, 141
  media misinformation on costs of, 95–97
  to prolong imminent death, 179–181
  proposed restrictions on new, 246–247
Teenage pregnancy
  in Canada versus United States, 125
  and infant mortality rate, 149
Teresa, Mother, 92
Tetanus, 135
Tetracyclines, 4
Texas, University of, Medical Center, 118
Thatcher, Margaret, 24
Thomas, Norman, 24, 25

Thurmond, Strom, 31
Toberoff, Max, 228
Toronto Hospital for Sick Children, 105
Tort liability, 5, 20
    effect of, on health care costs, 239–241,
        258
    joint and several liability, 237–238
    and medical malpractice suits, 222–224,
        226
Townsend, Francis E., 45
Townsend Plan, 45
Truman, Harry, 29–36
Truman Doctrine, 29, 39
Tuberculosis (TB), 135, 136, 150, 174
Tufts University School of Medicine, 44
Typhoid fever, 135, 150

U
Ultrasonography, 133
Un-American Activities, House Select Com-
    mittee on, 42
Uninsured, medical care for, 99–102
Union Colony (Colorado), 109, 111
Union for Democratic Action (UDA), 25–
    26, 52
United Auto Workers, 26, 32
United Nations, 33
United States
    average length of hospitalization in,
        126
    infant mortality rate in, 148–149, 150
    life expectancy in, 38, 148
    maternal mortality rates in, 149
    socialism in, 24–36
    teenage pregnancy rate in, 125
U.S. health care system
    cost comparison with Canadian health
        care, 120–127

after World War II, 20
Universal health care, 81, 83, 87
Utilization review, ineffectiveness of, 190–
    191

V
Vaccines, and tort liability, 223–224, 229
Veterans Administration, U.S., 101, 124
Vietnam War veterans, and health care
    costs, 124
Violent crime, effect of, on health care
    costs, 124–125, 146–148
Viral infections, 137
Virgin, Herbert, 20–21

W
Wallace, Henry, 29–32, 39
War on Poverty (Johnson), 156, 160
Washington Post, 82
Watts, Representative, 74
Weaver, George, 50
Webb, Beatrice, 23
Webb, Sidney, 22–23, 25, 254
Webbs, Barbara, 166
Whig Party, 110
Whitaker, Clem, 34
Whooping cough, 4, 135
    adverse effects from vaccine for, 223
Wicker, Tom, 73
Williams, Mennen, 50
Wofford, Harris, health care plan of, 85–86
World Medical Association, 89

Y
Young Communist International, 27
Young Workers League, National Executive
    Committee of, 27

DATE DUE